THE

PUBLICATIONS

OF THE

Lincoln Record Society

FOUNDED IN THE YEAR

1910

VOLUME 40

FOR THE YEAR ENDING 31ST AUGUST, 1943

The First Minute Book of the Gainsborough Monthly Meeting of the Society of Friends

1669—1719

EDITED BY

HAROLD W. BRACE

F.R.HIST.S.

Clerk of Lincolnshire Monthly Meeting

Volume II

1689—1709

PRINTED FOR

THE LINCOLN RECORD SOCIETY

BY

THE HEREFORD TIMES LIMITED, HEREFORD

1949

(v)

TABLE OF CONTENTS

	Page
TABLE OF CONTENTS	v
PREFACE	vii
THE MINUTE BOOK	1
APPENDIX	209
INDEXES :	
Persons and Places	211
Subjects	219

PREFACE

The text in this volume covers a period of consolidation ; the Toleration Act of 1689 enabled Meeting Houses to be built and licensed, so business concerning real property begins to appear in Monthly Meeting Minutes. Preoccupation with discipline, leading to the appointment of Overseers who were required to report formally ; structural elaboration as in the establishment of Preparative Meetings ; meticulous recording of names of Representatives, to Monthly and Quarterly Meetings, and of those appointed to inquire into the " clearness " of the parties to a marriage ; are all indicative of congelation from a movement into an organisation.

Severe persecution having ceased, except for isolated cases such as the one in the appendix to this volume, Quakers were no longer being bled financially, so cases requiring relief might have been expected to decline, but since they did not, the inference is that the benefits were attracting adherents whose circumstances rendered them likely to require such assistance. Suspicion of this lingered a long time, as shown in the report of the Friends appointed to interview a husband and wife " who jointly expressed a desire to be joined in Membership with us, declaring themselves free from any interested views, as to the outward ".[1] Probably, an analysis of the occupations of Friends would show a higher proportion belonging to the labouring classes in the 18th than in the 17th centuries. It is hoped to include in the Appendix to Volume 3, sufficient Biographical details to facilitate identification of the principal persons mentioned in the text.

Monthly Meeting began to control the activities of those numerous volunteers for the itinerant Ministry who replaced the original leaders, most of whom died during this period. Such deaths emphasised the desirability of putting on record first-hand accounts of the dynamic period before it was too late and the inquiries (pp. 164, 167–9) for the materials of a " General History " of the introduction of Quakerism were directed to Quarterly Meetings and such accounts as are extant have been published.[2] Unfortunately, the Lincolnshire return is missing, so an attempt will be made to present the evidence now available, relating to the compass of Gainsborough Monthly Meeting, for the period before the minutes begin, in the appendix to Volume 3.

The references to George Fox's writings (pp. 16–7) are in connexion with the Manuscript at Friends' House, London, entitled " The

---

[1] Gainsborough Monthly Meeting Minutes, under date 11 : 10 : 1805.
[2] *The First Publishers of Truth*, Norman Penney, supplements 1–5 of J.F.H.S., London, 1907.

Annual Catalogue of Geo : Fox, his Epistles, Doctrines, Books, Papers & Writings ".[1] Quarterly Meetings sent in lists of such writings by Fox as were copied into local Minute Books, &c., and these returns formed one of the sources of the compilation, made 1694–7.

HAROLD W. BRACE.

28 July, 1949.

---

[1] Edited by Henry J. Cadbury, Cambridge, Mass., 1939.

The First Minute Book of the Gainsborough Monthly Meeting of the Society of Friends 1669-1719

p. 145 continued.

ATT a Monthly Meeting held at Brigge the 10th of the 11th month 1689[1] :—

Ordered a contribution be collected & brought up to the next Monthly Meeting : which is to be at Brigge.

ATT a Monthly Meeting held at Brigg the 14th, 12th month 1689[2] :—

Henry Symson & Thomas Potter acquainted Friends of this Meeting with a child of Anthony Turners of Martin lately deceased that is left destitute & if speedy care be not taken the town will take her into there care, it is therefore the order of this Meeting that the Freinds of Gainsbrough Meeting take her into there care & this Meeting will see them indemnified.

p. 146.[3]

Informe at the least two of the most moderate Justices of the Peace of the County (Quorumunus) *that you* are presented & convicted upon the statute of 23 and 29 of Elizabeth and the 3d of King James against *papistry* which inflicteth £20 upon every papist absenting himselfe from his parish Church by *the space of* one month. Then acquaint those Justices that you are willing to take the test contai*ned in the* Act of Parliament made the 30th of this Kings reigne, that thereby it may appear you are no popi*sh recusant* and desire them to certify the King of your soe doeing. If the Justices question their authority *in this* behalfe, as if they were not concernd to take cognisance of thy takeing the test, or to certify the King thereon *then* you may show them the Act of Parliament and also the order lately obtained out of the Exchequer for the discharge of 13 Friends in Cambridgeshire, whereby it doth appear that those Friends did take the test in Cambridge last Lent Assizes, before the Lord Chiefe Baron Mountague, then Judge of the Assize who certified the King thereof upon which certificate the King ordered their discharge, & they are now dischargd accordingly, as appears by the said order. You may further informe the said Justices, that on the 17th of November last

---

[1] 10th January, 1690.   [2] 14th February, 1690.
[3] This page is in poor order, words in italics are conjectural.

past, severall people called Quakers appeared before Sir Charles
Croftsread, Knight and Thomas Holland, Esquire, Justices of
the Peace for the county of Suffolk who did certify the King
that the same persons had openly declared and subscribed
the said test or declaration, upon which certificate the King
ordered the discharge of severall persons. *The* main end of
making such application to the Justices to take the test before
them is the procuring their certificate thereof to the King,
without which all such proceedure would be fruitless.

The Certificate of the Rector & Neighbors to the Justices.
Wee the Rector, Churchwardens, with other inhabitants and
housekeepers within the parish of . . . . in the county
of . . . . doe hereby certify, that . . . . are our neighbors & fellow parishioners & persons of honest conversation,
living peacably & quietly amongst us . . . were never reputed
or suspected by any of us, as Popish Recusents, but are now
of that sort of protestants who are called Quakers. In witnesse
whereof wee have hereunto severally subscribed our names
this . . . . day of . . . . In the year of our Lord Christ
1681.

p. 147.

Contributions came in as followeth :

		£	s.	d.	
Imp.	Gainsbrough	00	13	10	
	Winteringham	00	12	00	
	Crowle	00	14	00	
	Brigg	00	14	00	Garthrope wanting
	Totall	02	13	10	
	Returnd to Gainsbrough	00	13	10	
	Returned to Butterwick	00	14	00	
	Rest yet in stock	01	06	00	

Ordered that a contribution be collected & brought into the next
Monthly Meeting which is to be at Thomas Wresles in Butterwick.

Signed by Joseph Richardson.

ATT a Monthly Meeting held at the house of Thomas Wresles
in Botterwick the 14th day of the first month 1690[1] :—

Whereas Gainsbrough Friends brought an account that they have
discoursed with Anthony Turner daughter about what shee
is willing to give to Friends out of what her father left her,
to the bringing up her sister, her answer was shee was willing
to give them £3, 20s. in hand, 20s. at Midsumer & 20s. at

[1] 14th March, 1690.

Martimas, soe that Friends of every Meeting is desired to inquire what Friends there is that are willing to take such a girl with that money & what Friends & they shall further agree on & bring an account to the next Monthly Meeting.

Whereas Robert Berrier of Ealand & his wife brought an account into this Meeting of the disposall of Appelline Brownes goods of Crowle, & of the payment of her debts, & has brought 25s. overplus into this meeting, Friends here haveing considered the trouble & care Robert & his wife have both had with the said children, have given them 15s. of the said money, with which they are both satisfied soe that 10s. remains of the said money.

Rested in Stock the last Monthly Meeting	01 : 06 : 00
the remainder of the Ile contribution	00 : 04 : 00
Garthrop last Monthly contribution	00 : 08 : 06
Totall	01 : 18 : 06
Disburst to John Pilsworth, senior towards the agreement with him for Widdow Browne son	01 : 10 : 00
alsoe allowed him for seavrall odd things for repairs the same time	00 : 03 : 08
Disburst to Michaell Beacock more towards the agreement with his apprentice ..	00 : 05 : 00

Contributions came into this meeting for the Quarterly Meeting service as followeth :—

p. 148.

	£	s.	d.
Imp. Gainsbrough	00 :	14 :	00
Butterwick	00 :	12 :	04
Winteringham	00 :	14 :	09
Brigge	00 :	14 :	00
Garthrop..	00 :	08 :	00
Totall	03 :	03 :	01

£ s. d.

Ordered to be carried up to the Quarterly Meeting : 03 : 00 : 00 the other 3s. 1d. disposed of to the Ile Meeting soe that nothing in stock.

The next Monthly Meeting appointed to be at Henry Symsons house in Gainsbrough.

ATT a Meeting held at the house of Henry Symsons in Gainsbrough the 11th of the 2d month 1690[1] :—

Ordered that Thomas Wresle, William Harrison & John Urrey see to the discharging of Mary Codd tabling with Jane Davis of Belton ; and what they disburse this Meeting will see them indemnified.

It is still desired that Freinds in there particular Meetings consider of a place convenient for Anthony Turner daughter.

The next Monthly Meeting appointed to be at the house of John Wresles in Thealby.

ATT a Monthly Meeting held at the house of John Wresles in Thealby the 9th of the 3d Month 1690[2] :—

Thomas Wresle brought an account into this Meeting that he with William Harrison & John Urrey has disburst to Jane Davis of Belton for Mary Codd tabling 30s., she being paid of before till the 16th day of the 11th Month 1689, & the said Mary Codd came from Jane Davis to John Pilsworth, senior the 18th of the 2d Month 1690.

And Friends of this Meeting has agreed with John Pilsworth, senior that his son Joseph of Epworth shall table the said Mary Codd for one year according to the agreement with Jane Davis of Belton being :

                                                                £   s.   d.
                                                               03 : 05 : 00

Inquiry being made for a setlement for Anthony Turner daughter among Friends but finding none, Freinds are willing that she should continue with her sister till a place present.

p. 149.

Ordered that John Pilsworth get such nessesaryes as is thought fitt for Mary Codd & bring the account to the next Monthly Meeting.

It is propounded by some Friends in this Meeting for the keeping of a Meeting one a month at David Crosbys in Gunhouse for the service of Truth & benifitt of Friends in there spiritual union & comunion one with another therein, & Friends have unanimously consented and agreed thereto, & that there be kept one this sumer every month begining the next 3d fourth day of this month & soe to continue the same day in every month, & that notice be given thereof accordingly.

It is alsoe desired by some Friends in this Meeting that the Woemens Meeting be further considered of & Friends have concluded that at the next Monthly Meeting, it be fully discoursed & setled to the satisfaction of Friends that desire it.

[1] 11th April, 1690.   [2] 9th May, 1690.

Ordered that a contribution be collected & brought up to the next Monthly Meeting from which Thomas Wresle is to have 30s. & John Howell 13s. 8d. & the rest to the Quarterly Meeting. Next Monthly Meeting ordered at Jane Morleys in Adlinfleet.

Signed by Joseph Richardson.

Att a Monthly Meeting held at the house of Jane Morleys in Adlinfleet the 13th day of the 4th month 1690[1] :—

The Woemens Meeting came under consideration in this Meeting & for some good causes it is thought convenient that the finall determination thereof be left to the next Monthly Meeting, where soe many Woemen Freinds as can with convenience are desired to be.

Contributions came in as followeth :—

	£	s.	d.
Winteringham	00	17	06
Gainsbrough	00	15	00
Crowle Meeting	00	16	03
Brigg	00	16	00
Garthrop	00	08	04
	03	13	01

	£	s.	d.
Disburst to John Pilsworth for nessesaries for Mary Codd by order of the last Monthly Meeting	00	07	10
Disburst to Thomas Wresle, William Harrison & John Orry upon Mary Codd account	01	10	00
Disburst to John Howell of Brigg being the remainder & full for an apprentice put to him by Friends of this Meeting ..	00	13	08

The remainder ordered for the service of the Quarterly Meeting.

Thomas Wresle & John Pilsworth are ordered to account with Jane Davis for Mary Codd tabling & bring an account to the next Monthly Meeting.

p. 150.

It is ordered by this Meeting that Thomas Wresle give to Jane Carnell & Cassandra Chapman six shillings for there present supply & this Meeting will see him indempnified.

It is ordered by this Meeting that the boy of Appelline Brownes be continued with Robert Berrier untill further order & in the mean time Friends are desired to see if they can finde a convenient place for him, & give notice to this Meeting.

[1] 13th June, 1690.

The next Monthly Meeting ordered at David Crosby house in
Gunhouse.

Signed by Joseph Richardson.

ATT a Monthly Meeting held at the house of David Crosbys
in Gunhouse the 11th of the 5th month 1690[1] :—

The refference of the Weomens Meeting came under consideration
in this Meeting & was fully debated & weightily considered
& Freinds unanimously consented & agreed, that the Woemens
Meeting be diligently kept with the Mens & that Freinds are
to take speciall care in each Perticular Meeting for the performance of that service, & when it is neglected, to be inquired
into the reasons thereof, that soe it may be kept & upheld to
the satisfaction of those that are weightily concerned therein.

The account with Jane Davis is yet referred to Thomas Wresle and
John Pilsworth & to bring it into the next Monthly
Meeting.

Thomas Wresle according to the order of the last Monthly Meeting
has laid down to Jane Carnell & Cassandra Chapman 3s. &
will lye down the other 3s. before the next Monthly Meeting
& bring an account thereof.

The next Monthly Meeting is appointed to be kept at John Urryes
in Epworth where both the men & woemen Friends are desired
to come up as much as in them lyes, for the performance of
both there services, & alsoe for the Worshipp of God as may
be had with convenience.

Signed by Joseph Richardson.

p. 151.

ATT a Meeting held at the house of John Urryes in Epworth
the 8th of the 6th month 1690[2] :—

Ordered by this Meeting that Thomas Wresle & Henry Hudson goe
& desire Widdow Stuttin of Burringham to come to the next
Monthly Meeting, in order for the setting forth, what shee
is willing to secure to Freinds for the use of her children in
this the time of her widdowhood.

	£	s.	d.
Thomas Wresle & John Pilsworth have accounted with Jane Davis of Belton for the tabling Mary Codd & there is yet oweing to her	00	07	09
Thomas Wresle has laid down the other 3s. to the 2 poor widdowes soe that this Meeting is indebted to him	00	06	00

[1] 11th July, 1690.   [2] 6th August, 1690.

The Generall Meeting for Worshipp is to be continued as first agreed at the house of David Crosbys the day that was formerly appointed.

The next Monthly ordered to be at Brigg & a contribution to be collected & brought up to it.

Signed by Joseph Richardson.

ATT a Monthly Meeting held at Brigge the 12th of the 7th month 90[1] :—

Contributions came in as followeth :—

	£	s.	d.
Imp. Gainsborough	01 :	01 :	06
Crowle	01 :	01 :	00
Winteringham	01 :	02 :	04
Brigge	01 :	02 :	00
Garthrop	00 :	08 :	00
In Stock	00 :	13 :	00
Totall	05 :	07 :	10

Disbursements :—

To Thomas Wresle for 2 poor widdows	00 : 06 : 00
To Thomas Wresle more for Jane Davis which clears of for Mary Codd	00 : 07 : 09
To John Pilsworth for ½ a year tabling of John Browne	01 : 10 : 00
To John Pilsworth more for shifts shoes & stockings for Browne	00 : 04 : 01
Ordered to the Quarterly Meeting	03 : 00 : 00
Makes up the abovesaid sum of	05 : 07 : 00

This money paid to John Pilsworth makes up for tabling John Brown a year the last first day of the 6th month 1690.

This Meeting has agreed with John Pilsworth, senior to give him the sum of four pound, for tabling John Browne next year, & John Pilsworth has promised to keep him that time at schooll.

[1] 12th September, 1690.

The business of Widdow Stuttin is reffered till next Monthly Meeting
& Thomas Wresle & Henry Hudson is desired to speak to
her to get ready & make her appearance the next Monthly
Meeting.

p. 152.

This day Thomas Wresle, Henry Simpson & Thomas Markham
was ordered by this Meeting to speak to John Odlin : which
accordingly they did, & had pretty much discourse with him
concerning his affairs & he has promised to soe order his affaires
as give them satisfaction at the next Monthly Meeting.

                                        £   s.   d.
This Meeting is indebted to Henry Simpson 00 : 04 : 00.
The next Monthly Meeting is to be at Brigge.

                    Signed by Joseph Richardson.

Att a Monthly Meeting held at Brigg the 10th of 8th month
1690[1] :—

Widdow Stuttin bussiness being neglected by those appointed :
Thomas Wresle & Henry Hudson are desired to speak to her
againe to get all things ready and make her appearance at
the next Monthly Meeting.

Freinds of Spalding Monthly Meeting haveing lately had under
there consideration the low estate of William Birkes belonging
to there Meeting & finding his condition to stand in need of
supplyes from Freinds of other Meetings, they have sent a
letter to this Meeting to request Freinds charity on his behalf,
which hath been read & considered of in this Meeting, but
reffered to the next Monthly Meeting what Freinds are free &
willing to doe in that matter.

Freinds of this Meeting are desired to acquaint Freinds in there
Perticular Meetings, what sufferings they have sustained by
priest or impropriator upon the account of tythe for this last
year & to make them ready & bring them up an account
thereof to the next Meeting.

Thomas Wresle of Winteringham & William West was ordered
by this Meeting to goe to John Odlin againe, to get his answer,
and accordingly did & he has ingaged to appeare at the next
Monthly Meeting & give Freinds full satisfaction as touching
his affaires.

The next Monthly Meeting ordered to be at Brigge.

                    Signed by Joseph Richardson.

[1] 10th October, 1690.

p. 153.

ATT a Monthly Meeting held at Brigge the 14th of the 9th month 90[1] :—

Thomas Wresle & Henry Hudson according to the order of the last Meeting spoke with Widdow Stuttin & her answer was that shee was not unwilling to settle something on her children soe Friends have ordered Thomas Wresle, Thomas Markham & David Crosby to goe to her before the next meeting & settle things as well as they can for the good of the children & give an account to the next Meeting.

William Birkes condition came under consideration in this Meeting & much debate was held about it, & at last it was agreed, in the first place to advise with some Friends at the Quarterly Meeting, to have a better understanding of things before Friends can tell what to doe in that matter tho there is not an unwillingnes in Friends to contribute to his assistance, after they are satisfied what kindness there charity will doe him.

The account of suffering for tythe for this present year was brought into this Meeting from all Meetings except Garthrop, & they have promised to take care to get theres ready & bring into the next Monthly Meeting, & soe ordered to be sent to John Whitehead to be recorded.

John Odlin being from home at this time, Edward Gilliat & Joseph Richardson are desired to speak to him once more to appear at the next Monthly Meeting, there to give Freinds satisfaction in things they have to propound to him.

Ordered that a contribution be collected & brought up to the next Monthly Meeting which is to be at Brigge.

Signed by Joseph Richardson.

ATT a Monthly Meeting held at the Meeting House at Edward Giliatts in Brigg the 12th of the 10th month 1690[2] :—

Widdow Stuttin bussines of Burringham being neglected against this Monthly Meeting, it is still desired that Thomas Wresle, Thomas Markham & David Crosby goe to her & setle things as well as they can for the good of the children & give an account thereof to the next Monthly Meeting.

No Friends coming from Garthrop meeting John Wresle is desired to put them in minde to bring up there suffering for tythe the next Monthly Meeting.

[1] 14th November, 1690.   [2] 12th December, 1690.

John Odlin being still from home & the consideration of his affaires comeing before Freinds of this Meeting, they have drawn up a paper of advice which is to be recorded, & ordered to be sent to him.

p. 154.

Here followes a true coppy which was sent to John Odlin & his wife & delivered by the hande of Thomas Markham.

To Freinds John Odlin & Sarah,

Wee being this day met together in the fear of God in relation to the affaires of Truth, & haveing under our consideration your present condition & being informed by Friends of Brigg Meeting, that you have seaverall times been both spoken & written too by them, & alsoe seaverall times sent too by order of this Monthly Meeting, advising you to regulate what hath been amiss both in yourselves & family, & alsoe to take some speedy care to satisfy what just debts are upon you according to your abillity, that Truth & Freinds may not be reproached, nor yourselves cut off from the body as a branch fruitless.

Therefore wee have upon weighty considerations come to this result once more to advise you to take a true account of what you owe & to whome, & to take a speedy course to get in what is oweing to you, and forthwith expose to saile all your estate that is in your possesion then offer to all your creditors what composition your estate will make to them, & if they agree thereto, to distribute it amongst them proportionably, that soe the clamour of your creditors may be stopped, your conscience discharged, Truth & Friends cleared as much as in you lye & you put into a capacity to earn bread for the sustenance of your selves & family, that both you & they perish not together.

But if you will still regard no councell neither adhere to our sober advice but put off & make delayes as heretofore you have done we hereby signify to you that we shall be nessessitated to disown you by giveing out a Testimony against you for the clearing of the Truth which we make proffession of, & that the world may know you have been faithfully warned.

Note alsoe that above 6 months agoe a paper of wholesome advice & councell was given him, but he like an unworthy man comited it imeadiately to the flames, a coppy of which may be seen at Edward Gilliats remaining as a Testimony against him.

Contributions came in as followeth :—

				£	s.	d.
Imp.	Buterwick	..	..		14 :	06
	Winteringham	..	..		17 :	09
	Brigg	..	..	..		17 :	00
	Garthrop..	..	..		08 :	00
	Totall	..	..	..	03 :	15 :	09

Disbusments :—

		£	s.	d.
To Joseph Pilsworth for half year for Mary Codd		01 :	12 :	06
To Thomas Wresle that he laid down to 2 widdowes ..		00 :	02 :	00
To Robert Colyer for close for young Browne ..		00 :	06 :	10
To Henry Symson which was oweing by the Meeting ..		00 :	04 :	00
To the Quarterly Meeting ..		01 :	10 :	02

The next Monthly Meeting to be at Brigge.

p. 155.

ATT a Monthly Meeting held at the Meeting House at Edward Gilliatts in Brigge the 9th of the 11th Month 1690[1] :—

Garthrop Freinds haveing brought into this Meeting an account of there suffering for tythe for this present yeare, are ordered forthwith to be sent by some of Gainsbrough Freinds to our dear freind John Whitehead in order to be ingrossed.

Thomas Markham has brought an account into this Meeting that he with Joseph Richardson, had been with Widdow Stuttin of Burringham & shee has promised them to take speedy care to answer Friends request in the setlement of her childrens portions, & Freinds of this Meeting desires David Crosby to see it be done, & give an account thereof to the next Monthly Meeting.

A paper was read in this Meeting which came from the Quarterly Meeting signifying the debts that are upon them & request of Freinds to make two contributions throughout the County against the next Quarterly Meeting, which was agreed too.

And this Meeting has ordered the first contribution be collected & brought up to the next Monthly Meeting which is to be at Brigge.

[1] 11th January, 1691.

Att a Monthly Meeting held at the house of Edward Gilliatt in Brigge the 13th of the 12th month 1690[1] :—

Thomas Markham & Joseph Richardson are ordered by this Meeting to get bonds drawn, for security of Widdow Stuttins childrens portions, & to send them to David Crosby to get signed against the next Monthly Meeting.

Some Freinds of Brigg Meeting are desired once more to reminde John Odlin, to answer Friends request before the next Monthly Meeting, else they are determined to give forth a Testimony against him.

Contributions came in as followeth :—

	£	s.	d.
Gainsbrough	00	16	00
Butterwick	00	16	09
Winteringham	00	16	00
Brigge	00	14	00

Disbursements as followeth :—   £   s.   d.

To Anthony Morrice for John Pilsworth tabling Browne which makes up half a year ending the first day of this present ..   ..   ..   02 : 00 : 00

To Thomas Wresle for 2 poor widdows of there Meeting   00 : 04 : 00

To Joseph Richardson for 2 poor widdows in there Meeting ..   ..   ..   00 : 07 : 00

Rests yet in stock in Joseph Richardson hands the sum of 01 : 01 : 09.

William Martin of Brigg came this day into our Monthly Meeting & published his intentions of marriage with Anne Mitchell of the same, & she with her father & mother being present gave there free consent, but it being the first time they are desired to wait Friends answer till the next Monthly Meeting.

Ordered that another contribution be collected & brought up to the next Monthly Meeting, when Friends nessessity being supplyed the rest to be carried up to the Quarterly Meeting.

Next Monthly Meeting to be at Brigg.

Signed by Joseph Richardson.

[1] 13th February, 1691.

p. 156.

ATT a Monthly Meeting held at the Meeting House at Edward Gilliats in Brigg the 13th of the first month 1691[1] :—

The busines of Widdow Stuttins children was discoursed in this Meeting, & left still to Thomas Wresle, Anthony Morrice & David Crosby to effect as an oppertunity with there good likeing presents.

John Odlins busines was this day seariously considered and weightily discoursed & in regard the Quarterly Meeting is near, Friends have agreed to take there advice how further to proceed with him.

Contributions came in as followeth :—

	£	s.	d.
Gainsbrough		13 :	06
Butterwick		13 :	06
Winteringham		13 :	06
Brigge		16 :	00
Garthrop		13 :	06
Totall	04 :	11 :	09

Disbursments as followeth :—

	£	s.	d.
Imps. to Michaell Beacock being in full for his apprentice the sum of	01 :	00 :	00
To John Pilsworth more being in full for ½ year.. ..	00 :	10 :	00
To Thomas Wresle, Butterwick for 2 poor widdows ..	00 :	01 :	09
Ordered to the Quarterly Meeting	03 :	00 :	00

It is desired that Joseph Richardson lye down 5s. for supplying the nessesities of a poor woman Friend in that Meeting, & bring an account thereof to the next Monthly Meeting.

John Pilsworth is alsoe desired to get some close for the repairs of Mary Codd & bring an account thereof to the next Monthly Meeting.

This day William Martin of Brigg & Anne Mitchell of the same came a second time into our Meeting, & signified the continuance of there purpose of marriage each with other, and Friends finding nothing to hinder there said proceedings, have left the consumation thereof to themselves with the advice of Friends according to the good order of Truth.

The next Monthly Meeting ordered to be at Henry Simpsons in Gainsbrough.

Signed by Joseph Richardson.

[1] 13th March, 1691.

ATT a Monthly Meeting held at the house of Henry Simpsons in Gainsbrough the 10th of the 2d month 1691[1] :—

The business of Widdow Stuttins is yet left to Thomas Wresle, Anthony Morrice & David Crosby.

Abraham Northen in Gainsbrough came into this Meeting & published his intentions of marriage with Martha Smith of the same, & shee being present gave her consent, & they alsoe brought 2 certificates one from his mother, & the other from her unkle, signifying both there willingnes thereunto, but it being the first time they are desired to wait Friends answer till the next Monthly Meeting.

It is ordered that a contribution be collected & brought to the next Monthly Meeting which is to be at Thomas Wresles in Beltoft.

Signed by Joseph Richardson.

p. 157.

ATT a Monthly Meeting held at the house of Thomas Wresles in Beltoft the 8th of the 3d month 1691[2] :—

It is agreed by this Meeting that a Meeting be kept once a month at the house of David Crosbys dureing this sumer season, to be held the 3d 4th day of this month, & soe to continue every 3d 4th day of every month, for this sumer time.

Abraham Northen of Gainsbrough came a second time into our Monthly Meeting and published the continuance of his intentions of marriage with Martha Smith of the same, & shee being present gave her consent, & Freinds haveing nothing against there proceedings, have left the consumation thereof to themselves with the advice of Freinds according to the good order of Truth.

Contributions came in as followeth :—

	£	s.	d.
Gainsbrough		12 :	06
Crowle		15 :	09
Winteringham		14 :	06
Brigge		14 :	06
Garthrop		00 :	00
In Stock		07 :	03
Totall	3 :	04 :	06

[1] 10th April, 1691.   [2] 8th May, 1691.

Disbursments :—	£	s.	d.
To Henry Simson for Oakly Shields	00	02	00
To John Pilsworth for his son Joseph for tabling Mary Codd for half a year	01	12	06
To John Wresle for releife of Dinah Wood..	00	05	00
To Joseph Richardson for Mary Goxhill ..	00	02	06
To Thomas Wresle for Jane Carnell & Cassandra Chapman	00	06	06
for letters	00	01	06
In Stock yet in Joseph Richardson hands ..	00	14	06

The next Monthly Meeting ordered to be at Thealby & a contribution collected & brought up thither.

p. 158.

ATT a Monthly Meeting held at the house of John Wresles in Thealby the 12th of the 4th Month 1691[1] :—

Francis Dent of Roxby came this day into our Monthly Meeting and published his intention of marriage with Sarah Champion of Blyth, & brought with him a certificate, from there Monthly Meeting, signifying he had done the same there, as a few lines he brought under her hand signifying her willingness & consent thereunto, but it being the first time, they are desired to wait Freinds answer till the next Monthly Meeting.

Contributions came in as followeth :—

	£	s.	d.
Gainsbrough		12	00
Crowle		16	00
Winteringham		15	06
Brigge		15	00
Garthrop		10	00
In Stock		14	06
	04	03	00

Disbursments :—

To Joseph Pilsworth of Epworth the sum of 8s. which we thinke will clear all the charge on her to him till the 19th of the 3d month 1691, att which time, Mary Codd left Joseph Pilsworth & went to table with John Potters of Lea, but have allowed but for a month must look the book to see if that clear all for Joseph Pilsworth.

The next Monthly Meeting ordered to be at John Clarks house in Garthrop.

Signed by Joseph Richardson.

[1] 12th June, 1691.

ATT a Monthly Meeting held at the house of John Clarks in Garthrop the 10th day of the 5th Month 1691[1] :—

Whereas complaint hath been made to this Meeting, that John Pilsworth, junior in Epworth & his wife, doth dishonour the Truth by there dishorderly walking, it is therefore ordered by this Meeting that there Meeting be removed from his house, untill they manifest repentance & amendment of life, & that Thomas Wresle & Anthony Morrice let them know, this Meeting desires there appearance at the next Monthly Meeting.

The care of the collecting George Fox books or paper printed or written according to the advice of the Yearly Meeting, is left to the consideration of the next Monthly Meeting.

p. 159.

Ordered by this Meeting that the care of the generall contribution be left to the consideration of the next Monthly Meeting.

This day Francis Dent of Thealby came a second time into our Monthly Meeting, & signified the continuance of his purpose of marriage with Sarah Champion of Blyth, & haveing brought with him a certificate from the Monthly Meeting to which she belongs, that all things are clear on her part & we also finding the same on his part, have left the consumation thereof to themselves with the advice of Freinds according to the good order of Truth.

The next Monthly Meeting ordered to be at the house of John Urryes in Epworth.

Signed by Joseph Richardson.

ATT a Monthly Meeting held at the house of John Urryes in Epworth the 14th of the 6th Month 1691[2] :—

It is desired by Freinds of this Meeting that Friends in there respective Meetings make search for all books, papers and manuscripts given forth by dear George Fox, & write the titles & dates of each perticular booke, and the first and last sentence of each perticular paper & manuscript.

Ordered that our ordenary contribution be collected & brought up to the next Monthly Meeting.

The next Monthly Meeting be held at the house of David Crosbys in Gunhouse.

Signed by Joseph Richardson.

[1] 10th July, 1691.   [2] 14th August, 1691.

p. 160.

ATT a Monthly Meeting held at the house of David Crosbys in Gunhouse the 11th of the 7th Month 1691[1] :—

The bookes & papers given forth by dear George Fox was brought into this Meeting, & the titles & dates was taken down & sent to London according to the desire of Freinds.

Contributions came in as followeth :—

	£	s.	d.
Gainsbrough		14	: 06
Crowle		12	: 00
Winteringham		13	: 06
Brigg		15	: 00
Garthrop		08	: 00
Stock		08	: 00
Totall	03	: 11	: 00

Disbursments :—

	£	s.	d.
First to Henry Simpson	00	: 00	: 11
To John Pilsworth, senior for half a year for young Brown the sum of	02	: 00	: 00
To Thomas Wresle of Beltoft for 2 poor widdowes in the Ile	00	: 02	: 11
To the Quarterly Meeting being all we have..	01	: 07	: 00

Ordered that the nationall contribution be collected & brought up to the next Quarterly Meeting.

This Meeting have unanimously agreed that a Meeting be kept the last 6th day in everey month at Thealby belonging to Winteringham Meeting for the worshipp of God & to begin the last 6th day of this month.

Ordered that the next Monthly Meeting be held at the house of Thomas Wresles in Beltoft.

Signed by Joseph Richardson.

p. 161.

ATT a Monthly Meeting held at the house of Thomas Wresles in Beltoft the 9th of 8br 1691[2] :—

It is desired by this Meeting that the Freinds of the respective Meetings, bring up there sufferings for tythes & all other sufferings upon Truths account to the next Monthly Meeting, which is ordered be at Brigge.

Signed by Joseph Richardson.

[1] 11th September, 1691.   [2] 9th October, 1691.

B

ATT a Monthly Meeting held at the Meeting House att Edward Gilliatts the 13th of the 9th month 1691[1] :—

In answer to Friends request at the last Monthly Meeting the Isle & Winteringham Meeting have brought up there sufferings for tythe, & Gainsbrough, Brigg & Garthrop Meeting is desired to have theres ready against the next Monthly Meeting.

This day Jabez Bethell of Brigg came into our Monthly Meeting & signified his purpose of marriage with Anne Theaker of Cunsby, & brought a certificate with him from Friends of the Monthly Meeting to which shee doth belong, signifying her willingness & consent thereunto, it being the first time they are desired to wait Friends answer till the next Monthly Meeting.

Ordered that a contribution be collected & brought up to the next Monthly Meeting which is to be at Brigge.

Signed by Joseph Richardson.

ATT a Monthly Meeting held at the Meeting House att Edward Gilliats the 10th of the 10th month 1691[2] :—

According to Friends desire Gainsbrough, Brigg & Garthrop have brought in there sufferings for tythe, and ordered Joseph Richardson to make them ready & send the first opportunity to John Whitehead.

This day Jabez Bethell of Brigge came a second tyme into our Monthly Meeting, & signified the continuance of his purpose of marriage with Anne Theaker of Cunsby, & brought with him a certificate from Friends of the Monthly Meeting to which shee doth belong, signifying that he had done the like with them, & that they had given there approbation (p. 162) and consent to the purpose of the said parties, & Freinds of this Meeting finding nothing to the contrary on his part have likewise left the consumation thereof to themselves with the advice of Freinds according to the good order of Truth.

Contributions came in as followeth :—   £   s.   d.

Gainsbrough	..	..	..	14	:	09
Crowle	..	..	..	14	:	03
Winteringham	..	..	..	15	:	06
Brigge	..	..	..	15	:	00
Garthrop	..	..	..	08	:	00
				03 : 07 : 06		

[1] 13th November, 1691.   [2] 10th December, 1691.

Disbursments :—   £   s.   d.

Imps. to Joseph Potter for his father tabling
    of Mary Codd half a year the sum of   01 : 12 : 06
to Henry Symson which he laid down for
    aprons   ..   ..   00 : 01 : 10½
to Joseph Richardson which he laid
    down last Quarterly Meeting   ..   00 : 00 : 10
to Easter Stephenson of Elsham   ..   00 : 02 : 03
the rest to the Quarterly Meeting being   01 : 10 : 00

Ordered that the next Monthly Meeting be at Brigg.

Signed by Joseph Richardson.

ATT a Monthly Meeting held at the Meeting House at Edward Gilliats in Brigge the 8th of the 11th Month 1691[1] :—

Joseph Richardson according to the order of the last Monthly Meeting drew up the account of Friends suffering for tythe & sent them away to John Whitehead.

The consideration of Ester Stephenson condition came before this Monthly Meeting, & the Woemen Friends of Brigge Meeting are desired it as touching her son, & give an account to the next Monthly Meeting.

This Monthly Meeting being informed that John Pilsworth wife, junior of Epworth hath at present left comeing to Meetings, by reason of some difference betwixt her & her husband, some Friends of there Meeting are desired to know of her the reason, & bring an account to the next Monthly Meeting.

Thomas Wresle of Winteringham has Elizabeth Bathurst booke & is desired to send it thro the Meetings till it get back to Brigg, & call of the Ile Freinds for John Hoggs book & the answer & another great book that was to goe through the Meetings.

The next Monthly Meeting ordered at Brigge.

Signed by Joseph Richardson.

p. 163.

ATT a Monthly Meeting held at the Meeting House att Edward Gilliats in Brigg the 12th of the 12th month 1691[2] :—

The consideration of Hester Stephenson business touching her son is reffered to the next Monthly Meeting.

The business touching the wife of John Pilsworth, junior in Epworth is refered to the next Monthly Meetinge.

Remember to make inquiry for John Hoggs booke & the answer with another great book that was to goe through the Meetings, it being concluded by Friends that where books comes amongst

[1] 8th January, 1692.   [2] 12th February, 1692.

us but one of a sort, that after Friends in there respective Meetings have had the perusall of them they be lodged in the Meeting House at Brigge, where Friends may have recourse to them upon any occasion that may offer.

Ordered that a contribution be collected & brought up to the next Monthly Meeting where Friends nescessityes being supplyed the rest to goe to the Quarterly Meetinge.

The next Monthly Meeting ordered to be at Brigge.

Signed by Joseph Richardson.

ATT a Monthly Meeting held at the Meeting House in Edward Gilliats at Brigg the 11th of the first month 1691/2[1] :—

John Pilsworth, senior of Epworth gave an account to this Meeting that Mary Morrice & Mary Berrier according to the order of the last Monthly Meeting, had spoke to his son John wife and that shee had promised them shee would satisfy Freinds by writeing soe this Meeting desires that John Pilsworth, senior & the 2 weomen Friends aforesaid goe & speak to her againe in order to perform her promise & bring an account to the next Monthly Meeting.

The inquiry after John Hoggs book & the answer with the other great bound book is left to the next Monthly Meeting.

Contributions came in as followeth :—

		£	s.	d.
Imps. Gainsbrough	.. ..	00	14	00
Crowle	.. .. ..	00	16	06
Winteringham	..	00	17	06
Brigge	.. .. ..	00	15	00
Garthrop not come	..	–	–	–
Totall	.. ..	03	03	00
In Stock	.. ..	00	11	00
Totall	.. ..	03	14	00

p. 164.

Disbursments :—

	£	s.	d.
To John Pilsworth for half a year for young Browne	02	00	00
more to John Pilsworth for shifts & stockings for same boy	00	04	00
To Joseph Richardson which he laid down at Quarterly Meeting soe that nothing remains in Stock	01	10	00

[1] 11th March, 1692.

The nescessities of Ester Stephenson of Elsham was laid before this meeting againe & some Friends of Brigg Meeting were ordered to lye down 10s. for her present supply till money be raised to reimburse them againe.

Godfrey Newbold, junior in Woodhouse lately a member of our Monthly Meeting came this day & signified his intentions of marriage with Hannah Atherton of Barnsley in Yorkshire & brought with him a certificate from there Monthly Meeting signifying he had done the same with them & alsoe 2 certificates more from his father & her father & mother, signifying there willingness & consent thereunto, & we knowing nothing here but that all things are clear on his part have left the further determination thereof to the advice of Friends he respectively belongs according to the good order of Truth.

The consideration of the settlement of a week day Meeting in each Meeting is left to be determined at the next Monthly Meeting which is to be at David Crosbys in Gunhouse.

Signed by Joseph Richardson.

ATT a Monthly Meeting held at the house of David Crosbys in Gunhouse the 8th of the 2d Month 1692[1] :—

Thomas Wresle & David Crosby is desired by this Meeting to goe & speak to John Pilsworth wife junior & desire her to perform her promise by writeing to give the Monthly Meeting satisfaction or make her personall appearance.

Thomas Wresle, Beltoft is desired to lye down 7s. 6d. for a coffin for Jane Carnill & to be reimbursed againe by the next Monthly Meeting.

It is concluded by Friends of this Meeting that the generall Meeting which is to be held at the house of David Crosbys dureing this sumer season, begin the 2d 4th day of the 3d Month next & soe the 2d 4th day in every month dureing the time.

The Ile & Gainsbrough Friends have taken into consideration the settlement of a weekly Meeting till the next Monthly Meeting, there to be fully resolved.

The inquiry after the bookes is referd to the next Monthly Meeting which is to be at Henry Symsons in Gainsbrough.

Signed by Joseph Richardson.

p. 165.

ATT a Monthly Meeting held at the house of Henry Symsons in Gainsbrough the 13th of 3d month 1692[2] :—

Thomas Wresle & David Crosby gave account to this Meeting that they could not get to speak to John Pilsworth wife junior

---

[1] 8th April, 1692.   [2] 13th May, 1692.

in Epworth but if any Friends have any thing in there mindes yet speak or write to her they are desired by this Meeting not to neglect it.

Thomas Wresle has laid down the money for Jane Carnill coffin & is to be reimbursed by the next Monthly Meeting.

Gainsbrough Friends have concluded to keep there Meeting on the week day the first 6th day in every month.

The Ile Friends have concluded to keep there weekly Meeting the first 3d day in every month.

The books that were inquired after are brought into this Meeting in order to be lodged at Brigg Meeting House.

The geting of some repaires for Mary Codd is left to Gainsbrough Friends & bring an account to the next Monthly Meeting.

Ordered that a contribution be collected & brought into the next Monthly Meeting which is to be at Thealby.

Signed by Joseph Richardson.

ATT a Monthly Meeting held at the house of John Wresles in Thealby the 10th of the 4th month 1692[1] :—

Joseph Richardson went to John Pilsworth house junior in order to speak to his wife, for the clearing of himself & the blessed Truth which we profess, but could not obtaine her company, nevertheless Friends of this Meeting, have yet left that concern to those who feells stirrings & drawings in there hearts in the love of God towards her.

Contributions came in as followeth :—

	£	s.	d.
Gainsbrough	00	18	66
Crowle	00	16	03
Winteringham	01	01	00
Brigge	00	19	00
Garthrop	00	07	00
before from Garthrop	00	09	00
Totall	04	10	09

Disburst as followeth :—

	£	s.	d.
to Joseph Richardson for Ester Stephenson		10	00
to Thomas Wresle for Jane Carnill coffin		07	06
to David Crosby for Widdow Bradhead		02	00
to Henry Symson for Mary Codd	01	12	06
to Henry more for a pair shoes	00	02	02
to Robert Colyer for young Brown	00	08	08
to the Quarterly Meeting	01	10	00

[1] 10th June, 1692.

The next Monthly Meeting ordered to be at Jane Morleys in Adlinfleet.

Signed by Joseph Richardson.

p. 166.

ATT a Monthly Meeting held at the house of Jane Morleys
in Adlinfleet the 8th day of the 5th month 1692[1] :—

Thomas Markham hath indeavourd to speak with the wife of John
Pilsworth, junior in Epworth, that Freinds might know the
cause wherefore shee withdraws her self from Freinds, but
shee absented her self & would not be speak withall, soe that
it is still left to Friends freedoms to seek another oppertunity
with her & give an account to the next Monthly Meeting.

It is ordered that the next Monthly Meeting be held at the house
of Thomas Wresles in Beltoft.

Signed by Joseph Richardson.

ATT a Monthly Meeting held at the houes of John[2] Wresles
in Beltoft the 13th of the 6th Month 1692[3] :—

Freinds not yet obtaining an oppertunity with John Pilsworth wife
junior in Epworth for the clearing of themselves & the blessed
Truth, it is yet left to such Friends as feells any thing yet in
there hearts towards her to use there indeavour therein, &
give an account to the next Monthly Meeting.

Anthony Westoby of Winteringham came into this Meeting &
published his intentions of marriage with Anne[4] Austine of
Lincolne, but brought no certificate with him either from
Friends or the party cheifly concernd for Friends satisfaction,
soe that this Meeting have writt to them desireing there care
& consideration in giveinge Friends more ample satisfaction
at our next Monthly Meeting.

It is desired that a contribution be collected & brought into the
next Monthly Meetinge which is to be at John Urryes in
Epworth.

Signed by Joseph Richardson.

p. 167.

ATT a Monthly Meeting held at the house of John Urryes in
Epworth the 9th of the 7th month 1692[5] :—

Whereas Jane Morley of Adlinfleet was desired to take an oppertunity
to speak with John Pilsworth wife junior in Epworth & bring
an account thereof to this Meeting we understand shee could
not obtaine the same with convenience, & therefore leaves
it still with her as time & oppertunity shall present.

---

[1] 15th July, 1692.   [2] *Sic: recte* Thomas.   [3] 13th August, 1692.
[4] *Sic: recte* Elizabeth.   [5] 9th September, 1692.

Contributions came in as followeth :—

	£	s.	d.
Gainsbrough	01 :	01 :	00
Crowle	00 :	17 :	06
Winteringham	00 :	18 :	06
Brigge	00 :	19 :	06
Garthrop	00 :	09 :	00
Totall	04 :	05 :	06

Disbursments :—

	£	s.	d.
to Brigg upon a generall account	00 :	10 :	00
to Crowle for Cassandra Chapman	00 :	05 :	00
to John Pilsworth for ½ year ending the first day of the 6th month 92 for young Brown	02 :	00 :	00
To Thomas Potter for repairs of Mary Codd..	00 :	10 :	11
Totall	03 :	05 :	11

	£	s.	d.
Rests yet in Joseph Richardson hands	00 :	19 :	07½

which he is desired to make up

	£	s.	d.
thirty shillings	01 :	10 :	00

& carry to the next Quarterly Meeting & this Meeting will see him indempnified.

The case of our suffering Freinds in Ireland touching a collection for there present releife has been under consideration in this Meeting and is referd to the Quarterly Meeting to have there advice in soe weighty & good a work.

This day Anthony Westoby of Winteringham came a second tyme into our Monthly Meeting, & signified the continuance of his purpose of marriage with Elizabeth Austine of Lincolne & brought a certificate with him from there Monthly Meeting signifying her willingness & consent thereunto, & Friends here finding nothing to object against there proceedings but that all things were clear on his part have left the consumation thereof to themselves with the advice of Friends according to the good order of Truth.

The next Monthly Meeting ordered to be at Brigge.

Signed by Joseph Richardson.

p. 168.

ATT a Monthly Meeting held att the Meeting House at Edward Gilliatts the 14th of the 8th month 1692[1] :—

An account was brought before Freinds in this Meeting that Jane Morley of Adlinfleet could not yet meet with an oppertunity conveniently to speak with John Pilsworth wife, junior in

[1] 14th October, 1692.

Epworth, but that shee intended to use her indeavour before the next Monthly Meeting & give an account of the same.

The case of suffering Friends in Ireland touching a collection for there present releife, was a second tyme under the consideration of this Meeting & Gainsbrough & the Ile Meeting have both collected and brought it into this Meeting but Winteringham, Brigg and Garthrop are yet to collect theres the next first day & send it the first oppertunity to Lincolne.

	£	s.	d.
Gainsbrough collection ..	08 :	14 :	06
The Iles was	05 :	00 :	00
	13 :	14 :	06

This Meeting desires that Friends in there Perticular Meetings bring in there severall accounts of suffering for tythes & bring them into the next Monthly Meeting.

This Meeting alsoe desires as by advice from the Quarterly Meeting that some Friends in every Meeting acquaint Friends to make there wills in time of health for preventing future inconveniency, & that they keep up the antient Testimony of Truth against the world, feastings, fastings & fachions.

Some Freinds in Brig Meeting have made complaint to this Meeting concerning Nickholas Wilkinsons dissorderly walking soe that they have desired Thomas Markham & Robert Colyer to wish him to appear at the next Monthly Meeting, to clear himself if he can of what Friends have to charge him withall & bring his answer to the next Monthly Meeting.

Some Friends of Brigg Meeting are desired to draw up a paper concerning Friends antient Testimony in many Perticular things & comunicate it to the next Monthly Meeting which is ordered to be at Brigg.

Signed in behalf of the Meeting

by Joseph Richardson.

p. 169.

ATT a Monthly Meeting held at the Meeting House at Edward Gilliats in Brigg the 11th of the 9th Month 1692[1] :—

The case of John Pilsworth wife junior in Epworth is yet refred & left to Jane Morley of Adlinfleet who is still desired to take the first convenient oppertunity to speak to her & bring in her answer to the next Monthly Meeting.

According to the order of the last Monthly Meeting Winteringham, Brigge & Garthrop Meetings have collected for the supply of the poor suffering Friends in Ireland & with what was collected

---

[1] 11th November, 1692.

before from Gainsbrough & the Ile made up in all from this
Monthly Meeting the sum of thirty pounds : & Thomas Markham
& Robert Colyer carried it to Lincolne in order to be sent
towards London for the service aforesaid.

Whereas the last Monthly Meeting ordered every Perticular
Meeting to bring in there account of suffering for tythe, Gainsbrough onely has brought theres into this Meeting, & the
Ile, Winteringham, Brigg & Garthrop are desired to have theres
ready against the next Monthly Meeting.

The nessesities of Hester Stephenson & Mary Goxhill was laid
before this Meeting, & they have ordered some of Brigg Freinds
to releive them with a present supply & this Meeting will see
them indempnified.

Brigge Freinds are still desired to draw up Friends antient Testimony
& many perticular things & comunicate it to the next Monthly
Meeting.

This Meeting desires that a contribution be collected & brought
into the next Monthly Meeting where Friends nessessities being
supplyed the rest to be carried up to the Quarterly Meeting.

Nickolas Wilkinson not appearing at this Meeting as Friends desired
they have drawn up the following paper & have ordered it
to be given unto him.

p. 170.

Nickholas Wilkinson,

Whereas Thomas Markham & Robert Colyer with some
others have divers times spoken to thee about thy disorderly
walking in seaverall respects, and instead of amendment
thou hast rather grown worse, to the reproach of Truth &
greife of honest harted Friends. Therefore complaint was
made against thee at our last Monthly Meeting, & they ordered
Thomas Markham & Robert Colyer to speak to thee & desire
thy appearance at this Meeting to answer to such thing as
Friends have to charge thee withall, but wee understand thy
answer was to them thou did not intend to appear as thou
hast manifested it this day, whereby thou shuns the oppertunity
of clearing thy self or comeing under condemnation if thou
be found guilty. Therefore wee doe once more in love to thy
soule, & for clearing of the blessed Truth of which wee make
profession & for discharge of our consciences to the same,
desire thy appearance at our next Monthly Meeting to give
Friends such satisfaction as they & the Truth requires in
such cases, otherwise wee doe signify by these few lines that
wee shall be constrained then & there to give forth a Testimony
against thee & let the world know our christian indeevours
have not been a wanting towards thee.

Given forth at our Monthly Meeting held at Brigg the 11th day of the 9th month 1692.[1]

Subscribed by

William Smith.	Robert Coakes.	
William West.	Joseph Berrier.	Joseph Richardson.
Thomas Wresle	William Williamson.	
William Browne.	Thomas Nainby.	John Howell.
Francis Dent.	Jabez Bethell.	

Next Monthly Meeting ordered at Brigge.

Signed in behalf of the Meetinge

by Joseph Richardson.

p. 171.

ATT a Monthly Meeting held at the Meeting House at Edward Gilliats the 9th day of the 10th month 1692[2] :—

Jane Morley of Adlinfleet is yet desired to take an oppertunity to speak with John Pilsworth wife junior of Epworth & bring her answer to the next Monthly Meeting.

Brigg Friends are yet desired some of them to draw up a paper of Friends antient testimony in many perticular things, & comunicate it to the next Monthly Meeting.

According to the order of the last Monthly Meeting the Ile, Brigg, Winteringham & Garthrop brought in there accounts of suffering for tythe & Joseph Richardson is desired to draw them up together & send them the first oppertunity to our dear Freind John Whitehead.

Contributions came in as followeth :—

	£	s.	d.
Gainsbrough	00	18	09
Crowle	00	13	00
Winteringham	00	15	06
Brigg	00	17	00
Garthrop	00	08	00
Totall	03	12	03

Disbursments as followeth :—

	£	s.	d.
For half a year for Mary Codd table	01	12	06
more for repaires for her	00	04	00
to Mary Goxhill & Ester Steenson	00	15	00
Rests in Joseph Richardsons hands	01	00	01

& he is desired to make it up 30s. for the service of the Quarterly Meeting, & this Meeting will repay it againe.

[1] 11th November, 1692.   [2] 9th December, 1692.

Peter Naylor of Gainsbrough is desired to lye down 5s. for the
    releife of Mary Broadhead & this Meeting will see him indemni-
    fied.

Whereas a paper was writt from the last Monthly Meeting & delivered
    to Nickalos Wilkinson of Brigg concerning his disorderly walking
    he appeared at this Meeting & after Friends had pretty much
    debate with him, & manifested to him many errors he had
    done & comited he seemed to sorry & promised to amend &
    take Friends advice wherby he had brought a reproach upon
    the Truth & proffessors thereof which Friends was willing
    to accept & see if he performed his promises before the next
    Monthly Meeting.

Next Monthly Meeting ordered to be at Brigge.

                            Signed by Joseph Richardson.

        ATT a Monthly Meeting held at Brigg the 13 day of 11 Month
1692/3[1] :—

Jane Morley spoak to John Pilsworth wife to know wherfore she
    came not to our Meetings as formerly & her answer was that
    Freinds left her by takeing the Meeting from there house—
    soe it is left to the next Monthly Meetings care what further
    is to be done in order to her recovery.

Complaint was made to this Meeting by Brigg Freinds against
    Nickolas Wilkinson for breach of his promise to Freinds at
    the last Monthly Meeting soe it is left to the care of Freinds
    of the next Monthly Meeting to deal with him as in the wisdome
    of God they shall see cause.

It is ordered that ther be a contribution made and brought up
    to the next Monthly Meeting which is to be at Edward Gilliatts
    in Brigg.

p. 172.

        ATT a Monthly Meeting held at the house of Edward Gilliatt
in Brigg the 11th 12th month 1692[2] :—

Brigg Freinds are yett desired to draw up a paper of the busines
    of Monthly Meetings and comunicate it to the next Monthly
    Meeting.

This Meeting hath had the business of John Pilsworth wife under
    ther further consideration and finding her yet obstinate does
    desire that Freinds of the Isle Meeting or any other Freinds
    doe yet speak or write to her as they feel there hearts opned
    towards her in the love of God for her recovery.

[1] 13th January, 1693.   [2] 11th February, 1693.

This Meeting has ordered the paper of condemnation that is drawn up against Nickolas Wilkinson to be recorded in our Monthly Meeting booke and alsoe to write to Freinds at London & else where and give them an account of him.

Contributions came in as followeth :—

	£	s.	d.
Gainsbrough		11 :	06
the Isle		13 :	00
Wintringham		15 :	00
Brigg		15 :	00
Garthorp		08 :	00

03 : 02 : 06

Disbursments :—

	£	s.	d.
to John Pilsworth for 2 years table for John Brown	02 :	00 :	00
to Peter Naylor for what he laid down to Mary Broadhead	0 :	05 :	00
to John Pilsworth for shooes & stockings for John Brown	0 :	07 :	06
to Joseph Richardson that he laid down	00 :	10 :	00

The next Monthly Meeting to be att Brigg.

To all people to whome this writeing shall come know yee that Nicholas Wilkinson, cordwiner of Glamford Briggs haveing been convinced of the blessed Truth, and hath had conversation with us the people of God in scorn called Quakers for some years by past but haveing been unfaithfull to the Lord and that blessed principle of divine grace which the Lord in mercy bestowed on him, & which we doue make proffession of, have turned aside out of the right way & walked disorderly to the shame of religeon the dishonour of God his Truth and people, And whereas divers Freinds whose spiritts have been greived for those things have sought his return for a long time, & in there godly care for the Truth sake, and his everlasting welfair have often spoaken to him, and when that would take noe effect, his condition was laid before the Monthly Meetings, and Freinds from thence ordred to speak to him, alsoe to advise him to come to the Monthly Meeting to receive the advice of Freinds in the Truth, which he did accordingly and seemed to hearken to there councell and promised amendment, but instead of a reformation he is grown worse, his conversation more debauched then before, not only in running from one woman to another under pretence of marryage but in frequenting the company of loose weomen, that his name is become a reproach, besides his running into debt, and taking noe care

to pay what he owes, to the injury of many, and to the great
damage of those that are not able to give him creditt, and
other ungodly practices as lyeing for which he is soe notorious,
that his word in any case cannot be taken, all which are against
the Truth we proffess, which leads to injure noe man ther fore
we doe testifie & declare to all the world that we have noe
fellow shippe with him.

Given forth at our Monthly Meeting the 11th day of the 12 Month
1692/3 subscribed in the behalfe of the said Meeting by

Joseph Richardson.

p. 173.

ATT a Monthly Meeting held att the Meeting House at Edward
Gilliatts in Brigg the 10th of the first month 92/3[1] :—

This Meeting has ordered the paper draw up by Friends of Brigge
Meeting to be recorded in the Meeting book.

This Meeting desires that some Friend of Brigg Meeting would lye
down 40s. for the service of the Quarterly Meeting & to be
reimbursed by the next Meetinge.

James Coakes of Butterwick came this day into our Monthly
Meeting & published his intentions of marriage with Anne Clark,
Garthrop, shee being present gave her consent, but it being
the first time they are desired to wait Friends answer till
the next Monthly Meeting, where they are both desired to
be present.

Ordered that a contribution be collected & brought up to the next
Monthly Meeting which is ordered to be at Henry Symsons
in Gainsbrough.

ATT a Monthly Meeting held at the house of Henry Symsons
in Gainsbrough the 14th of 2nd month 1693[2] :—

The condition of Mary Northen was laid before this Meeting, &
it was left to Gainsbrough Friends to administer something
to her necessity, & this Meeting will see them indempnified.

James Coakes of Butterwick came this day a 2d time into our
Monthly Meeting with Anne Clarke of Garthrop, & both of
them signified the continuance of there purpose marriage, &
all things being found clear on behalf of both parties the
consumation thereof is left to their own conveniency according
to the good order of Truth.

John Clark, junior, Garthrop came this day into our Monthly Meeting
& signified his intentions of marriage with Rachell Hicks of
Sticknam[3] belonging Multon[4] Monthly Meeting & brought a

[1] 10th March, 1693.   [2] 14th April, 1693.
[3] *Sic: recte* Stittenham.   [4] *Sic: recte* Malton, co. York.

certificate from thence of there appearance there & the consent
of relations & Friends, but it being the first time they are
desired to wait Friends answer till the next Monthly Meeting.

Contributions came in as followeth :—

				£	s.	d.
Garthrop	..	..	..	00 :	07 :	00
Gainsbrough	..	..	..	00 :	11 :	06
Ile Meeting	..	..	..	00 :	14 :	06
Winteringham	..	..	..	00 :	18 :	00
Brigge	..	..	..	00 :	15 :	06

		£	s.	d.
Totall	..	03 :	06 :	06

		£	s.	d.
To Joseph Richardson which he laid down to the Quarterly Meeting	.. .. ..	02 :	00 :	00
To John Pilsworth for repairs	.. ..	00 :	05 :	02
To Henry Symson for a poor Frend there Meeting	.. ..	00 :	02 :	06
To Robert Colyer for woolsey & triming for young Brown	.. ..	00 :	05 :	06

	£	s.	d.
	00 :	14 :	04

It is concluded by this Meeting that there be 2 contributions collected
this quarter one for Tumby Meeting House repaires the other
for the Monthly & Quarterly Meeting service, the first to be
collected & brought into the next Monthly Meeting which is
to be at Thealby.

Signed by Joseph Richardson.

p. 174.

ATT a Monthly Meeting held at the house of John Wresles
in Thealby the 12th of the 3d month 1693[1] :—

Contributions came in as followeth :—

				£	s.	d.
Gainsbrough	..	..	..	00 :	11 :	09
Ile	..	..	..	00 :	10 :	00
Winteringham	..	..	..	00 :	12 :	00
Brigge	..	..	..	00 :	15 :	06
Garthrop	..	..	..	00 :	00 :	00

			£	s.	d.	
Totall	..	..	02 :	09 :	03	in Joseph Richardsons hands.

This day John Clark, junior in Garthrop came into our Monthly
Meeting, the second time & signified the continuance of his

---

[1] 12th May, 1693.

purpose of marriage with Rachell Hicks & brought with him a certificate of there appearing at the Monthly Meeting to which shee doth belong, and Friends here upon examination finding nothing against it on his part, have given him a certificate thereof & left the consumation thereof to themselves with the advice of the Monthly Meeting to which shee doth belong, to perfect the same as may be seen meet according to the good order of Truth.

The next Monthly Meeting ordered to be at Robert Reeders of Cotle Hall, & that a contribution be collected & brought up thither.

Signed in behalfe of the Meeting by

Joseph Richardson.

ATT a Monthly Meeting held at the house of Robert Reeders of Cotlehall the 9th day of the 4th month 1693[1] :—

Contributions came in as followeth :—

	£	s.	d.
Gainsbrough	00	12	06
Crowle	00	12	09
Winteringham	00	16	03
Brigge	00	13	00
Garthrop duble..	00	13	00
Colected before & in stock ..	03	02	07
Totall	05	10	01

Disbursments out of the same as followeth :—

	£	s.	d.
To P. N.[2] for half a year for Mary Codd : ..	01	12	06
To Bridget Mosley for her releife	00	05	00
Ordered to the Quarterly Meeting	01	12	06
Ordered for the repaires of Tomby Meeting House	02	00	00
Totall	05	10	00

It is ordered that a Meeting for the worshipp of God be held at the house of David the 2d fourth day of every month dureing this sumer time & to begin the next 4th day.

Ordered that the next Monthly Meeting be held at the house of John Orryes in Epworth.

Signed by Joseph Richardson.

[1] 9th June, 1693.   [2] Sic: for Peter Naylor.

p. 175.

ATT a Monthly Meeting held at the house of John Urryes in Epworth the 14th of the 5th month 1693[1] :—

The nessessities of Mary Codd is left to Gainsbrough Freinds to doe as they shall see meet & to be reimbursed againe by this Meeting.

Freinds at this Meeting haveing acquainted Mary Berrier with removeing the aforesd Mary Codd to there house shee has taken time till the next Monthly Meeting to advise with her husband & return an answer accordingly.

The next Monthly Meeting ordered to be at Brigge.

Signed by Joseph Richardson.

ATT a Monthly Meeting held at Brigg the 11th of 6th month 93[2] :—

Robert Berrier wife of Ealand gave this Meeting to understand that her husband & shee had considered about takeing Mary Codd but is not willing to receive her soe that shee is still left to Friends care to inquire for her a place.

Friends of Gainsbrough Meeting have taken care to get Mary Codd such nessaries as was fitting & this Meeting is to see them indemnified.

It is ordered that a contribution be collected & brought up to the next Monthly Meeting which is to be at the house of Thomas Wresle in Beltoft.

Signed by Joseph Richardson.

ATT a Monthly Meeting held at the house of Thomas Wresles in Beltoft the 8th of the 7th month 1693[3] :—

Friends of this Meeting are informed that George Atkinson of Roxby is willing to take Mary Codd soe that it is left to Winteringham Meeting & Brigg to agree with him for keeping her.

Contributions came in as followeth :—

	£	s.	d.
Gainsbrough		12 :	09
Brigg		14 :	00
Crowle		13 :	00
Garthrop		08 :	00
	03 :	04 :	03

[1] 16th July, 1693.   [2] 11th August, 1693.   [3] 8th September, 1693.

c

	£	s.	d.
Disburst for Mary Codd repaires	00	10	06
to John Pilsworth for repairs of John Brown	00	02	00
to John Pilsworth for keeping John Brown ½ year	02	00	00

Rests in stock yet 11s. 9d. which Brigg Friends are desired
  to make up to 40s. & carry to the Quarterly Meeting &
  this Meeting will see them indempnified.

	£	s.	d.
Joseph Richardson laid down to the Quarterly Meeting	02	00	00
& upon another Friend account	00	04	00
Received in stock before	00	11	09
& from the Quarterly Meeting	00	05	00
Soe that this Meeting is indebted to him the sum of	01	07	03

p. 176.

This day John Williamson of Wrawby came into our Meeting and
  publisht his intention of marriage with Elizabeth Pease of
  Brigge shee being present gave her consent, but this being
  the first time they are desired to wait Friends answer till the
  next Monthly Meeting.

It is ordered that a contribution be collected & brought upp to
  the next Monthly Meeting which is ordered to be at Brigge.

It is ordered by the Quarterly Meeting that 2 Friends be chosen
  by this Meeting to take care to carry up Friends sufferings
  for tythe & other things to the next Quarterly Meeting which
  is to be the 27th of the tenth Month 1693.

Signed by Joseph Richardson.

ATT a Monthly Meeting held at Brigg the 13 of the 8th month
1693[1] :—

Mary Codd was brought hither according to the order of the last
  Monthly Meeting & is to goe & live with George Atkinson of
  Roxby for one year upon the same tearmes shee hath lived
  with John Potter of Lea.

It is desired by Friends of this Meeting that Friends in the seaverall
  Meetings bring up an account of there sufferings for tythes
  & other matters to the next Monthly Meeting & Thomas
  Markham & Peter Nayler are appointed to see they be carefully
  coppyed & carried up to the next Quarterly Meeting.

[1] 13th October, 1693.

Contributions came in as followeth :—   £   s.   d.
- Gainsbrough   ..   ..   ..   11 : 08
- The Ile ..   ..   12 : 00
- Winteringham ..   ..   ..   15 : 00
- Brigge   ..   ..   14 : 00
- Garthrop   ..   ..   ..   09 : 06

Totall   ..   ..   ..   03 : 02 : 08

  £   s.   d.

To Joseph Richardson which he laid down at
  Quarterly Meeting   ..   ..   ..   01 : 07 : 03
for Mary Codd shoes & stockings   ..   ..   00 : 03 : 09
To the Ile Meeting for Bridget Mosley   ..   00 : 05 : 00
To Brigg Meeting for Ester Stephenson   ..   00 : 05 : 00
To Thomas Potter for Mary Codd tabling at his
  fathers   ..   ..   01 : 01 : 08½
which clears all till this day but for 4s. 6½d. upon
  her account soe that nothing remains in
  stock all being disposed of.

This day John Williamson of Wrawby & Elizabeth Pease of Brigge came into our Monthly Meeting a second tyme, & signified the continuance of there purpose of marriage each with other, & Freinds finding nothing against it to hinder there said proceedings, have left the consumation thereof to themselves with the advice of Freinds according to the good order of Truth.

The next Monthly Meeting ordered to be at Brigge.

Signed by Joseph Richardson.

p. 177.

ATT a Monthly Meeting held at the Meeting House at Edward Gilliats Brigg the 10th of the 9th month 1693[1] :—

According to order of the last Monthly Meeting, Gainsbrough, the Ile & Winteringham Meetings have brought in there sufferings for tythe for this present year, & notice is desired to be given to Garthrop Friends to have theres ready against the next Monthly Meeting.

This day Anthony Morrice of Beltoft came into our Monthly Meeting & published his intentions of marriage with Mary Godfrey of Cotle Hall, & shee being present gave her consent, but it being the first time, they are desired to wait Friends answer till the next Monthly Meeting.

Ordered that a contribution be collected & brought up to the next Monthly Meeting which is to be at Brigge.

Signed by Joseph Richardson.

[1] 10th November, 1693.

ATT a Monthly Meeting held at the Meeting House at Edward Gilliatts in Brigg the 8th day of the 10th month 1693[1] :—

George Atkinson came into this Meeting & signified his unwillingness to continue Mary Codd for a year, according to a former contract with Friends & therefore desires that Friends would take care to dispose of her, & in the mean time he is willing shee should continue with him till a convenient place be found out.

Contributions came in as followeth :—

	£	s.	d.
Gainsbrough	12	:	00
the Ile	14	:	03
Winteringham	15	:	00
Brigg	15	:	03

Disbursments :—	£	s.	d.
To John Potter	00	: 04	: 06
To William Smith for Mary Goxhill & Ester	00	: 08	: 00
Remains in Joseph Richardson hand	00	: 04	: 00
Left in Joseph hand for Quarterly Meeting ..	02	: 00	: 00

This day Anthony Morrice came a second time into our Meeting and signified the continuance of his purpose of marriage with Mary Godfrey & brought with him a certificate from her self her father & mother signifying there willingness & consent & Friends of this Meeting finding nothing against it have left the consumation thereof to themselves with the advice of Friends to perfect the thing as may be seen meet according to the good order of Truth.

This day John Wresle came into our Monthly Meeting & published his intentions of marriage with Elizabeth Browne of Brigge, shee being present gave her consent but it being the first time they are desired to wait Friends answer till the next Monthly Meeting.

Next Meeting ordered to be at Brigge.

Signed by Joseph Richardson.

p. 178.

ATT a Monthly Meeting held at the Meeting House at Edward Gilliatts in Brigg the 12th of the 11th month 1693[2] :—

This day an account was made with George Atkinson for Mary Codd tabling and buryall as alsoe what Joseph Richardson has received from Garthrop & what he had in his hand, & there remains yet oweing to George Atkinson the sum of £00 : 12 : 02 besides what was paid him this day.

[1] 8th December, 1693.   [2] 12th January, 1694.

This day John Wresle of Brigg came a second time & signified the continuance of his purpose of marriage with Elizabeth Browne of the same & shee & her father being present gave there consent, Friends here haveing nothing against it, have left the consumation thereof to themselves with the advice of Friends according to the good order of Truth.

This day John Howell of Brigg came into our Monthly Meeting and published his intentions of marriage with Mary Duckworth at Thomas Lowers house in London & brought severall testimonialls under the hands of her father, herself, her master & mistress signifying her clearness & there willingness unto the same, but it being the first time they are desired to wait Friends answer till the next Monthly Meeting.

Next meeting ordered to be at Brigg.

Signed by Joseph Richardson.

ATT a Monthly Meeting held at the Meeting House at Edward Gilliatts in Brigg the 9th of the 12th month 1693[1] :—

This day an account was given of the departure of our dear & antient Friend Thomas Wresle of Beltoft, & that he has left to the Friends of this Meeting the sum of three pounds to be disposed of at there discretion, for which this Meeting have given the executors a discharge, & it is put into the hands of Joseph Richardson untill it be disposed of by this Meeting.

The sum of 12s. 2d. oweing to George Atkinson payment thereof is deffered untill the next Monthly Meeting, & Mary Codds apparell is left with Robert Colyer till they be disposed of.

This day John Howell came a second time into our Meeting & signified the continuance of his purpose of marriage with Mary Duckworth & hath brought with him a certificate from the Monthly Meeting at Lancaster to which shee doth at present belong signifying they have both done the like there. Now there being nothing found here but that all things are clear on his part, we have returned it with our certificate to the said Monthly Meeting for there approbation & accomplishment.

It is ordered that a contribution be collected for the service of the Truth & brought into the next Monthly Meeting which is ordered to be at Henry Symsons house in Gainsbrough.

Signed by Joseph Richardson.

[1] 9th February, 1694.

p. 179.

ATT a Monthly Meeting held at the house of Henry Symsons in Gainsbrough the 9th day of the first month 1694[1] :—

Contributions came in as followeth :—

	£	s.	d.
Gainsbrough	00	11	08
Epworth	00	15	00
Winteringham	00	15	06
Brigge	00	15	00
Garthrop	00	00	00
	02	17	02

Disbursments :—

	£	s.	d.
to John Urry for John Browne	02	00	00
to Friends belonging Gainsbrough Meeting	00	03	00
& they are desired to lye down more to be paid the next Monthly Meeting to George Atkinson the sum of	00	12	02

which make streight with him for Mary Codd.

The cloathes of Mary Codd lyes yet in Robert Colyer hands to dispose of.

The aforesaid John Browne is desired to be at the next Monthly Meeting where Friends will take further care for his settlement.

Freinds of Brigge Meeting is desired to carry up to Lincolne two pounds for the Quarterly Meeting service, & is to be paid againe out of the money given by Thomas Wresle of Beltoft to Freinds of this Meeting.

Next Monthly Meeting ordered at Elizabeth Wresle house in Beltoft.

ATT a Monthly Meeting held at the house of Widdow Wresles in Beltoft the 13th of 2d month 1694[2] :—

It is ordered by this Meeting that Peter Naylor & Thomas Wresle, goe to speak to John Urry & his wife about takeing of John Browne.

Ordered that John Pilsworth & William Browne buy close for John Browne & bring an account thereof to the next Monthly Meeting.

Ordered that Mary Berrier & Anne Foster take care to get some close for Bridget Mosley, & bring an account to the next Monthly Meeting.

This day William Taylor of West Halton came into our Monthly Meeting & published his intentions of marriage with Judeth

[1] 9th March, 1694.   [2] 13th April, 1694.

Chapman of Epworth shee being present gave her consent, but it being the first time they are desired to waite Friends answer till next Monthly Meeting.

This day Thomas Recket of Lea came into our Monthly Meeting & published his intentions of marriage with Susanna Turner of Thealby, & she being present gave her consent, but it being the first time they are desired to wait Freinds answer till the next Monthly Meeting.

Next Monthly Meeting ordered to be at the house of John Wresles in Thealby.

p. 180.

ATT a Monthly Meeting held at the Meeting House in Thealby the 11th of the 3d month 1694[1] :—

According to the order of the last Monthly Meeting Peter Naylor & Thomas Wresle has spoke to John Urry of Epworth, but findes Mary Berrier of Hurst Hall willing to take John Browne for a year, & Friends at this Meeting have agreed to give her three pound this year, & he is to begin the 14th day of the second month 1694.

An account was brought into this Meeting what stock remaines & there yet rests in Joseph Richardson hands the

	£	s.	d.
sum of	02	08	00
besides disbursments to Henry Symson ..	00	02	00
to Mary Berrier for Bridget Mosley	00	05	00
to John Pilsworth for tabling John Browne up	01	03	00

And received this day of Thomas Wresle of Winteringham the sum of 20s. being a legacy given to this Meeting by our Friend William Harrison late of Hull a litle before his death for which this Meeting has given a discharge & yet rests in Joseph Richardson hands but .. .. 02 : 08 : 00

This day William Taylor of West Halton & Judeth Chapman of Epworth came a second time into our Monthly Meeting & signified the continuance of there purpose of marriage each with other, & Friends finding nothing against it have left the consumation thereof to themselves with the advice of Friends to perfect the same as may be seen meet according to Truths order.

This day Thomas Recket of Lea & Susanna Turner of Thealby came a second time into this Meeting & signified the continuance of there purpose of marriage each with other, & Friends haveing nothing to object against it, have left the consumation thereof to themselves with the advice of Friends according to the good order of Truth.

[1] 11th May, 1694.

This day Thomas Wresle of Beltoft came into our Meeting and published his intentions of marriage with Mary Turner of Thealby & shee being present gave her consent, but it being the first time they are desired to wait Friends answer till next Monthly Meeting.

This day William Berrier of Ealand came into our Meeting & published his intentions of marriage with Joan Clark of Butterwick & shee being present gave her consent but it being the first time they are desired to wait Friends answer till next Monthly Meeting.

This day John Nainby of Castlethorp came into our Meeting & published his intentions of marriage with Sarah Browne of Partney Mills & brought with him a certificate under her own (*p. 181*) hand signifying her willingness & consent thereunto but it being the first time they are desired to wait Freinds answer till the next Monthly Meeting.

The next Monthly Meeting ordered to be at John Clarkes in Garthrop & that a contribution be collected & brought thither.

Signed by Joseph Richardson.

ATT a Monthly Meeting held at the house of John Clarkes in Garthrop the 8th day of the 4th month 1694[1] :—

It is agreed upon by this Meeting that a Meeting for Worshipp be kept once a month att David Crosbys house dureing this sumer season, & to begin the 13th of this month.

Contributions came in as followeth :—

	£	s.	d.
Gainsbrough		13 : 00	
Brigg		15 : 00	
Winteringham		16 : 00	
the Ile		15 : 00	
Garthrop		08 : 00	
Totall	03 : 07 : 06		

Disbursments :—

	£	s.	d.
To John Pilsworth for close for John Brown..		16 : 00	
To Garthrop Meeting for Doll Pickhaver		07 : 00	
To William Berrier for Bridget Mosley		03 : 06	
Ordered to the Quarterly Meeting	02 : 00 : 00		
Robert Colyer brought into this Meeting for close he sould of Mary Codds		07 : 00	
Remains yet in stock in Joseph Richardson hand		08 : 00	

[1] 8th June, 1694.

This day Thomas Wresle of Beltoft & Mary Turner of Thealby came a second time & signified the continuance of there purpose of marriage each with other & all things being found clear on behalf of both parties the consumation thereof is left to themselves with the advice of Friends according to the good order of Truth.

This day William Berrier of Ealand & Joan Clark of Butterwick came a second time into our Meeting, & signified the continuance of there purpose of marriage each with other, & all things being found clear on behalf of both parties the consumation thereof is left to themselves & Friends according to Truths order.

p. 182.

This day John Nainby of Castlethorp came into our Meeting with Sarah Browne of Partney Mills, & signified the continuance of there purpose of marriage each with other, & all things being found clear on behalf of both parties, the consumation thereof is left to themselves according to the good order of Truth.

Next Monthly Meeting ordered at John Urrys house in Epworth.

Signed by Joseph Richardson.

Att a Monthly Meeting held at the house of John Urryes in Epworth the 13th of the 5th month 1694[1] :—

The nessessities of Thomas Browne of Epworth being laid before this meeting, Friends of there Meeting is desired to supply his need & give an account thereof to the next Monthly Meeting.

Mary Berrier gave an account to this Meeting that John Browne wanted repaires, shee is desired to doe it & give account to next Monthly Meeting.

According to order of last Quarterly Meeting, Friends of this Meeting have had it under consideration, & have appointed Edward Gilliatt & Thomas Markham to speak to Edward Ascogh & informe him what Friends requests to him is on there behalf as formerly.

Next Monthly Meeting ordered to be at David Crosbys in Gunhouse & that the Meeting for Worshipp be kept alsoe the same day for Friends convenience.

Signed by Joseph Richardson.

[1] 13th July, 1694.

ATT a Monthly Meeting held at David Crosbys in Gunhouse the 10th day of the 6th month 1694[1] :—

John Brown nessesities came to 5s. which John Urry laid down according to order of last Monthly Meeting.

It is thought meet by Friends of this Meeting, that the Meeting for Worshipp be discontinued till the next year.

Ordered that a contribution be collected, & brought up to the next Monthly Meeting which is ordered to be at the house of Henry Hudson of Butterwick.

Signed by Joseph Richardson.

p. 183.

ATT a Monthly Meeting held att the house of Henry Hudson of West Butterwick the 12th day of the 7th month 1694[2] :—

Contributions came in as followeth :—

				£	s.	d.
Gainsbrough	..	..	..	00	12	00
Epworth..	..	..	..	00	14	06
Garthrop	..	..	..	00	08	06
Winteringham..	..	..	..	00	16	00
Brigge ..	..	..	..	00	17	06
Totall ..	..	..		3	08	06

	£	s.	d.
disburst to Gainsbrough Friends which they have laid down		10	00
to John Urry which he laid down		05	00
to Mary Berrier for John Browne repairs ..		05	04
to William Browne for releife of Bridget Mosley		05	00
to Thomas Wresle for releife of Elizabeth Oyle		03	02
ordered to the Quarterly Meeting	02	00	00

The difference between Mary Pilsworth of Epworth & John Pilsworth her father in law is refered to 6 freinds to hear both & to put an end to it Henry Simson, Robert Earott, Robert Colyer, Joseph Richardson & Edward Gilliatt, is to meet at John Urryes in Epworth next 6th day come a week to see it perfected if possible.

Next Monthly Meeting ordered to be at Brigge.

Signed by Joseph Richardson.

The 21th of the 7th month 94.[3]

Whereas complaint was made at the last Monthly Meeting about a difference betwixt John Pilsworth & wife senior & John

---

[1] 10th August, 1694.   [2] 12th September, 1694.   [3] 21st September, 1694.

Pilsworth & wife junior all of Epworth, it was agreed by the said Meeting & the parties concerned that Henry Symson, Robert Earott, Thomas Wresle, Edward Gilliatt, Robert Colyer & Joseph Richardson should meet at John Urryes in Epworth as this day to hear & determine all matters & things in difference among them & wee the aforesaid parties John Pilsworth & his wife senior & John & his wife junior doe hereby sollemly prommiss to acquiess & stand to the judgment of the above named Friends. In testimony whereof wee have hereunto set our hands the day & year abovesaid.

> John Pilsworth, senior.
> John Pilsworth, junior.
> Alice Pilsworth, senior.
> Mary Pilsworth, junior.

p. 184.

According to Agreement as on the other side wee have this day heard and determined all matters & things in difference betwixt the above named parties & doe find upon examination of accounts depending that John Pilsworth, senior is indebted to his son John Pilsworth, junior the sum of eight pounds which we have awarded shall be paid as followeth Imprimis upon the 21th 8th month next the sum of forty shillings, & the other six pounds to be paid in 3 years after viz twenty shillings at Mayday ninety five, & twenty shillings more at Martimas ninety five, & soe at Mayday & Martimas forty shillings accordingly in ninety seaven, to which award wee that are chosen have hereunto set our hands the day & year above written.

Henry Symson. Robert Earott. Edward Gilliatt. Thomas Wresle. Robert Colyer. Joseph Richardson.

This may certify whome it may concern that wee John Pilsworth, senior & John Pilsworth, junior of Epworth doe stand to & approve of the award of our Friends as abovesaid In witness whereof we have hereunto put our hands the day & year above-said.

> John Pilsworth, senior. John Pilsworth, junior.

ATT a Monthly Meeting held at Brigg the 12th of the 8th month 94[1] :—

The sufferings for tythe for this present year was brought in from the Ile Meeting & Winteringham & from Gainsbrough, Brigge & Garthrop they are desired to be ready against the next Monthly Meeting.

---

[1] 12th October, 1694.

It is ordered by this Meeting that the securities of all the burying
   places belonging this Monthly Meeting be brought into the
   next to be recorded in the book in whose hands they are lodged,
   that Friends may have recourse to them as need shall require.
Next Monthly Meeting ordered to be at Brigge.

Signed by Joseph Richardson.

ATT a Monthly Meeting held at Brigg the 9th of the 9th month
1694[1] :—

The suffering for tythe came into this Meeting from Gainsbrough &
   Garthrop Meeting according to order of the last Monthly Meeting.
It is still desired that an inquiry be made in the seaverall Meetings
   where the securities of the burying places are lodged & brought
   up to the next Monthly Meeting to be recorded as desired.
It is ordered that a contribution be collected & brought up to the
   next Monthly Meeting from whence Friends nessesities being
   suplyed the rest to be sent to the Quarterly Meeting.
Next Meeting at Brigge.

Signed by Joseph Richardson.

p. 185.

ATT a Monthly Meeting held att the Meeting House at Edward
Gilliatts in Brigg the 14th of the 10th month 1694[2] :—

According to the order of the last Monthly Meeting Thomas
   Wresle of Winteringham gave an account that the writeings
   for there burying place are lodged in his hands which Freinds
   may see & have recourse unto as need shall require.
Wee are also informed that the writeings for the burying place
   belonging to Gainsborough are lodged in the custody of Peter
   Naylor of the same.
Adlinfleet Friends are desired to give an account what they have
   done about there burying place to the next Monthly Meeting.
And the Ile Freinds are desired to doe the same, & give an account
   to the next Monthly Meeting.
Contributions came in as followeth :—

		£	s.	d.
Gainsbrough	.. .. ..	00	12	06
the Ile ..	.. .. ..	00	16	00
Winteringham ..	.. ..	00	15	00
Brigg ..	.. .. ..	00	15	00
Garthrop	.. .. ..	00	09	00
Totall ..	.. ..	03	07	06

[1] 9th November, 1694.　　　　[2] 14th December, 1694.

Disburst to Joseph Berrier for his mother Mary Berrier for half a year tabling of John Browne the sum of thirty shillings.

Ordered to the Quarterly Meeting thirty shillings & them that carryes it are desired to lye down more if need require.

Disbursed for 2 poor widdowes belonging Brigg Meeting seaven & six pence which is in full of this collection, & Joseph Richardson is desired to lye down more if occasion be & to be reimbursed againe by this Meeting.

The next Monthly Meeting ordered to be at Brigge.

Signed by Joseph Richardson.

ATT a Monthly Meeting held at the Meeting House at Edward Gilliatts in Brigge the 11th of the 11th month 1694[1] :—

Remember to reminde Adlinfleett Meeting & the Ile Meeting about the deeds of there burying places that they may be recorded.

Ordered that a contribution be collected & brought into the next Monthly Meeting for the releife of Richard Theaker in his present nessesity haveing sustained great damage by fire, & to be sent with the first convenience to him—or to Abraham Skerme.

The next Monthly Meeting ordered to be at Brigge.

p. 186.

ATT a Monthly Meeting held at the Meeting House at Edward Gilliatts in Brigge the 8th day of the 12th month 1694[2] :—

Friends of Adlinfleet Meeting are desired to get there antient burying place fenced off for there own service & give an account thereof to the next Monthly Meeting.

The collection for Richard Theaker loss by fire came in as followeth :

	£	s.	d.
Gainsbrough ..	00 :	11 :	09
The Ile	00 :	15 :	00
Winteringham ..	00 :	17 :	06
Brigge	00 :	15 :	06
Garthrop ..	00 :	08 :	00

Totall .. 03 : 07 : 09 which was then ordered & accordingly sent to Richard Theaker by Joseph Richardson.

Ordered that a contribution be collected for Truths service, from whence Friends nessessities being supplyed the rest to goe to the Quarterly Meeting.

[1] 11th January, 1695.   [2] 8th February, 1695.

Next Monthly Meeting ordered to be at Henry Symsons in Gainsbrough.

Signed by Joseph Richardson.

Att a Monthly Meeting held at the house of Henry Symsons in Gainsbrough the 8th day of the first month 1694/5[1] :—

Friends of Adlinfleet Meeting are still desired to get there antient burying place fenced & give an account thereof to the next Monthly Meeting.

Contributions came in as followeth :—

	£	s.	d.
Gainsbrough		12	00
the Ile		14	06
Winteringham		17	00
Brigg		14	06
Garthrop		09	00
Totall	03	07	00

Disburst as followeth :

	£	s.	d.
To the Ile by Joseph Pilsworth	00	05	00
To Brigg by Robert Colyer	00	05	00
To Garthrop by Thomas Morley	00	05	00
To Quarterly Meeting	02	00	00
Rests yet in stock in Joseph Richardson hand	00	12	00

Next Monthly Meeting ordered to be at Thealby.

Signed by Joseph Richardson.

p. 187.

Att a Monthly Meeting held at the house of John Wresles in Thealby the 12th of the 2d month 95[2] :—

This Meeting nominated Christopher Wilson, John Clark & Thomas Morley with the consent of there Meeting to see to the geting of there antient burying place fenced, & give ann account thereof to the next Monthly Meeting.

Complaint being made to this Meeting of the dissorderly carridge & dress of Mary Haslehurst of Gainsbrough, whereby Freinds & Truth has suffered & been reproached ; it is concluded & agreed by this Meeting that Henry Symson & Peter Naylor speak to her & watch over her in much tenderness, to see if there be any hopes of her return & amendment, & give there sence to Friends at the next Monthly Meeting, & if any Friends finde it upon them to speak to her ; that they doe it, for the clearing of the Truth & themselves before that time.

[1] 8th March, 1695.   [2] 12th April, 1695.

Whereas the matter depending betwixt Joseph Berrier of Ealand & his sister in law was laid before this Meeting & much debate & discourse had about the same, it is concluded by this Meeting, that Robert Earott, John Urry, senior, Thomas Wresle of Beltoft & Thomas Winder of Crowle, goe to them at some convenient oppertunity, & warn them to proceed no further in that matter, & to acquaint them with the sence of Friends.

Concerning the same, & alsoe discourse with his mother or any other Friends that may privately or publickly give any encouragment thereto, it being not consistant with Truth, & which Friends can have no fellowship withall, & alsoe both they & his mother are desired to appear at the next Monthly Meeting to give Friends satisfaction therein.

Friends haveing under there consideration in this Meeting the disposall of John Browne, have now discoursed & agreed with Jabez Bethell of Brigge for one year & Jabez is to have with him 50s. & if they like of each other, he is to be continued with him as an apprentice 7 years more, & then the 50s. to be made up £8.

It is agreed next Monthly Meeting be held at John Urryes in Epworth & then to be considered of appointing a day once a month for Worshipp at David Crosbys in Gunhouse.

Signed by Joseph Richardson.

p. 188.

ATT a Monthly Meeting held at the house of John Urrys in Epworth the 10th day of the 3d month 1695[1] :—

Adlinfleet Friends according to the order of the last Monthly Meeting bought wood for the fencing there antient burying place & this Meeting has desired they will see to get it done & give an account to the next Monthly Meeting.

The case of Mary Haslehurst of Gainsbrough comeing before this Meeting, Henry Symson acquainted Friends that he had spoke to her as desired, but found not her answer very acceptable, Friends therefore have thought meet if possible they may prevaile with her for her own good to defer a litle longer, & Henry Symson, Peter Nayler & Thomas Potter are desired to speak to her againe, & see if she be willing to give Friends satisfaction in these things they & the Truth are offended with & give an account to the next Monthly Meeting.

[1] 10th May, 1695.

They alsoe desire to know whether shee has received Joseph
    Richardson letter & what answer shee returnes to the
    same.

According to the order of the last Monthly Meeting Robert Earott,
    John Urry, Thomas Wresle acquainted this Meeting that they
    had spoke to Joseph Berrier, his sister & mother, & had such a
    satisfactory answer from them, as has comforted Friends
    harts in this Meeting, & Joseph Berrier being here present
    declares the same before us all.

Joseph Berrier is desired to carry John Browne to Jabez Bethell
    of Brigge the 12th day of this month.

It is ordered that the Monthly Meeting for Worshipp, begin to be
    held at David Crosbys in Gunhouse the last 4th day of this
    month & to be continued the last 4th day of every month soe
    long as Freinds shall see meet.

It is ordered that a contribution be collected, & brought up to the
    next Monthly Meeting, from which Freinds nessessities being
    first supplyed the rest to goe to the Quarterly Meeting.

Next Monthly Meeting ordered to be at Jane Morleys in Adlinfleet.

                            Signed by Joseph Richardson.

p. 189.

ATT a Monthly Meeting held at Jane Morleys in Adlinfleet
the 14th day of the 4th month 1695[1] :—

According to Friends desire Adlinfleet Meeting have gott there
    antient burying place fenced to the sattisfaction of this Meeting.

According to the desire of Friends Henry Symson & Thomas
    Potter spoke to Mary Haslehurst & had a deliberate discourse
    with her, but found her much averse to give Friends any
    satisfactory answer, soe that Friends have writt a few lines
    to her for the clearing of the Truth & themselves & waites
    her answer till the next Monthly Meeting.

Friends of Brigge Meeting are desired to putt John Brown of Brigg
    that lives with Jabez Bethell into repaires & give an account
    to the next Monthly Meeting.

Friends of this Meeting haveing under there consideration some
    temptations that Joan Berrier widdow lyes under, by reason
    of one of the world makeing suite to her in order for marriage
    it is desired that David Crosby or some other Friend would
    goe & speak to her that shee give no entertainment to any
    such motion as not being consistant with Truth, & to give an
    account to the next Monthly Meeting.

[1] 14th June, 1695.

Contributions came in as followeth :—

	£	s.	d.
Gainsbrough Meeting		12	06
Ile Meeting		16	00
Winteringham Meeting ..		15	06
Brigg Meeting		16	06
Garthrop Meeting		08	00
In Stock		12	00
Totall	04	01	00

Disbursments :—

	£	s.	d.
to Mary Berrier which clears of for John Browne	01	10	00
to Robert Earott which he laid down to Bridgett Mosley	00	01	06
to Christopher Wilson for Doll Pickhaver ..	00	03	00
to Joseph Berrier for Bridget Mosley now ..	00	04	00
Ordered to the Quarterly Meeting	02	00	00
Rests yet in stock in Joseph Richardson hand	00	03	00

The next Monthly Meeting ordered to be at Brigge.

Joseph Richardson.

ATT a Monthly Meeting held att the Meeting House at Edward Gilliatts in Brigg the 12th of the 5th month 1695[1] :—

Henry Symson acquaints this Meeting that Thomas Potter has spoke & delivered the writeing to Mary Haslehurst, but findes her to refuse all Friends indeavours for her return & amendment, soe that this Meeting from the sence they have of her present state & condition, as alsoe finding themselves pretty clear in there indeavours concerning her, thinkes meet to proceed in giveing forth a Testimony against her as in the wisdome of God Friends shall be directed.

The case of Thomas Reckit being laid before this Meeting, it is left to Gainsbrough Friends to use there discretion about him, & this Meeting will be assistant to them.

p. 190.

According to the order of the last Monthly Meeting, David Crosby & Robert Earott spoke to Joan Berrier widdow not to entertaine any motion in order for marriage with one that is not a Friend to Truth, & her answer was to them, shee owned there love, nor would consent to any such thing. Yet notwithstanding her promise has been prevailed upon to marry with him, to her own condemnation & Friends greefe & trouble.

[1] 12th July, 1695.

D

Complaint being made to this Meeting that John Wresle of Brigge
walkes very dissorderly to the reproach of Truth & Friends,
this Meeting therefore desires William Smith & Robert Colyer
goe to admonish him & bring his answer to the next Monthly
Meeting.

This Meeting desires upon complaint of John Pilsworth, senior in
Epworth that John Pilsworth, junior his son & he appear at
the next Monthly Meeting which is ordered to be at the house
of widdow Wresles in Butterwick.

Signed by Joseph Richardson.

ATT a Monthly Meeting held at the house of widdow Wresles
in Butterwick the 9th of the 6th month 1695[1] :—

Henry Symson acquainted this Meeting that he has spoke to Mary
Haslehurst about the paper Friends sent to her from the
Monthly Meeting but her answer was she had made it
away.

According to the last Monthly Meeting order William Smith &
Robert Colyer did speake to John Wresle concerning his dissorderly walking, & he did here them with tenderness hopeing
of amendment, its still desired that Thomas Nainby & Robert
Colyer have an eye towards him for good.

The case of Joan Berrier came before this Meeting concerning her
marriage with one that is no Friend, contrary to Friends advice
& her own promise, its therefore ordered that Jane Morley
& Sarah Crosby goe & speake to her concerning the same &
bring her answer to the next Monthly Meeting.

According to the order of the last Monthly Meeting John Pilsworth,
senior and John Pilsworth, junior did both appear at this
Meeting & are willing to let the difference fall.

Ordered that a contribution be collected & brought up to the next
Monthly Meeting which is ordered to be at the house of Henry
Symsons in Gainsbrough.

Signed by Joseph Richardson.

ATT a Monthly Meeting held at the house of Henry Symson
in Gainsbrough the 13th of the 7th month 1695[2] :—

The case of Mary Haslehurst is referred to our next Monthly Meeting
at the request of our dear Friend John Whitehead, who desires
to advise with her, before Friends proceed in giveing forth a
Testimony against her.

[1] 9th August, 1695.   [2] 13th September, 1695.

p. 191.

The case of John Wresle of Brigg being laid before this Meeting, Friends have thought meet in there tender care for his preservation if possible to order Edward Gilliatt & Joseph Richardson to advise & councell him to beware in runing evill courses, & to appear at the next Monthly Meeting to give Friends satisfaction in matters & things they have to lay to his charge.

According to the last Monthly Meeting order Jane Morley, David Crosby & his wife has spoke to Joan Stovin of Crowle late Joan Berrier, but gott little answer from her concerning her marriage out of the Truth, but this Meeting still desires that John Urry, senior of Epworth & Thomas Cutsforth take a convenient oppertunity to speak to her againe, that if possible shee may be brought to a sence wherein shee has offended, & give Friends satisfaction therein, & that John & Thomas return her answer to the next Monthly Meeting.

Contributions came in as followeth :—

	£	s.	d.
Gainsbrough Meeting	00 :	12 :	04
the Ile Meeting	00 :	14 :	06
Winteringham Meeting ..	00 :	15 :	00
Brigg Meeting	00 :	14 :	06
Garthrop Meeting	00 :	08 :	00
	03 :	04 :	10

Disbursments :—

To Jabez Bethell boy upon the account of repairs .. .. 01 : 05 : 10½
To the Quarterly Meeting by Peter Naylor 01 : 15 : 00 & if he see need to lye down 5s. more & then there will be 1s. oweing or else he will have 4s. in his hand.

The nessessities of Bridget Mosley was laid before this Meeting & the charge shee has been att in getting her turves : this Meeting desires John Urry, senior and Joseph Berrier speak to her, & see what shee can pay towards that charge, & give an account to the next Monthly Meeting.

The next Monthly Meeting ordered to be at the house of David Crosbys in Gunhouse.

ATT a Monthly Meeting held at the house of David Crosby in Gunhouse the 11th day of the 8th month 1695[1] :—

This Meeting desires Joseph Richardson to write to our dear Friend John Whitehead for a coppy of what he judges meet to be

---

[1] 11th October, 1695.

drawn up as a Testimony against Mary Haslehurst, for & by reason of her dissorderly walking, & refuseing the good councell & advice given her by Friends of the Truth.

John Wresle of Brigg not appearing at this Meeting as he promised to Joseph Richardson, it is desired his father & unckle Thomas Wresle, father[1] Browne & Joseph Richardson goe to advise him & to wish him to appear at the next Monthly Meeting.

This Meeting desires that Joseph Berrier & Robert Coakes with some other Friends goe againe to Joan Stovin of Crowle, & see if they can reach Gods witness to an acknowledgment wherein shee has offended, & that shee may condemn her marriage out of the Truth, by some Testimony from under her own hand to be brought up to the Monthly Meeting.

The leading of Bridget Mosley turves is referred to the next Monthly Meeting.

It is desired by this Meeting that Friends bring in an account of there suffering for tythe to the next Monthly Meeting.

Friends are desired to speak to those Parliament that lives near them which may be chosen, in Friends behalf, when matters may be brought before them in Parliament.[2]

p. 192.

Robert Earott & Robert Coakes are desired to speak to Mary Moody of Gunthorp about her leaveing Friends & walking contrary to Truth & bring her answer to the next Monthly Meeting.

Ordered that a contribution be collected & brought up to the next Monthly Meeting which is to be at Brigge.

> Signed by Joseph Richardson.

Att a Monthly Meeting held att the Meeting House at Edward Gilliatts in Brigge the 8th day of the 9th month 1695[3] :—

According to the order of the last Monthly Meeting Joseph Berrier & Robert Coakes spoke to Joan Stovin of Crowle & found her willing to signe a paper of condemnation for marrying with a man out of Truth, soe that this Meeting desires some of them to get a paper drawn up : ready for that purpose, & if possible to get her signe it before next Monthly Meeting. John Urry, junior, Thomas Wresle & Joseph Berrier is desired to see it done.

---

[1] *Sic : recte* father in law.　　　　　[2] A reference to the 'Affirmation.'
[3] 8th November, 1695.

According to the order of the last Monthly Meeting Thomas Wresle of Winteringham & brother John went to visit John Wresle of Brigg as alsoe some Friends of this Meeting, who says he ownes Friends love & tenderness towards him, in seeking his everlasting welfare, but is ashamed to appear at the Meeting because of guilt, but is in hopes of amendment as he saith, soe that this Meeting desires Friends in Brigge, would have a watchfull eye over him for good, and give there sence of him to the next Monthly Meeting.

Friends are desired in the seaverall Meetings belonging to this Monthly Meetting that have not brought an account of there suffering for tythe, to acquaint Friends to make them ready & bring them up to the next Monthly Meeting.

Friends have taken care to speak to those Parliament newly chosen on Friends behalf.

Robert Earott with Joseph Rogers spoke to Mary Moody of Gunthorp & found her in a pretty low frame of spirit & was in hopes that shee would more frequent Friends Meetings than formerly. Soe that Friends of that Meeting are desired to have an eye over her for good. John Urry, senior & Henry Hudson is desired to take care in it & bring there sence of her to the next Monthly Meeting.

Contributions came in as followeth :—

		£	s.	d.
Imps.	Gainsbrough	13	:	00
	the Ile	14	:	06
	Winteringham ..	15	:	00
	Brigg	15	:	00
	Garthrop	08	:	06
	Totall	03	: 06 :	00

Disbursments :— £   s.   d.

To John Urry & Robert Earott which they laid down .. ..   07 : 00

to Anthony Westoby for releif Elizabeth Oyle .. ..   03 : 00

To Joseph Berrier for releif Bridget Mosley ..   02 : 00

Remaines yet in stock in Joseph Richardson hands the sum of .. .. ..   02 : 14 : 00

Ordered that a contribution be collected & brought up to the next Monthly Meeting which is to be at Brigge.

Signed by Joseph Richardson.

ATT a Monthly Meeting held at the Meeting House at Edward Gilliatts the 13th of the 10th month 1695[1] :—

Whereas John Urry, junior Thomas Wresle & Joseph Berrier was desired by the last Monthly Meeting to get a paper of condemnation signed by Joan Stovin of Crowle, for marrying with a (*p. 193*) man out of the Truth, but could not yet meet with a convenient oppertunity, this Meeting desires there care to get it effected against the next Monthly Meeting.

Whereas Brigg Friends was desired to have an eye over John Wresle of there town, & he haveing in the mean time, left his wife & family, this Meeting still desires that Friends in Brigg, would advise & assist his wife in what is convenient & also to speak to him if he come againe before the next Monthly Meeting.

Friends haveing brought in an account of there suffering for tythe, Joseph Richardson is desired to take in carying or sending them to John Whitehead.

This Meeting still desires that John Urry, senior & James Coakes goe & speak to Mary Moody of Gunthrop, & in tenderness to acquaint her with desires for her own good & bring in her answer to the next Monthly Meeting.

Whereas this Meeting is acquainted with the indegency & poverty of Hester Barrow in Haxey parish that formerly frequented Friends Meetings when shee was able as this Meeting is informed. It is desired by Friends at this Meeting, that John Urry & Robert Earott give her a visit, & see how it is with her both as to her inward & outward condition, & give in there sence to the next Monthly Meeting.

Joshua Reeder of Cotle Hall came into the Meeting & published his intentions of marriage with Hannah Parish of Selby, & shee being present gave her consent but it being the first time they are desired to wait Friends answer till the next Monthly Meeting.

Contributions came in as followeth :—

	£	s.	d.
Gainsbrough		13 :	03
the Ile		12 :	06
Winteringham		14 :	09
Brigg		14 :	06
Garthrop		08 :	00
Totall :	3 :	03 :	00 to be carried

to Lincolne Quarterly Meeting for a perticular service.[2]

[1] 13th December, 1695.   [2] To repay money borrowed from a legacy.

	£	s.	d.
In stock in Joseph Richardson hand	02	14	00
Disburst to Jabez Bethell for repairs of young				
Browne	00	04	04
to Jabez Bethell more in part for ½ year for				
young Browne	00	12	00
to 2 poor widdowes in Brigg Meeting	00	05	09
for another service	00	02	00
To the Quarterly Meeting by Joseph Richardson	01	10	00

soe that no stock remaines in Joseph Richardson.

Next Monthly Meeting ordered at Brigg.

Signed by Joseph Richardson.

ATT a Monthly Meeting held at the Meeting House at Edward Gilliatts the 10th of the 11th month 1695[1] :—

Friends haveing been with Joan Stovin of Crowle as desired by the last Monthly Meeting, have obtained a paper of condemnation under her own hand to clear Friends & the Truth which is here set down for Friends satisfaction.

To Friends, I being sencible of the godly & christian care you have had over me in labouring with me from tyme to tyme in order to have preserved me in unity & fellowship with the Lord & his people, & under the government of his blessed Truth of which I was a proffessor. Yet notwithstanding I am bound in conscience to confess that I sleighted your labours of love & displeased the Lord in takeing my now husband, wherein I acted contrary to your wholesome advice & alsoe against my own knowledge wherefore I finde it my duty to give forth this Testimony, first to signify your clearness on my behalf, Secondly (p. 194) to condemn my contumatious act of impiety given under my hand the 15th day of the 10th month 1695.[2]

Joan Stovin.

It is still desired that John Wresle relations & friends of Brigg Meetinge have an eye over his wife for good, & write to him as may be thought meet.

Joseph Richardson has given Friends suffering for tythe to John Whitehead as desired.

Friends of this Meeting still desires that John Urry, senior & James Coakes goe & speak to Mary Moody in much tenderness towards her for Truth sake, & bring in her answer to the next Monthly Meeting.

---

[1] 10th January, 1696.   [2] 15th December, 1695.

This Meeting desires John Urry, senior acquaint Friends of there
Meeting about Hester Barrow & see who of them is willing
to goe with him to her, & advise with her about her inward
& outward condition & bring there sence to the next Monthly
Meeting.

Friends in this Meeting haveing under there consideration the
nessesity of our Friend Richard Grantham, that has suffered
very much for his Testimony beareing for the blessed Truth,
have nominated Henry Symson of Gainsbrough, John Urry,
senior, of Epworth, John Wresle of Thealby, Edward Gilliatt
of Brigg & Thomas Morley of Adlinfleet to acquaint Friends in
there respective Meetings, & collect among the most able
Friends something towards his releife & bring it up to the
next Monthly Meeting.

Friends in this Meeting haveing received a few lines from our dear
Friend John Whitehead signifying that Robert Stanley, junior
of Waddinton & Elizabeth Parsons did both appear at there
last Monthly Meeting & signified there intentions of marriage
each with other. It is therefore desired that Friends of Brigg
Meeting consider of the matter & give them at some convenient
time before the next Monthly Meeting a certificate, as they
upon an inquiry shall see meet.

Joshua Reader of Cotle Hall came a second time into our Meeting
& signified the continuance of his purpose of marriage with
Hannah Parish of Selby, & brought a certificate from Friends
of that Meeting of her clearness from all other persons, as alsoe
a few lines under her own hand of her willingness thereunto,
and Friends of this Meeting haveing nothing against it have
left the consumation thereof to themselves with the advice
of Friends according to the good order of Truth.

Next Monthly Meeting ordered to be at Brigg.

Signed by Joseph Richardson.

ATT a Monthly Meeting held at the Meeting House at Edward
Gilliatts the 14th day of the 12th month 1695[1] :—

Its still desired that John Wresle relations & Friends have an
eye of tender regard to his wife dureing his absence.

Its desired by this Meeting that Henry Symson & Peter Nayler
speak to Mary Moody of Gunthorp in tenderness towards her
for Truth sake & bring her answer to the next Monthly
Meeting.

This Meeting desires that Thomas Wresle of Beltoft, & John Urry,
junior of Epworth take care to speak in good tyme to the

[1] 14th February, 1696.

assessors at Haxey in behalf of Easter Barrowe, that her assessment be taken of by reason of her poverty, & alsoe to discourse her about her inward condition, & bring in there sence to the next Monthly Meeting.

p. 195.

Contributions came in as followeth for Richard Grantham :—

	£	s.	d.
Gainsbrough	01	01	04
the Ile	00	18	00
Winteringham	01	05	00
Brigge	00	18	03
Garthrop	00	12	06

£   s.   d.

Totall 04 : 15 : 07 that is collected for Richard Grantham releife to be carryed up to Lincolne Quarterly Meeting for him by Peter Nayler.

Peter Nayler of Gainsbrough, acquainting this Meeting with the misserable state & condition[1] of Thomas Recket of Lea, upon consideration thereof Friends of this Meeting, desires that Gainsbrough Friends concern themselves to use there discretion about him & bring an account thereof to the next Monthly Meeting.

Ordered that a contribution be collected & brought up to the next Monthly Meeting which is to be at Brigg & its desired that as many weomen Friends as can conveniently come up to the said Meeting.

Signed by Joseph Richardson.

ATT a Monthly Meeting held at the Meeting House at Edward Gilliatts the 13th day of the first month 1695/6[2] :—

According to order of last Monthly Meeting Henry Symson & Peter Nayler spoke to Mary Moody of Gunthrop, & had some friendly & seasonable conference with her, insomuch as shee cleares Friends & Truth & seemes to be more loveing than formerly, & Henry Symson & Peter Nayler are still desired to have an eye over her for good, & bring in there sence to the next Monthly Meeting.

Its left still to John Urry, senior of Epworth & Thomas Wresle of Beltoft to take care in speaking to the assessors of Haxey in good time about takeing of Easter Barrowes assessment as alsoe about her inward condition & give an account to the next Monthly Meeting.

---

[1] Insanity.   [2] 13th March, 1696.

Its still left to Gainsbrough Friends the care of Thomas Recket
with the advice of the Quarterly Meeting, & give an account
to the next Monthly Meeting.

Contributions came in as followeth :—

	£	s.	d.
Gainsbrough		12 : 06	
the Ile		12 : 00	
Winteringham		18 : 00	
Brigg		14 : 06	
Garthrop		08 : 06	

Disbursments :—

	£	s.	d.
to Henry Symson for releif of widdow Marshall	00	04	00
to Jabez Bethell which makes up for ½ a year for Brown		14	02
to Jabez more for another quarter of last ½ year		12	06
to the Quarterly Meeting	01	15	00

being all in stock we have.

This day Thomas Hutchisson of Fockerby came into our Meeting &
published his intentions of marriage with Mary Morrice of
Buterwick & shee being present gave her consent but it being
the first time they are desired to wait Friends answer till next
Monthly Meeting.

Ordered that next Monthly Meeting be at Henry Symsons in Gainsbrough.

Signed by Joseph Richardson.

p. 196.

ATT a Monthly Meeting held at the house of Henry Symsons
in Gainsbrough the 16th day of the 2d month 1696[1] :—

According to Friends desire Henry Symson spoke againe to Mary
Moody & findes yet something further in his minde towards
her, which Friends desires he with others may clear themselves
as tyme & oppertunity presents & give an account to the
next Monthly Meeting.

Freinds of Gainsbrough Meeting have divers times had discourse
with the neighbourhood at Lea about Thomas Recket, & the
neighbours have wholly taken him upon themselves, & putt
him into the House of Correction at Gainsbrough, intending
to make his estate pay the charge soe long as it will last,
& his wifes relations are desired to have an eye towards her
& releive her as nessesity shall require, Robert Colyer & Joseph
Richardson are desired to acquaint them with it.

[1] 16th February, 1696.

This day Thomas Hutchisson of Fockerby came a second tyme into our Meeting & signified the continuance of his purpose of marriage with Mary Morrice, & all things appearing clear on the behalf of both parties the consumation thereof is left to themselves with the advice of Friends according to the good order of Truth.

Friends of this Meeting haveing under there consideration the settlement of a Meeting for Worshipp once a month this sumer time, have concluded that it be kept the last 4th day of this month & soe of every month for this sumer without other reason be rendered for the contrary.

Ordered that the next Monthly Meeting be kept at Winteringham.

Signed by Joseph Richardson.

Att a Monthly Meeting held at the Meeting House at Anthony Westobys in Winteringham the 8th day of the 3d month 1696[1] :—

The care of Thomas Recket & his wife is left to Friends in Gainsbrough Meeting & to give an account to the next Monthly Meeting.

Ordered that a contribution be collected & brought up to the next Monthly Meeting from which is to be paid 12s. for books oweing to John Whitehead on the publick account.

The further consideration of the state & condition of Mary Moody came before this Meeting & an account was given & Isabell Gilliatt that they had been with her, & had cleared there spirits to her, which owned to be in great love, but there appears not much hope of her recovery since & therefore if Henry Symson or any other Friend have still any thing in there mindes towards her they are desired to clear themselves & give an account to the next Monthly Meeting.

The consideration for security for the burying place at Crowle & another at Thealby & one at John Nainbys house in Caistrop, and alsoe about the Meeting House at Anthony Westobys, came before this Meeting, & Friends in there seaverall Meetings concerned are desired to take care therein & give an account to the next Monthly Meeting which is to be att widdow Reeders at Cotle Hall.

Signed by Joseph Richardson.

p. 197.

Att a Meeting held at Cotle Hall the 12th of the 4th month 1696[2] :—

The care of Thomas Recket & his wife is still left to Gainsbrough Friends for them to give an account to the next Monthly Meeting.

[1] 8th May, 1696.   [2] 12th June, 1696.

The continuance of the care for security of Crowle burying place
& another at Thealby & that at John Nainbys as also the
Meeting House at Anthony Westobys is still left to Friends of
each Meeting, & to give an account to the next Monthly
Meeting.

Contributions came in as followeth :—

				£	s.	d.
Gainsbrough	..	..	..	13 :	06	
the Ile ..	..	..	..	14 :	00	
Winteringham ..	..	..	..	17 :	06	
Brigge ..	..	..	..	13 :	04½	
Garthrop	..	..	..	08 :	00	
Totall ..	..	..	03 : 06 :	04½	

Disbursments :— £ s. d.

to Gainsbrough Friends for John Marshall	
burying	: 15 : 00
to Bridget Mosley	: 02 : 00
to John Whitehead for Books	: 12 : 00
to the Quarterly Meeting	01 : 17 : 04½

The further consideration about Mary Moody is left to be discourst
with Sarah Nainby & Phebe Dent, & to give an account
thereof to Henry Symson who alsoe has it in minde to speak
to her.

In regard the Quarterly Meeting falls about the same time that
the Meeting for Worshipp is to be at David Crosbys, Friends
have thought meet to dismiss it for this Month.

Next Monthly Meeting ordered to be at John Urrys in Epworth.

Signed by Joseph Richardson.

ATT a Monthly Meeting in the 5th month 96[1] held at the house
of John Urrys in Epworth.

The care of Thomas Recket & his wife is still left to Gainsbrough
Friends & for them to give an account to the next Monthly
Meeting.

Friends are desired in there respective Meetings to inquire who
of them may want a boy, & Friends of Winteringham Meeting
are desired to ask David Crosby when he comes home if he be
willing to take one, and give an account to the next Monthly
Meeting.

Its desired by Friends of this Meeting that the writeings of the
seaverall burying places & the donors names be sought out

[1] July, 1696.

& brought up to the next Monthly Meeting in order that they may be recorded in the Monthly Meeting booke appointed for that service.

Its desired that either the Monthly Meeting book or the matter to be inquired into of Monthly Meeting business, be read att the next Meeting.

Joseph Berrier of Hurst Hall came into this Meeting and published his intention of marriage with Susanna Rockhill (*p. 198*) And shee being present gave her consent, but it being the first time they are desired to wait Friends answer till the next Monthly Meeting.

Thomas Hopkins of Keelby, came into this meeting & published his intention of marriage with Elizabeth Nickesson of Grimsby & shee being present gave her consent, but it being the first time they are desired to wait Friends answer till the next Monthly Meeting.

Its desired by Friends of this Meeting that the Meeting for Worship be kept the last 4th day of this month at David Crosbys & that they & Friends have generall notice.

Next Monthly Meeting appointed to be at Brigge.

Signed by Joseph Richardson.

Owing to Jabez Bethell for one quarter of John Browne 12 : 06 with other things laid out for him

& to Joseph Richardson for 2 stamp paper indentures .. 02 : 06

Friends agreement with Jabez Bethell at Thealby the 12th of the 2d month 95 to putt John Browne an apprentice with him for 8 year & if they liked of each other after one year was expired then Jabez was to have for the first year 50s. to be made up £8, the 2d. year 30s., the 3d. year 40s. & the 4th year 40s., which makes up the £8.

Att a Monthly Meeting held at Edward Gilliatts at Brigg the 14 of the 6th month 1696[1] :—

Henry Simpson acquainted Friends of this Meeting that there burying place is kept in good order, & the writeings given for the place by Thomas Fisher of Kexby was lodged in the hands of Peter Nayler in Gainsbrough.

The writeings given for Brigg burying place by Robert Richardson of Wootton are lodged in the hand of Jane Markham widdow in Brigg & the same is kept in good order.

[1] 14th August, 1696.

And the coppy given for the burying place in Crowle by William
Berrier are lodged in the hands of John Urry in Epworth.

And the will made by Anne Hobson widdow, for the burying place
in Garthrop is in the hands of Christopher Wilson, & it is kept
in good order.

p. 199.

And the burying place at Winteringham given by William Harrison
of the same is kept in good order, & the writeings are lodged
in the hands of Thomas Wresle in Winteringham, they were
made over to Friends the 3d of 3d month 69.

The continuance of the care of Thomas Recket & his wife is left
to Gainsbrough Friends.

Friends haveing had some conference with David Crosby in this
Meeting about takeing widdow Marshall son, have agreed
for David to take him the next voyage to London, after which
to treat about teaching, & Friends of Gainsbrough are desired
to put him into some repairs for sea.

Joseph Berrier of Hurst Hall came a second tyme & signified the
continuance of his purpose of marriage with Susanna Rockill,
and shee being present gave her consent, & brought a certificate
of her relations & Friends willingness thereunto, & Friends
of this Meeting haveing nothing against it have left the consumation thereof to themselves with the advice of Friends
according to the good order of Truth.

Thomas Hopkins of Keelby came a second time into our Meeting
& signified the continuance of his purpose of marriage with
Elizabeth Nickesson of Great Grimsby, & shee being present
gave her consent & brought with them 2 certificates from there
parents signifying there consent thereunto & Friends haveing
nothing against it have left the consumation thereof to themselves with advice of Friends according to the good order
of Truth.

Next Monthly Meeting ordered to be at David Crosbys in Gunhouse
& that a collection be brought up thither.

Signed by Joseph Richardson.

ATT a Monthly Meeting held at the house of David Crosbys
in Gunhouse the 11th day of the 7th month 1696[1] :—

The continuance of the care of Thomas Recket & his wife is
still left to Gainsbrough Friends.

[1] 11th September, 1696.

Contributions came in as followeth :— £ s. d.

Gainsbrough	..	..	..	13 : 00
the Ile ..	..	..	..	16 : 00
Brigg ..	..	..	..	15 : 00
Winteringham ..	..	..		16 : 00
Garthrop	..	..	..	09 : 06

Totall .. .. .. 03 : 09 : 06

Disbursments £ s. d.

To Henry Symson which he laid out by order of
this Meeting .. .. 00 : 09 : 00
To Robert Everatt .. .. 00 : 04 : 00
To Thomas Wresle, Winteringham .. .. 00 : 02 : 00
being 00 : 12 : 00
to the Quarterly Meeting .. .. .. 02 : 00 : 00
Rests in Stock .. .. 00 : 14 : 06

Ordered that a Meeting for Worshipp be held at David Crosby house the first 4th day of the next Month.

Ordered that the next Monthly Meeting be held at the house of Henry Hudsons in Butterwick.

Signed by Joseph Richardson.

p. 200.

ATT a Monthly Meeting held at the house of Henry Hudsons in Butterwick the the 9th day of the 8th month 1696[1] :—

The case of Mary Moody came againe under the consideration of this Meeting & Friends have ordered Henry Symson & Peter Nayler to goe to her once more or David Crosby & bring her answer to the next Monthly Meeting.

The case of Thomas Recket is still left to Gainsbrough Freinds, ordered that the next Monthly Meeting be at Brigge.

Signed by Joseph Richardson.

The writeings belonging the grave yard at Thealby are lodged in the hands of John Dent of Roxby.

George Frow, Joseph Wresle, John Dent & Thomas Wresle are trustees concerning the Meeting House at Anthony Westobys of Winteringham & have taken a surrender in court for it.

ATT a Monthly Meeting held at the Meeting House at Edward Gilliatts in Brigge the 13 of the 9th month 1696[2] :—

Its desired that Friends in each Perticular Meeting take care to bring an account of what sufferings has happened there for tythe or otherwayes unto the next Monthly Meeting.

[1] 9th October, 1696. [2] 13th November, 1696.

John Torr of Scrooby in Nottinghamshire & Phebe Dent of Roxby
     came into this Meeting & published there intentions of marriage
     each with other, but it being the first time they are both desired
     to wait Friends answer till next Monthly Meeting.

Ordered that a contribution be collected & brought up to the next
     Monthly Meeting which is to be at Brigge.

                         Signed by Joseph Richardson.

ATT a Monthly Meeting held at the Meeting House at Edward
Gilliatts in Brigg the 11th of the 10th month 1696[1] :—

According to order of the last Monthly Meeting seaverall Friends
     brought in there account of suffering for tythe, & the rest have
     promised to make them ready & carry or send them up to the
     Quarterly Meeting.

Whereas Thomas Potter gave an account to this Meeting of the
     nessesity of Abraham Northern wife, its left to Friends of
     Gainsbrough Meeting what is convenient to be done & give
     an account to the next Monthly Meeting.

John Torr of Scrooby in Nottinghamshire came a second time into
     this Meeting & signified the continuance of his purpose of
     marriage with Phebe Dent of Roxby, & shee being present gave
     her consent, & brought a certificate of his publishing the same
     at the Monthly Meeting to which he belongs as alsoe two
     certifficates under relations hands signifying there consent, &
     Friends here haveing nothing to object against it on her part
     finding all things clear have left the consumation to there
     Monthly Meeting with the advice of Friends to perfect the
     thing as may be seen meet.

p. 201.

Thomas Potter of Gainsbrough came into this Meeting & published
     his intentions of Marriage with Mary Barlow of Waddingham[2]
     & brought a certificate under her & her relations hand signifying
     there consent thereunto, but it being the first time they are
     desired to wait Friends answer till the next Monthly Meeting.

Contributions came in as followeth :—

		£	s.	d.
Gainsbrough	.. .. ..	00	17	00
the Ile	.. ..	00	15	08
Winteringham	.. .. ..	01	04	00
Brigg	.. ..	00	18	00
Garthrop	.. .. ..	00	12	00
Totall	.. .. ..	04	06	08
Stock	.. .. ..	00	17	00

[1] 11th December, 1696.   [2] *Sic: recte* Waddington.

Disbursments :—

to Henry Symson for Marshall repaires ..	13 : 00	
to Jabez Bethell for quarter of John Browne..	16 : 06	
which makes up for the first year 50s.		
to Joseph Richardson which he laid down ..	04 : 00	
to Edward Gilliatt which he laid down ..	02 : 06	
to John Urry for 2 poor widdowes	05 : 00	
to Brigg for 2 poor widdowes	05 : 00	

wanted in weight soe that all is disposed as
   above & to the Quarterly Meeting. To the
   Quarterly Meeting ..   ..   03 : 00 : 00
soe that nothing remaines in stock.

Next Monthly Meeting ordered to be at Brigge.

Signed by Joseph Richardson.

ATT a Monthly Meeting held at the Meeting House att Edward Gilliatts in Brigge the 8th of the 11th month 1696[1] :—

According to order of last Monthly Meeting Gainsbrough Friends laid down 5s. for releife of Abraham Northern wife.

The care of Thomas Recket is still left to Gainsbrough Friends.

This day Thomas Potter of Gainsbrough came into the Meeting and signified a second time the purpose of marriage with Mary Barlow of Waddinton & brought with him a certificate of her clearness & consent with relations alsoe, & Friends here haveing nothing to object against it on his part have left the consumation thereof to themselves with advice of Friends that belongs Lincolne Monthly Meeting according to the good order of Truth.

Next Monthly Meeting ordered at Brigg.

Signed by Joseph Richardson.

ATT a Monthly Meeting held at Brigg the 12th of the 12th month 1696[2] :—

Information was given to this Meeting that John Wresle of Brigge is returned to his wife, & therefore this Meeting desires Robert Colyer & Thomas Nainby would give him a visit & desire his appearance at our next Monthly Meeting.

Its ordered that a contribution be collected & brought up to the next Monthly Meeting, from whence Friends nessesities here being supplied the remainder to goe to the service of the Quarterly Meeting.

Next Monthly Meeting ordered to be at Brigge.

Signed by Joseph Richardson.

[1] 8th January, 1697.   [2] 12th February, 1697.

E

p. 202.

ATT a Monthly Meeting held at Edward Gilliatts in Brigge the 12th of the first month 1697[1] :—

The continuance of the care of Thomas Recket is left to Gainsbrough Friends.

This day Robert Rumley of Crowle came into our Monthly Meeting & published his intention of marriage with Hannah Mexber of Heck belonging Warnsworth Monthly Meeting, & she being present gave her consent, & brought a certificate they had done the like at Warnsworth Monthly Meeting, but it being the first they are both desired to wait Friends answer till next Monthly Meeting.

Robert Colyer & Thomas Nainby went & spoke to John Wresle of Brigge according to order, & desired his appearance at this Meeting which he promised he would, but shame ariseing from his evill practises has made him decline his promiss soe that Friends of this Meeting desires Robert Colyer & Thomas Nainby would give him another visitt, & discourse him as the Lord shall put it into there harts & bring his answer to the next Monthly Meeting.

Contributions came in as followeth :—

	£	s.	d.
Gainsbrough		14	00
Ile Meeting		19	00
Winteringham		18	00
Brigge		15	00
Garthrop		09	06
Totall	03	15	06

Disbursments as followeth :—

	£	s.	d.
to Gainsbrough Friends which they laid down	00	07	06
To John Urry for Easter Barrows releife	00	07	06
to William Smith which he laid down	00	01	00
to Edward Gilliatt which he laid down	00	02	06
to Henry Symson for Mary Northen	00	02	06
to Jabes Bethell towards this year for Browne	01	00	00
ordered to the Quarterly Meeting	01	10	00
Rests in stock in Joseph Richardson hand	00	04	00

Next Monthly Meeting ordered at Henry Symsons house in Gainsbrough.

Signed by Joseph Richardson.

[1] 12th March, 1697.

ATT a Monthly Meeting held at the house of Henry Symsons in Gainsbrough the 9th of the 2d month 1697[1] :—

Robert Colyer acquainted Friends that he with Thomas Nainby had spoke with John Wresle againe, but could get little from him, save that he writt a few lines to Friends which gave little satisfaction its therefore desired that William Smith & Robert Colyer give him another vissitt, & understand his minde what they can & give an account to the next Monthly Meeting.

The care of Thomas Reckett & his wife is still left to Gainsbrough Freinds.

This day Robert Rumley of Crowle came a second tyme & signified the continuance of his purpose of marriage with Hannah Mexber & brought a few lines from her signifying that shee joynes with him in the matter & upon deliberate discourse with Friends about him, findes not matter to object against it on his part & therefore leave it to Friends concernd of Warmsworth Meeting to which shee belongs according to the good order of Truth.

p. 203.

This day John Dent of Roxby came into this Meeting and published his intention of marriage with Ruth Lambert of Tickhill & brought with him a certificate from Blyth Monthly Meeting that they had done the same with them, & shee being present gave her consent as alsoe another certificate under her own hand to this Meeting of her willingness thereunto, but it being the first time they are both desired to wait Freinds answer till next Monthly Meeting.

Next Monthly Meeting ordered at John Wresles in Thealby.

Signed by Joseph Richardson.

ATT a Monthly Meeting held at Thealby the 14th day of the 3d month 97[2] :—

According to the order of last Monthly Meeting William Smith & Robert Colyer spoke to John Wresle of Brigge, but could get litle from him, yet for the clearing of ourselves & the Truth this Meeting has ordered John Nainby of Caistrop and Edward Gilliatt of Brigge, to give him another visit & bring in his answer to the next Monthly Meeting.

This day John Dent of Roxby came a second time into our Meeting & signified the continuance of his purpose of marriage with Ruth Lambert of Tickhill & brought with him a certificate from there Monthly Meeting that he had done the like with

---

[1] 9th April, 1697.   [2] 14th May, 1697.

them, & that it is with her & her relations consent & this Meeting haveing nothing against it on his part, have left the consumation thereof to themselves with the advice of Friends & relations concernd according to the good order of Truth.

Upon some debate in this Meeting about Thomas Recket & his wife Friends leaves the care thereof to Gainsbrough Friends.

Ordered that a contribution be collected & brought up to the next Monthly Meeting which is ordered to be at John Clarkes in Garthrop.

Signed by Joseph Richardson.

ATT a Monthly Meeting held at John Clarks in Garthrop the 11th day of the 4th month 97[1] :—

Whereas John Nainby of Caistrop is willing to give Friends belonging to Brigge Meeting a burying place, this meeting desires Brigge Friends would take care to get it fenced with all convenient speed.

According to order of last Monthly Meeting Edward Gilliat & John Nainby that they had been with John Wresle, & had desired Friends patience with him till the next Meeting & then he would appear before them, however this Meeting orders John Wresle his father & Thomas Wresle his unckle to speak to him & give an account to the next Monthly Meeting.

Contributions came in as followeth :—

	£	s.	d.
Gainsbrough Meeting	00	13	00
Ile Meeting	00	16	00
Winteringham Meeting ..	00	17	06
Brige Meeting	00	16	00
Garthrop Meeting ..	00	09	06
	03	12	00

Disbursments as followeth :—

	£	s.	d.
To Gainsbrough Friends which they laid down	00	01	06
To John Urry in the Ile	00	05	00
to Thomas Wresle for Elizabeth Oyle, Winteringham	00	02	00
To Christopher Wilson of Adlinfleet	00	02	06
To Jabez Bethell, Brigge due May last ..	00	10	00
to Edward Gilliat for 2 poor widdowes ..	00	05	00
to the Quarterly Meeting	01	10	00
Rests in stock in Joseph Richardson hand ..	00	16	00

[1] 11th June, 1697.

p. 204.

Its considered & agreed on by this Meeting, that a Meeting for Worshipp be held dureing the sumer season at David Crosbys in Gunhouse the last 4th day in the week in every month.

Ordered that the next Monthly Meeting be at John Urryes in Epworth.

Signed by Joseph Richardson.

ATT a Monthly Meeting held at John Urryes in Epworth the 9th day of the 5th month 1697[1] :—

This Meeting still desires Friends of Brigg Meeting to take care the getting the ground fenced which John Nainby has given them for a burying place.

This Meeting desires Robert Colyer & Joseph Richardson to speak to John Wresle of Brigg for neglect of his promise & to clear there own spiritts with him & bring his answer to the next Monthly Meeting.

The care of Thomas Recket wife is continued upon Gainsbrough Freinds.

Upon some debate & serious consideration of advice from our last Quarterly Meeting to the Monthly Meetings Friends here have appointed Edward Gilliatt & Joseph Richardson with the assistance of Thomas Wresle of Winteringham & Robert Colyer, to draw up a paper, what Freinds are to inquire into in Perticular Meetings, & show Henry Symson of Gainsbrough a coppy thereof, & with his advice to comunicate it to the next Monthly Meeting.[2]

Whereas Henry Hudson of West Butterwick has offered a Meeting House for Friends belonging the Ile Meeting, Friends accepts kindly thereof & desires he would make the same ready for the purpose, & that the Ile Friends keep ther week day Meeting as formerly appointed the first 4th day in every month at John Urrys & Henry Hudsons.

Friends finding Robert Earott not to frequent our Meetings as formerly desires that John Urry, senior of Epworth with some other Friends would goe & speak to him & know his reason & bring his answer to the next Monthly Meeting.

Ordered that the next Monthly Meeting be at Brigge.

Signed by Joseph Richardson.

[1] 9th July, 1697.   [2] Appointment of Overseers.

ATT a Monthly Meeting held at the Meeting House at Edward
Gilliatts in Brigge the 13th of 6th month 97[1] :—

The care is continued on Brigg Friends to get the burying place
fenced which John Nainby has given them.

The care of Thomas Recket wife is continued with Gainsbrough
Friends.

Henry Hudson of Butterwick has answered Friends request and
got the house ready for Friends & a Meeting was held the
first 4th day in this month.

p. 205.

A debate in this Meeting hapening about some miscarriages of late
in the Ile Meeting, Friends desires that John Urry, senior of
Epworth would speak to Robert Earott, & Richard Turner,
& that Robert Coakes likewise speak to Henry Hudson to make
there appearance at the next Monthly Meeting.

John Bishop of Uslett[2] came into this Meeting & published his
intentions of marriage with Mary Berrier of Ealand & shee
being present gave her consent, but it being the first time they
are desired to wait Friends answer till next Monthly Meeting.

Robert Colyer & Joseph Richardson are still desired to speak to
John Wresle to make his appearance at next Monthly Meeting.

Its left to Brigg Friends to fill the paper & send it the first oppertunity
to Abraham Morrice of Lincolne.

Ordered that a contribution be collected & brought up to the next
Monthly Meeting which is to be at David Crosbys in Gunhouse.

Signed by Joseph Richardson.

ATT a Monthly Meeting held at David Crosbys in Gunhouse
the 10th day of the 7th month 1697[3] :—

The care is continued on Brigg Friends of getting the burying
place fenced that John Nainby has given.

The care of Thomas Recket wife is continued with Gainsbrough
Friends.

Joseph Richardson & Robert Colyer are still desired to reminde
John Wresle of his promise to appear at next Monthly Meeting.

The Ile Friends not appearing Robert Coakes is desired to speak
to Henry Hudson & Richard Turner to come to the next
Monthly Meeting & to desire Richard Turner procure a certificate under faithfull Friends hands of the Meeting to which
he belongs concerning him & bring it up to the next Monthly
Meeting.

[1] 13th August, 1697.   [2] *Sic : recte* Ousefleet, Co. York.   [3] 10th September, 1697.

Contributions came in as followeth :— £   s.   d.

Gainsbrough Meeting	13 :	6
Ile Meeting	13 :	6
Winteringham Meeting ..	16 :	00
Brigg Meeting	15 :	00
Garthrop Meeting	09 :	00

Totall .. .. ..   3 : 07 : 00

Disbursments as followeth :—   £   s.   d.

to Henry Symson for E. Northen	05 : 00
to Jabez for John Brown	10 : 00
to the Quarterly Meeting	01 : 10 : 00

Rests in stock in Joseph Richardson hand ..   1 : 02 : 00

This day John Bishop of Uslett came a second time into our Meeting & signified the continuance of his purpose of marriage with Mary Berrier, shee being present gave her consent & Friends finding nothing to object against them have left the consumation to themselves with Friends advice according to the good order of Truth.

Next Monthly Meeting ordered to be at Thomas Wresles in Beltoft.

p. 206.

ATT a Monthly Meeting held at the house of Thomas Wresles in Beltoft the 8th day of the 8th month 1697[1] :—

The continuance of the care of getting the burying place fenced which John Nainby has given is left to Brigge Friends,

Whereas Gainsbrough Friends has given this Meeting to understand that Thomas Recket wife stands in need of some assistance Friends desires they would take care in the matter & give an account to the next Monthly Meeting.

According to order Robert Colyer spoke to John Wresle who promises to appear at the next Monthly Meeting at Brigg.

The nessesities of Bridget Mosley was laid before this Meeting & Friends have left the care thereof to the Ile Meeting & to give an account to the next Monthly Meeting.

Friends are desired to bring an account to there sufferings for tythe to the next Monthly Meeting.

According to order Robert Earott, Henry Hudson & Richard Turner came to this Meeting, & after long debate with them Friends made as good a conclussion as could be obtained.

Next Monthly Meeting ordered to be at Brigg.

Signed by Joseph Richardson.

[1] 8th October, 1697.

ATT a Monthly Meeting held at the Meeting House at Edward
Gilliatts in Brigg the 12th of the 9th month 97[1] :—

The care of getting John Nainby burying place fenced is still left
to Brigge Freinds.

The care of Thomas Recket wife is continued with Gainsbrough
Friends.

The Ile Friends are desired to take care about Bridget Mosley of
Crowle & give an account to the next Monthly Meeting.

Whereas John Wresle of Brigg has divers times promised to appear
att this Meeting, but never yet performed his promiss, not-
withstaning Friends patience for a long time, Friends therefore
desires that Edward Gilliat & Thomas Nainby to goe once
more to him & acquaint him, that if he neglect to come to the
next Monthly Meeting, Friends intends to proceed in giveing
forth a Testimony against him.

Friends of Gainsbrough, Winteringham & Adlinfleet Meetings have
brought in there accounts of suffering for tythe, & the Ile
Meeting has promised to have theres ready against the next
Monthly Meeting.

Ordered that the next Monthly Meeting be at Brigg & that a contribution be collected & brought up thither.

Signed by Joseph Richardson.

p. 207.

ATT a Monthly Meeting held at the Meeting House at Edward
Gilliatts in Brigg the 10th of the 10th month 1697[2] :—

The continuance of the care in getting the burying place at John
Nainbys is left with Brigg Freinds.

David Crosby of Gunhouse acquainted Friends in this Meeting,
that he was willing to take Thomas Marshall, son of Widdow
Marshall in Gainsbrough, for seaven yeares as an apprentice
to seafaring, & that if Friends would finde him with all sortes
of close for the first 4 yeares, he would finde all needfull
things the rest of his time, which Friends have greed to &
ordered David next time he goes to Gainsbrough to acquaint
Widdow Marshall therewith & get his indentures drawn &
sealed.

Friends in this Meeting haveing still under there consideration a
care for John Wresle who has hitherto sleighted there love &
forbearance towards him, have ordered Joseph Richardson
to write a few lines to him, & signe it in behalf of the Monthly
Meeting, & bring in a coppy to the next Monthly Meeting.

---

[1] 12th November, 1697.   [2] 10th December, 1697.

Contributions came in as followeth :—

	£	s.	d.
Gainsbrough		14 :	00
the Ile		15 :	00
Winteringham		15 :	00
Brigge		14 :	00
In stock	01 :	00 :	00
Totall	03 :	18 :	00

Disbursments :—

	£	s.	d.
To Gainsbrough Friends, Thomas Reckett wife releife	00 :	19 :	03
to the Ile Friends by Peter Nayler for B. Mosley	00 :	07 :	00
To Robert Colyer for Jabez Bethell boy close	00 :	09 :	02
To Peter Naylor for Martha Northen	00 :	05 :	00
To the Quarterly Meeting	01 :	10 :	00

Rests in stock in Joseph Richardson hand ..   00 : 08 : 07

Next Monthly Meeting ordered to be at Brigge.

Signed by Joseph Richardson.

ATT a Monthly Meeting held at the house of Edward Gilliatts in Brigg the 14th of 11th month 1697[1] :—

The continuance of the care in geting the burying place fenced which John Nainby of Caistrop has given them is still left to Brigg Friends.

The paper Joseph Richardson drew up & signed by order of the Monthly Meeting was delivered to John Wresle ; & this day read in our Meeting, & Friends have ordered John Nainby & Robert Colyer to goe once more to him & bring in his answer to the next Monthly Meeting.

The next Monthly Meeting ordered to be at Brigge.

Signed by Joseph Richardson.

p. 208.

ATT a Monthly Meeting held at the Meeting House at Edward Gilliatts in Brigg the 11th of 12 month 1697[2] :—

This Meeting desires that Brigg Freinds would take care in getting the burying place well fenced which John Nainby has given them.

Isaack Davis of Belton came this day into our Monthly Meeting & published his intentions of marriage with Anne Petty of

---

[1] 14th January, 1698.   [2] 11th February, 1698.

Fishlock & brought with him a certificate under her hand signifying her consent alsoe another under his mothers hand signifying hers alsoe with two certificates from the Monthly Meeting at Warnsworth & Sikehouse that he had done the like with them, but it being the first time they are desired to wait Friends answer till the next Monthly Meeting.

Upon some further discourse in this Meeting about John Wresle of Brigg his unckle Thomas Wresle has desired that Friends would wait till next Monthly Meeting to see how farr that they his relations can prevail with him before his condemnation for his transgression pass.

The next Monthly Meeting ordered to be at Brigg & a contribution to be collected & brought up thither.

Signed by Joseph Richardson.

ATT a Monthly Meeting at Edward Gilliatts Brigg 11th first month 98[1] :—

Brigg Friends are takeing care to get the burying place fenced.

Whereas at our last Monthly Meeting it was desired that those papers that was given forth by Friends wherein are divers things to be observed & care taken by those appointed in each Perticular Meeting, they were read accordingly & Friends unanimous therein, & made choice in each Meeting of men & woemen Friends for the service aforesaid as followeth which was approved by this Meeting.

Gainsbrough for the men Henry Symson & Peter Naylor, & for the woemen Sarah Nayler & Mary West.

Ile Meeting for the men John Urry, senior & James Coakes & for the woemen Mary Bishop & Ellen Hudson.

Winteringham Meeting for the men Thomas Wresle & John Wresle & Francis Dent & for the woemen Elizabeth Westoby & Susanna Wresle.

Brigg Meeting for the men William Smith & Joseph Richardson & for the woemen Sarah Nainby & Isabell Gilliatt.

Garthrop Meeting for the men Robert Vessey & Thomas Hutchison & for the woemen Jane Morley & Elizabeth Cornwell.

p. 209.

Isaak Davis of Belton came a second time into our Monthly Meeting & signified the continuance of his purpose of marriage with Anne Petty of Fishlock, but brought no certificate from her nor her mother, soe that Friends here can only signify to those

<hr>
[1] 11th March, 1698.

cheifly concerned that upon inquiry we finde nothing upon his part to hinder there joyning in marriage, & have intrusted our Friend Thomas Wresle of Beltoft to see that all things be clear on her part before they proceed further according to the good order of Truth.

Thomas Wresle acquainted this Meeting that he had spoke to his kinsman John Wresle, & had eased his spirit in a good sence of the Truth upon him, to the clearing of his conscience as a Friend & relation & David Crosby & Edward Gilliatt signified they had something upon there spirits to him soe this Meeting will wait till the next Monthly Meeting before they proceed to give forth a Testimony against him.

Contributions came in as followeth :—

	£	s.	d.
Gainsbrough Meeting ..		14 :	06
The Ile		13 :	00
Wintringham Meeting ..		16 :	00
Brigge Meeting		15 :	00
Garthrop Meeting		08 :	06
in Stock		12 :	00
Totall	03 :	19 :	00

Disbursments :—

	£	s.	d.
To Gainsbrough Friends for Thomas Recket wife		12 :	6
To Thomas Wresle, Beltoft for Bridget Mosley		02 :	6
To Thomas Wresle, Wintringham for widdow Walker		06 :	0
To Brigg widdows by Joseph Richardson ..		05 :	0
To Gervis Cornwell for Doll Pickhaver ..		02 :	6
To the Quarterly Meeting by Thomas Potter ..	01 :	05 :	0
Rests in stock	01 :	5 :	6

Next Monthly Meeting ordered to be at Gainsbrough.

Signed by Joseph Richardson.

ATT a Monthly Meeting held at Henry Simpsons in Gainsbrough the 8th day of the 2d month 1698[1] :—

Friends are taking care to get the burying place fenced at John Nainbys with all convenient speed.

David Crosby gives an account to this Meeting that he hath been with John Wresle of Brigg, & had a pritty time with him, & promised to appear at this Meeting, but haveing got some hurt of a legg could not come, soe David Crosby signifies he hath still something upon his minde & desires Edward Gilliatt

[1] 8th April, 1698.

may accompany him, & bring an account of his answer to the next Monthly Meeting.

Whereas the case of Martha Northen eldest son came under consideration of Friends in this Meeting, & it was left to Gainsbrough Friends to doe as they should see needfull & give an account to the next Monthly Meeting.

p. 210.

Henry Symson gives account to Friends in this Meeting of a certaine sum of money, left in Mathew Jackson hand, but will give further account thereof to the next Monthly Meeting.

This day Gervis Cornwell of Adlinfleet & Elizabeth Nainby of Caistrop came into this Meeting & signified there intentions of marriage each with other, but it being the first time they are desired to wait Friends answer till next Monthly Meeting.

Ordered that John Urry & James Coakes speake to Richard Turner to procure a certificate from the place where he formerly lived to give satisfaction to Friends concerning him, otherwayes Friends must doe it for there own satisfaction.

Next Monthly Meeting ordered to be at Thealby Meeting House.

Signed by Joseph Richardson.

ATT a Monthly Meeting held at the Meeting House in Thealby the 13th day of the 3d month 1698[1] :—

Brigge Friends have taken such care about the burying plaice at Caistrop that its now fenceing.

Gainsbrough Friends acquaints this Meeting that they have agreed with John Smith of Nottingham for 12d a week to mainteaine Martha Northern son for one year beginyng the first of this 3d month 1698.

Henry Symson gives an account that there is 6s. 8d. in Mathew Jackson hand, & will give a further account thereof to the next Monthly Meeting.

James Coakes & John Urry, senior hath spoken to Richard Turner, but he hath not given this Meeting such satisfaction as they desire therefore this Meeting desires they would deall with him againe & bring his answer or a certificate of his life & conversation to the next Monthly Meeting.

John Wresle of Brigg did this day appear at our Monthly Meeting & is sorry for his disorderly walking in times past, & doth promise to walk more orderly for the future & frequent Friends Meetings, & doth alsoe declare that he doth beleive in Friends love to him to deall thus with him.

[1] 13th May, 1698.

Ellinor Hudson & Mary Bishop are ordered to see what widdow Barrow stands in need of, & disburse the same & give account to the next Monthly Meeting.

p. 211.

Thomas Hutchison & Thomas Morley is desired to inquire after a convenient place for a bed to stand in for John Halliwell & give an account to the next Monthly Meeting.

This day Gervis Cornwell came into our Monthly Meeting & signified the continuance of his purpose of marriage with Elizabeth Nainby, & all things appearing clear on behalf of both parties, leaves the consumation thereof to themselves with the advice of Friends according to the good order of Truth.

Its disired that Friends take care that a contribution be collected & brought to the next Monthly Meeting which is ordered to be at Widdow Morleys in Adlinfleet.

Signed by Joseph Richardson,

ATT a Monthly Meeting held at Widdow Morley in Adlinfleet the 10th of 4th month 1698[1] :—

Brigg Friends gives an account that the burying place is fenceing but not wholly fenced.

This Meeting desires that Joseph Potter & Henry Symson make further inquiry about the 6 : 8 in Matthew Jackson hand & bring an account to the next Monthly Meeting.

John Urry & James Coakes have spoke to Richard Turner, but got no satisfactory answer from him soe that this Meeting desires Joseph Richardson & Edward Gilliatt doe what they can to procure a certificate from where he came concerning his life & conversation against the next Monthly Meeting.

Thomas Morley gives account to this Meeting that they had not yet found a place for John Halliwell but he with Robert Vessey are desired to look for one gainst the next Monthly Meeting.

Contributions came in as followeth :—

	£	s.	d.
Gainsbrough		13 :	6
Epworth..		13 :	6
Brigge		15 :	0
Winteringham ..		16 :	6
Garthrop		08 :	0
Totall	3 :	6 :	6

[1] 10th June, 1698.

Disbursments :—

	£	s.	d.
To Joseph Potter for Susan Recket	00	10	05½
To Francis Dent for Gervis Banton	00	05	00
to Mary Bishop for Widdow Barrow	00	3	6½
To John Bishop for Bridget Mosley	00	6	00
To Robert Vessey for Doll Pickhaver ..	00	2	00
for Quarterly Meeting	01	10	00
Remains in John Nainby hand in stock ..	00	9	6

p. 212.

This day William Huntsman of Epworth & Mary Nainby of Caistrop signified there intentions of marriage each with other, but it being the first time they are disired to wait Friends answer till the next Monthly Meeting.

The next Monthly Meeting ordered to be at the house of John Urrys in Epworth.

Signed by Joseph Richardson.

Att a Monthly Meeting held at the house of John Urrys in Epworth the 8th of the 5th month 1698[1] :—

Joshua Reeder gives account to this Meeting that he had spoke to John Halliwell who promisd he would amend his life & setle with him soe Friends left it till next Monthly Meeting.

Its still desired that Joseph Richardson, Robert Colyer & Edward Gilliatt procure a certificate about Richard Turner against next Monthly Meeting.

Joseph Richardson is desired to informe himself what contribution is to be collected for the poor distressed Friends in Scotland against the next Monthly Meeting.

Complaint in this Meeting hath been made that some Friends are not clear upon account of tythe soe that its desired that speciall care be taken to inquire who they are in each Meeting by the Friends appointed for such services to give an account to the next Monthly Meeting.

William Huntsman came this day a second time & signified the continuance of his purpose of marriage with Mary Nainby & brought a certificate signifying her consent, & Friends haveing nothing against it, have left the consumation thereof to themselves with Friends advice according to the good order of Truth.

Ordered that the next Monthly Meeting be at John Nainbys in Caistrop.

Signed by Joseph Richardson.

[1] 8th July, 1698.

ATT a Monthly Meeting held at John Nainbys in Caistrop the 12th of the 6th month 1698[1] :—

Thomas Morley & Thomas Hutchison acquainted Friends in this Meeting that they had procured a lodging place at Nicholas Bradley in Haudenby & they are desired to acquaint John & bring his answer to the next Monthly Meeting.

p. 213.

Friends as yet have got no certificate out of Darbyshire about Richard Turner but are in hopes to procure one against next Monthly Meeting,

Its desired that Friends who are chosen as overseers inquire of each perticuler Friend in there Meeting, about there clearness in paying tythe & bring an account to the next Monthly Meeting.

Contributions came in as followeth :—

	£	s.	d.
Gainsbrough	00 :	15 :	00
The Ile	00 :	14 :	00
Brigg	00 :	14 :	00
Wintringham	00 :	15 :	00
Garthrop	00 :	08 :	06
Totall	03 :	07 :	00

Disbursments :—

	£	s.	d.
To Henry Symson for Abraham Northen table with the 6 : 8 before made streight for 15 weekes	00 :	8 :	6
Rests in stock in Peter Nayler hand ..	2 :	18 :	8

Thomas Gibson of Haxey in the Ile came this day with Mary Pilsworth widdow of Epworth & published there intentions of marriage each with other but it being the first time they are desired to wait Friends answer till next Monthly Meeting.

Ordered that a generall contribution be collected for the nationall stock & brought to the next Monthly Meeting which is ordered to be at David Crosbys in Gunhouse.

Signed by Joseph Richardson.

ATT a Monthly Meeting held at the house of David Crosbys in Gunhouse the 9th of the 7th month 98[2] :—

Gervis Cornwell acquaints Friends that they had provided a bed for John Halliwell of Haudenby, & they are desired to see if he make use of it & give an account to the next Monthly Meeting.

According to order of the last Monthly Meeting Friends concerned have made inquiry in there Meetings of Friends clearness in

---

[1] 12th August, 1698.   [2] 9th September, 1698.

paying tythe & finds that Friends are pretty clear in the matter, & Friends that are overseers are still desired to use the same care and inquiry & to admonish such as are not faithfull in there Testimony therein.

p. 214.

Gainsbrough Friends are still desired to use there care that Susanna Recket suffer not want.

Gainsbrough Friends gives an account that a Meeting for Worshipp is setled amongst them every 3d sixt day in each month besides, besids the first 6th day which was setled before.

The nationall contribution came in as followeth :—

		£	s.	d.
Imps. Gainsbrough	.. ..	02 : 15 : 00
The Ile ..	.. ..	02 : 10 : 06
Brigge ..	.. ..	03 : 01 : 00
Winteringham	..	02 : 10 : 00
Garthrop..	.. ..	01 : 06 : 00
Totall ..	.. ..	12 : 02 : 06

Gainsbrough Friends are desired to take care in carrying this contribution to the next Quarterly Meeting at Lincolne.

The stock that remains is in Gainsbrough Friends	£	s.	d.
hand is	2 : 18 : 8
paid to Crowle for Bridget Mosley	00 : 05 : 00
to Thomas Wresle for Gervas Bainton ..	00 : 6 : 00
to the Quarterly Meeting	02 : 00 : 00
to Joseph Berrier	00 : 02 : 06

Rests in Edward Gilliatt hands in stock .. .. 00 : 04 : 6

This day Thomas Gibson of Haxey in the Ile of Axholme & Mary Pilsworth of Epworth came a second time & signified the continuance of there purpose of marriage each with other, & Friends finding not to withstand it have left to themselves with Friends advice according to the good order of Truth.

Next Monthly Meeting ordered to be at Brigge.

Signed by Joseph Richardson.

The 14th of the 8th month 98. Att a Monthly Meeting held at the Meeting House at Edward Gilliatts in Brigge[1] :—

Thomas Morley acquainted Friends that John Halliwell had not made use of the room they had provided for him.

Rests in stock in Peter Naylers hand 10s.

[1] 14th October, 1698.

p. 215.

The loss that Aquilla Scottney & Francis Hastings, Friends in Spalding suffered by fire came under Friends consideration in this Meeting, where Friends unanimously consented and agreed to raise £5 in this Monthly Meeting for there releife.

David Crosby is desired to give an account to the next Monthly Meeting what conclusion is made with widdow Marshall about her son being apprentice with him.

Its desired that Friends be carefull to bring in an account of there suffering from tythes to the next Monthly Meeting.

Its desired that Edward Gilliatt get a license from the Justices for Anthony Westabys Meeting House at Winteringham & for Thomas Foster house in Crowle.

Next Monthly Meeting ordered to be att Brigge.

Signed by Joseph Richardson,

ATT a Monthly Meeting held at the Meeting House att Edward Gilliatts in Brigg the 11th of 9th month 1698[1] :—

The contributions brought in for those Spalding Friends that suffered loss by fire :—

	£	s.	d.
Gainsbrough Friends	01	00	00
Winteringham	01	00	00
Brigge	01	00	00
Garthrop	00	11	00
Totall	3	11	00

all in Joseph Richardson hand.

David Crosby being not here is desired to give an account what he has done about taking widdow Marshalls son apprentice.

Its disired that all Friends take speciall care in bringing up there sufferings for tythe to the next Monthly Meeting.

This Meeting desires that Robert Colyer & Thomas Nainby goe to speak with John Wresle of Brigg, & desire his appearance at our next Monthly Meeting to give Freinds satisfaction why they may not proceed to give forth a Testimony against him.

Ordered that a contribution be collected & brought up to the next Monthly Meeting which is to be at Brigge.

Signed by Joseph Richardson.

[1] 11th November, 1698.

F

p. 216.

Friends of Winteringham Meeting have setled another Meeting for Worshipp at Winteringham the first 4th day in every month, the other being at Thealby the last 6th day in every month.

ATT a Monthly Meeting held at the Meeting House at Edward Gilliatts in Brigge the 9th day of the 10th month 98[1] :—

The Ile Friends brought in there collection being 20s. to this Meeting for those Friends that suffered loss by fire in Spalding ; which with what was collected before makes up five pounds which is desired to be carried up to the Quarterly Meeting for the service aforesaid.

David Crosby acquaints Friends that for some reasons he findes that widdow Marshall son is not fitt for him. Gainsbrough Friends are desired to consult with his mother for some place & employment for him against the next Monthly Meeting till which time David Crosby is willing he shall stay at his house.

Friends have brought in there suffering for tythe from the seaverall Meetings save the Ile Meeting & they intend to make theres ready & carry them to the Quarterly Meeting.

Robert Colyer & Thomas Nainby acquaints Friends in this Meeting that they have spoke to John Wresle, who desires another monthes time, & Friends desires that Edward Gilliatt & Joseph Richardson speak to him & put him in minde of his promiss.

Contributions came in as followeth :—

	£	s.	d.
Gainsbrough	00	15	00
The Ile	00	13	06
Winteringham	00	17	0
Brigg	00	15	00
Garthrop	00	08	06
	03	09	00

Disbursments as followeth :—

	£	s.	d.
To Peter Nayler towards a bill of charges brought into this Meeting	01	09	00
To the Quarterly Meeting	02	00	00

Next Monthly Meeting ordered to be at Brigge,

Signed by Joseph Richardson.

[1] 9th December, 1698.

p. 217.

Att a Monthly Meeting held at the Meeting House at Edward Gilliatts in Brigg the 13th of the 11th month 1698[1] :—

Friends in this Meeting have had some further discourse about widdow Marshall son that is with David Crosby at present, and have agreed, that David Crosby get him to his mother at Gainsbrough to remaine there till Freinds find an oppertunity to present to putt him out to another.

According to the order of the last Monthly Meeting Joseph Richardson & David Crosby spoke to John Wresle of Brigge, and after some discourse, prevailed with him soe much as he came to this Meeting, where Friends spoke to him what was upon there spirits for the clearing of themselves & the Truth, & he seemed to be low in his minde, & promised to frequent Friends Meetings and indeavour to amend his life, as alsoe to make his appearance at our next Monthly Meeting.

Robert Vesse acquainted Friends that they had been at some charge about John Halliwell & was like to be at more, & Friends has desired him to take care thereof & bring an account to the next Monthly Meeting.

Upon some discourse about John Browne, Jabez Bethells apprentice Friends advised Jabez his master to deliver his indentures to Friends which he has done accordingly & Friends have desired Joseph Berrier to see for a place for John Browne & give an account to the next Monthly Meeting.

Joseph Berrier acquainted this Meeting that Widdow Snowdall was in some nessesity, & Friends have desired that he with Friends would look after it & give an account to the next Monthly Meeting.

Ordered that a contribution be collected & brought up to the next Monthly Meeting which is ordered to be at Brigge.

Signed by Joseph Richardson.

Att a Monthly Meeting held at the Meeting House the 10th day of the 12th month 98[2] :—

The care of Thomas, widdow Marshall son is left to Gainsbrough Freinds, David Crosby bill of charges concerning him came to 02 : 07 : 02.

[1] 13th January, 1699.   [2] 10th February, 1699.

Thomas Morley acquainted Friends that Robert Vesse paid on John Halliwell account 00 : 14 : 00 and the further care about him is left to there Meetinge.

p. 218.

Jabez Bethell acquainted Friends in this Meeting that he is not satisfied about delivering John Browne indentures in.

James Coakes acquainted Friends of the nessisities of widdow Snowdell of Ealand, & Friends desires that Mary Bishopp & another Friend goe and advise with her & her son & daughter, to see what most needfull to be done in the matter & give an account to the next Monthly Meeting.

Abraham Morrice sent a letter which was read in this Meeting which signified the nessessitious condition of Richard Theaker, & Friends are desired in each Perticular Meeting to stirr up the most able amongst them to collect something for his releife & bring it up to the next Monthly Meeting.

Contributions came in as followeth :—

	£	s.	d.
Gainsbrough	00	15	6
The Ile	00	12	0
Winteringham	00	14	6
Brigge	00	14	6
Garthrop	00	09	0
Totall	03	05	06

which is in Joseph Richardson hand.

John Wresle came againe to this Meeting, & promises to frequent Friends Meeting as alsoe to answer there care & love towards him.

Next Monthly Meeting ordered to be at Brigge & a contribution to be collected & brought up thither as alsoe that Friends in each Perticular Meeting that are able contribute something to the releife of Richard Theaker & his poor family.

Signed by Joseph Richardson.

ATT a Monthly Meeting held at Brigg the 10th of the first month 1699[1] :—

The care of Thomas Marshall is still continued with Gainsbrough Friends.

The care of John Halliwell is continued upon Garthrop Meeting.

Jabez Bethell proposall is left to futher consideration about John Brown.

[1] 10th March, 1699.

Contributions came in as followeth :—

	£	s.	d.
Gainsbrough	00	15	06
The Ile	00	12	00
Winteringham	00	12	00
Brigg	00	14	00
Garthrop	00	08	00
In stock Joseph Richardson..	03	05	06

Disbursments :—

	£	s.	d.
to Robert Vesse which he paid on John Halliwell account	00	14	00
to Joseph Berrier for widdow Snowdall ..	00	03	06
to Peter Nayler which cleares of for Abraham Northen	00	13	00
till the 12th of this first month 99 more upon Thomas Recket wife account	00	11	00
Ordered to the Quarterly Meeting	03	00	00
& for Richard Theaker	04	10	00
Rests in Joseph Richardson hand	00	03	00

David Crosby bill remaines yet unpaid comes to   02 : 07 : 02

Next Monthly Meeting ordered at Gainsbrough.

Signed by Joseph Richardson.

p. 219.

ATT a Monthly Meeting held at Henry Symsons in Gainsbrough the 14th day of the 2d month 1699[1] :—

Gainsbrough Friends acquaints this Meeting that they had taken some care about Thomas Marshall & had some discourse with Richard Cockerill of there town hempdresser in order to putt him an aprentice, & Friends have left it to them to make as good a bargaine as they can with him & give an account to the next Monthly Meeting.

Friends desires Garthrop Meeting would continue there care over John Halliwell, & imploy him as oppertunity presents.

Jabez Bethell is desired to acquaint Friends at the next Monthly Meeting what his dissatisfaction is about John Browne.

Ordered that a contribution be collected, & brought up to the next Monthly Meeting which is to be at Anthony Westobys in Winteringham.

Signed by Joseph Richardson.

[1] 14th April, 1699.

ATT a Monthly Meeting held at the house of Anthony Westobys in Winteringham the 12th of 3d month 99[1] :—

Gainsbrough Friends acquainted this Meeting that they had discoursed with Richard Cockerill of there town hemp dresser about takeing Thomas Marshall apprentice & alsoe with his & his mother consent had bound him for 5 yeares to enter the 17th day of the 2d month 99 & paid him 30s. at his entrance & was by contract to pay 20s. more at 12 months end—which is to be in full of what he is to have with him for learning the aforesaid employment, his mother with Freinds assistance is to finde him apparell & other conveniences.

Its still desired that Friends of Garthrop Meeting would have an eye over John Halliwell, & give him lodging & put him upon some employment as much as they can, & give an account to the next Monthly Meeting.

Upon some further discourse with Jabez Bethell about John Browne Friends have agreed to deliver him his indentures in againe provided he will take care to seek him out & imploy him according to the contract Friends at first made with him.

Upon some discourse with Gainsbrough Friends about Thomas Recket, Friends of this Meeting have left it to them to discourse with the neighbourhood at Lea, & give an account at the next Monthly Meeting.

Contributions came in as followeth :—

				£	s.	d.
Gainsbrough	..	..	..	00 :	15 :	6
The Ile ..	..	..	..	00 :	15 :	0
Winteringham ..	..	..	..	00 :	16 :	0
Brigge ..	..	..	..	00 :	15 :	0
Garthrop	..	..	..	00 :	08 :	6
Totall	..	..	..	03 :	10 :	00

Disbursments :—

	£	s.	d.
to Francis Dent for help of Judith Tayler ..	00 :	15 :	00
to Robert Vesse which he paid on John Halliwells account	00 :	05 :	00
to David Crosby toward his disbursments ..	01 :	00 :	00
to Gainsbrough towards ther disbursments ..	01 :	10 :	00
Remains yet to Gainsbrough Friends of what they have laid down	00 :	18 :	00
& rests to David Crosby still	01 :	07 :	2
oweing to Joseph Richardson for 2 certificates	00 :	05 :	0

[1] 12th May, 1699.

p. 220.

This Meeting has agreed & concluded to hold a Meeting for Worshipp
at David Crosby house in Gunhouse, to begin the last 6th
day in this month & soe to continue the last 6th day in every
month dureing this sumer season as Friends shall see meet.

Next Monthly Meeting ordered to be at Joshua Reeders at Cotle
Hall, & a contribution to be collected & brought up thither.

> Signed by Joseph Richardson.

ATT a Monthly Meeting held at Joshua Reeders, Cotle Hall
the 9th day of the 4th month 1699[1] :—

It is still desired that Friends Garthrop Meeting continue there
care over John Halliwell that he want not such convenient
lodging as they shall see meet & give an account to the next
Monthly Meeting.

Upon discourse with Gainsbrough Friends about Thomas Reckett
Friends of this Meeting have left it to them to do for him as
they shall see meet & this Meeting will see them indempnified.

This Meeting still agrees to continue the Meeting for Worshipp at
David Crosbys in Gunhouse.

Contributions came in as followeth :—

	£	s.	d.
Gainsbrough	00	18	00
Brigge	00	15	00
The Ile	00	15	00
Winteringham	00	14	00
Garthrop	00	09	06
Totall	03	11	06

Disbursments :—

	£	s.	d.
To the Quarterly Meeting	02	17	00
to Joseph Richardson which he laid down	00	05	00
To Thomas Foster for Bridget Mosley & Margaret Snowdall	00	06	00
To Thomas Wresle, Wintringham	00	03	06

Next Monthly Meeting ordered to be at John Urrys house in Epworth,

> Signed by Joseph Richardson.

ATT a Monthly Meeting held at the house of John Urrys in
Epworth the 14th of the 5th month 1699[2] :—

Friends still agrees to continue the Meeting for Worshipp at David
Crosbys house as formerly.

[1] 9th June, 1699.   [2] 14th July, 1699.

Ordered that a contribution be collected & brought up to the next
Monthly Meeting which is ordered at John Nainbys in Castlethorp.

Signed by Joseph Richardson.

p. 221.

ATT a Monthly Meeting held at the house of John Nainbys
in Castlethorp the 10th of the 6th month 1699[1] :—

This Meeting desires that Brigg Friends would take care in getting
the writeings drawn & sealed before the next Monthly Meeting
for the burying place at John Nainbys.

John Clark of Garthrop came into this Meeting & published his
intentions of marriage with Sarah Walker daughter of William
Walker of Heck in the County of Yorke, & brought with him a
certificate under her fathers hand signifying his & his wifes
consent thereunto, but this Meeting desires that he would
take speciall care to get a certificate alsoe under the hand of the
aforesaid Sarah Walker signifying not only her consent but the
continuance of her purpose of marriage with him, & alsoe of
her being clear from all other persons, this being the first time
they are desired to wait Friends answer till the next Monthly
Meeting.

Contribution for bookes came in as followeth :—

				£	s.	d.
Gainsbrough	..	..	..	14	:	0½
The Ile ..	..	..	..	12	:	1½
Wintringham	..	..	..	12	:	5½
Brigg ..	..	..	..	13	:	06½
Garthrop	..	..	..	09	:	9½

Totall .. .. .. 03 : 01 : 1½ left with Peter
Nayler to be sent to Lincolne.

Ordered that the next Monthly Meeting be at David Crosbys house
in Gunhouse, & that a contribution be collected & brought
up thither.

Signed by Joseph Richardson.

ATT a Monthly Meeting held at the house of David Crosby
the 8th of the 7th month 1699[2] :—

Its still desired Brigg Friends take care to get the burying place
writeings made & sealed with John Nainby of Castlethorp.

Whereas complaint has been made in this Meeting about some
difference that has lately hapened betwixt Robert Earott
& Richard Turner, this Meeting desires that Richard Clark

[1] 10th August, 1699.   [2] 8th September, 1699.

would please to speak to Robert Earott to appear at the next Monthly Meeting & that John Urry would alsoe speak to Richard Turner to appear alsoe, & if they appear not to bring in there answer.

p. 222.

Contributions came in as followeth :—

	£	s.	d.
Gainsbrough		18 :	0
The Ile		14 :	0
Winteringham		17 :	0
Brigg		16 :	6
Garthrop		08 :	6
Totall	03 :	14 :	0

Disbursments :—

	£	s.	d.
To the Quarterly Meeting	01 :	10 :	00
To Gainsbrough for Thomas Recket wife ..	00 :	11 :	00
To Doll Pickhaver	00 :	02 :	00
To Margret Snowden	00 :	02 :	00
In Joseph Richardson hand	01 :	09 :	00

Next Monthly Meeting at Gainsbrough.

Signed by Joseph Richardson.

ATT a Monthly Meeting held at the house of Henry Symson in Gainsbrough the 13 of the 8th month 1699[1] :—

Brigg Friends are yet desired to take care to get the burying place writeings sealed at John Nainbys.

Joseph Richardson has paid into this Meeting the 29s. & its disburst as followeth :—

	£	s.	d,
To Bridget Mosley	00 :	04 :	00
to Marget Snowdell	00 :	03 :	06

Brigg Friends are to buy John Halliwell a coat with remainder of the money in John Nainby hand.

The difference between Robert Earott & Richard Turner came before Friends of this Meeting, & upon examination found Richard Turner much to blame, & agreed that a letter of condemnation should be drawn up before next Monthly Meeting against Richard Turner which he has promised to signe.

This day Amor Empson of Redness came into our Monthly Meeting & published his intentions of marriage with Mary Morley of Adlinfleett & shee being present gave her consent but it being

[1] 13th October, 1699.

the first time they are desired to wait Friends answer till the next Monthly Meeting, & the said Amor Empson is desired to bring his father consent or his reasons to the contrary.

Upon some reasons given the Meeting has ordered the Monthly Meeting to be the 3d 6th day in each Month dureing this winter.

Ordered the next Monthly Meeting to be at Brigg.

Signed by Joseph Richardson.

p. 223.

ATT a Monthly Meeting held at the Meeting House at Edward Gilliatts in Brigg the 17th of the 9th month 1699[1] :—

This Meeting desires Joseph Richardson, William Smith & Robert Colyer & Edward Gilliatt & Thomas Nainby advise with John Nainby to get the writeings made & sealed against the next Monthly Meeting.

The business betwixt Robert Earott & Richard Turner came this day againe before Friends & a paper was drawn up of matter & things betwixt them as alsoe something of condemnation for Richard Turner to signe, but he being not here John Urry, senior of Epworth is desired to speak to Richard Turner to appear at the next Monthly Meeting to performe the promiss he made to Friends.

Amor Empson bussiness is refered to the next Monthly Meeting.

Ordered the next Monthly Meeting be the 3d 6th day of next month.

Signed by Joseph Richardson.

ATT a Monthly Meeting held at the Meeting House at Edward Gilliatts in Brigg the 15th of the 10th month 1699[2] :—

Friends have according to order got the writeings & hopes to get them drawn & sealed before next Monthly Meeting.

In regard Richard Turner came not to this Meeting according to his promiss John Urry, senior & William Reed are desired to speak to him to know the cause, & alsoe to desire his appearance at next Monthly Meeting.

Amor Empson appeared at this Meeting & signified his fathers unwillingness in consenting to mary with Mary Morley soe that he with Mary Morley are both willing to wait time till the matter be more cleared to his father & Friends satisfaction.

This Meeting has ordered that Peter Nayler take care that sufferings be brought into the Quarterly orderly & John Urrye for the Iles, Francis Dent for Winteringhams, Thomas Morley & Robert Vesse for Adlinfleet & Joseph Richardson for Brigg.

[1] 17th November, 1699.   [2] 15th December, 1699.

Contributions came in as followeth :—

	£	s.	d.
Gainsbrough		19 :	6
The Ile		18 :	0
Winteringham		15 :	6
Brigg		16 :	0
Garthrop		09 :	6
stock	01 :	1 :	6

Disbursments :—

	£	s.	d.
To David Crosby in full	01 :	00 :	0
To Robert Colyer	00 :	11 :	0
To Peter Nayler for Susan Recket	00 :	08 :	0
To John Urry for Widdow Mosley & William Wright	00 :	04 :	00
to Thomas Morley for Doll Pickhaver ..	00 :	01 :	00
to Peter Nayler for Matthew Jackson on Abraham Northen account	00 :	18 :	00
To Peter Nayler for Quarter Meeting ..	01 :	10 :	00
To Robert Vesse for Doll Pickhaver	00 :	02 :	00
To Joseph Richardson for 2 poor widdows ..		04 :	11

Ordered next Monthly Meeting be held the 3d 6th day of next month at Brigg.

Signed by Joseph Richardson.

p. 224.

ATT a Monthly Meeting held at the Meeting House att Edward Gilliatts in Brigg the 19th of 11th month 1699[1] :—

Friends have got the writings drawn & will get them sealed against next Monthly Meeting.

Richard Turner appeared at this Meeting, & has promised to draw up a paper of condemnation & signe it for Friends satisfaction & clearing the Truth & bring it to next Monthly Meeting.

Something being spoken to in this Meeting about Amor Empson & Mary Morley, Its the judgment of Friends that whereas there has been proceedings in this Meeting between them in order to marriage, that the parties concerned draw up a paper each to other for the setting each other at liberty, because they cannot obtaine parents consent as alsoe for Friends satisfaction.

Sufferings for tythe was carried up to Lincolne by all the Meetings save Winteringham & Brigg, & they are desired to get theres fairly drawn over & send them to Thomas Robinson.

[1] 19th January, 1700.

Next Monthly Meeting ordered to be the 2d 6th day at Brigg as
formerly.

                                    . Signed by Joseph Richardson.

ATT a Monthly Meeting held at the Meeting House at Edward
Gilliatts in Brigg the 9th of 12th month 1699[1] :—

Friends have got the writeings about the burying place, sealed.
at John Nainbys & lodged them in Joseph Richardson hand.

Richard Turner sent 2 letters which was read in this Meeting, but
Friends not being satisfied therewith have sent him a few
lines to desire his appearance at our next Monthly Meeting.

Friends desires that Thomas Hutchisson would accompany Thomas
Morley to goe to Amor Empson to procure some few lines from
him to set Mary Morley free from all former engagements with
him as alsoe to get her to doe the like to him & bring an account
to the next Monthly Meeting.

Friends have brought in there sufferings for tythe & Brigg Friends
intends to get theres ready & send to Thomas Robinson,

Ordered that the next Monthly Meeting be at Brigg & that as many
weomen Friends come as conveniently can, & that a contribution
be collected & brought up thither.

                                    Signed by Joseph Richardson.

ATT a Monthly Meeting held at the Meeting House at Edward
Gilliatts in Brigg the 8th of the first month 1700[2] :—

Contributions came in as followeth :—

	£	s.	d.
Gainsbrough		18 :	0
the Ile		18 :	0
Winteringham		19 :	0
Brigge		16 :	0
Garthrop		09 :	0
Totall	04 : 00 :		0

Disbursments :—

	£	s.	d.
to Matthew Jackson for Abraham Northen ..		07 :	6
with 15s. before makes up one year			
3 bushels coales for Susan Recket		03 :	3
to James Coakes for Widdow Snowdell ..		02 :	9
to Doll Pickhaver by Thomas Morley ..		03 :	0
to the Quarterly Meeting	01 :	10 :	0
Rests in stock in Joseph Richardson hand ..	1 :	14 :	0

[1] 9th February, 1700.   [2] 8th March, 1700.

Richard Turner sent another letter to this Meeting but it being
to no satisfaction have writt to him againe, desireing the
performance of his promiss made to Friends at Gainsbrough
Monthly Meeting.

Thomas Morley according to order obtained a few lines under Amor
Empson hand, that cleares all former engagements betwixt
him & Mary Morley, & shee has promised to doe the like to
him when oppertunity presents.

Joseph Potter of Gainsbrough came this day into the Meeting &
published his intention of marriage with Mary Simpson of the
same, & brought a certificate from her father & another from
herself signifying both there consent to the matter but it
being the first they are desired to wait Friends answer till
next Monthly Meeting.

Thomas Williamson of Searby came this day into our Monthly
Meeting & published his intentions of marriage with Mary
Holmes of Midle Rasen & shee being present gave her consent
but it being the first they are both desired to wait Friends
answer till next Monthly Meeting.

Ordered the next Monthly Meeting be at Gainsbrough,

Signed by Joseph Richardson.

ATT a Monthly Meeting held at the house of Henry Symson
in Gainsbrough the 12th of 2d month 1700[1] :—

Its desired that the paper concerning Robert Barclay Apologies
be sent to Garthrop & from Brigg to Winteringham, that they
may subscribe what number they will take & bring an account
to the next Monthly Meeting.

Gainsbrough Meeting has subscribed to take of 13
Brigg Meeting has subscribed to take of 20

p. 225.

Joseph Potter & Mary Simson of Gainsbrough came a second time
& signified the continuance of there purpose of marriage each
with other, & Friends haveing nothing against it, have left
the consumation thereof to there own conveniency according
to the good order of Truth,

Thomas Williamson of Searby came a second time into this Meeting
& signified the continuance of his purpose of marriage with
Mary Holmes of Midle Rasen & brought a certificate from
her self & another from her mother signifying there willingness
& alsoe a letter from Partney Monthly Meeting that they left
the matter to us & Friends here haveing nothing against it

[1] 12th April, 1700.

have left the consumation thereof to themselves with Friends
advice according to the good order of Truth.

Ordered that the next Monthly Meeting be held at John Wresles
in Thealby.

Signed by Joseph Richardson.

ATT a Monthly Meeting held at the Meeting House at Thealby
the 10th day of the 3d month 1700[1] :—

The Ile Meeting subscribed to take of Robert Barclay's Appologies 21
Winteringham Meeting   21
Garthrop Meeting   5

Totall in this Monthly Meeting   80

Something being opened in this Meeting concerning David Crosby
daughter being married with a young man at London upon a
diblrate[2] consideration of the matter Thomas Wresle of Winteringham & Joseph Richardson of Brigg declare there willingness
to goe to Davids house & discourse the parties concerned &
give an account thereof to the next Monthly Meeting which
this Meeting approves of.

Upon some discourse about John Halliwell, Friends desires that
Robert Vesse with the advice of other Friends in that Meeting,
to see if they can take a room for him with conveniences for
lodging, & give an account to the next Meeting,

Ordered that a contribution be collected & brought to the next
Meeting which is to be at Jane Morleys in Adlinfleet.

Signed by Joseph Richardson.

p. 226.

ATT a Monthly Meeting held at the house of Jane Morley
in Adlinfleett the 11th of 4th month 1700[3] :—

William Smith & Robert Colyer was ordered from this Meeting
to goe to David Crosbys, & discourse him about the disorder
of his daughter & bring his answer to the next Monthly Meeting.

This day John Symson of Gainsbrough came into the Meeting
& published his intention of marriage with Margret Morley
of Adlinfleet & shee being present gave her consent, but it being
the first time they are desired to wait Friends answer to the
next Monthly Meeting.

This day came John Marshall son of John Marshall of Yorke &
published his intention of marriage with Rebecka Symson of
Gainsbrough & shee being present gave her consent but it being
the first time they are desired to wait Friends answer till next
Monthly Meeting.

[1] 10th May, 1700.   [2] *Sic* for deliberate.   [3] 11th June, 1700.

This day contributions came in as followeth :—

	£	s.	d.
Imps. from Gainsbrough		17 :	6
Brigg		15 :	6
Wintringham		15 :	0
The Ile		17 :	6
Garthrop		08 :	6
Totall	03 :	14 :	6

Disbursments :—

	£	s.	d.
To Thomas Potter for young Marshall apprentice	01 :	00 :	00
To Thomas Potter for Thomas Reckit	00 :	08 :	00
for 2 widdows in the Ile	00 :	08 :	00
for Doll Pickhaver	00 :	04 :	00

	£	s.	d.
Rests in Thomas Potter hands for Quarterly Meeting	01 :	12 :	08
Remains in Robert Colyer hands	00 :	02 :	06

Next Meeting ordered at John Urrys in Epworth.

Signed by Joseph Richardson.

ATT a Monthly Meeting held at John Urrys in Epworth the 12th day of the 5th month 1700[1] :—

Whereas William Smith & Robert Colyer was ordered to give David Crosby a vissitt about his daughter ; but he being from home they are desired to wait an oppertunity to answer Friends request before the next Monthly Meeting.

The Friends appointed for collecting a contribution for the poor Friends that suffered loss by fire are as followeth :—

p. 227.

Thomas Wresle & John Dent for Winteringham.
Robert Colyer & John Barlow for Brigge.
Peter Nayler & William West for Gainsbrough.
Thomas Hutchinson & Thomas Morley for Marshland.
Thomas Cutsforth, Richard Clark & John Urry for the Ile Meeting.

This Meeting desires that the 2 men & weomen Friends of each Meeting that are appointed to inspect into Truths affairs doe attend next Monthly Meeting or send in there answer.

The intention of marriage betwixt John Marshall and Rebecka Symson deffered by reason of some indisposition of body & other things till next Monthly Meeting.

[1] 12th July, 1700.

This day John Symson & Margret Morley came a second & signified
the continuance of there purpose of marriage each with other :
& Freinds finding nothing but clearness by both parties have
left the consumation to themselves with Friends advice according to the good order of Truth.

Next Monthly Meeting ordered at John Nainbys & a contribution
to be collected & brought up thither.

                         Signed by Joseph Richardson.

ATT a Monthly Meeting at John Nainbys in Castlethorp the
9th day of the 6th month 1700[1] :—

Its desired by this Meeting that the most able Friends doe contribute
freely for supply of Mumby Monthly Meeting, and for that
Friend that suffered loss by fire.

The Meeting being cald over, Friends belonging each Meeting to
inspect into Truths affaires gave an account to Friends satisfaction.

The further publication of marriage betwixt John Marshall and
Rebecka Symson is still deffered for divers reasons.

The Friends appointed to speak to David Crosby have had a pretty
time with him to there satisfaction, when his daughter has given
a Testimony against her disorderly proceedings in marriage.

Next Monthly Meeting ordered at David Crosbys & that collection
for Mumby Meeting & the Friend that suffered by fire be brought
thither.

p. 228.

ATT a Monthly Meeting held at the house of David Crosbys
in Gunhouse the 13th of the 7th month 1700[2] :—

The further publication of marriage betwixt John Marshall &
Rebecka Symson is deffered to the next Meeting at Gainsbrough.

This day Mordeca Westoby of Winteringham came into the Meeting
& published his intentions of marriage with Elizabeth Austine,
& brought with him a letter from her, her father & mother
signifying there willingness, but it giving not such satisfaction
to Freinds as they desire, Thomas Wresle is desired to speak
to Anthony Westoby & his wife, to obtaine better satisfaction
against next Monthly Meeting & alsoe of clearnes in all other
matters.

Next Monthly Meeting ordered at Gainsbrough.

                         Signed by Joseph Richardson.

[1] 9th August, 1700.   [2] 13th September, 1700.

ATT a Monthly Meeting held at Henry Symsons in Gainsbrough the 11th day of the 8th month 1700[1] :—

This day John Marshall late of Lime Street grocer in London came a second time & signified the continuance of his purpose of marriage with Rebecka Symson & shee being present gave her consent, and upon examination of matters having found all things clear on behalf of both parties have left the consumation thereof to there own discretion with Friends advice according to the good order of Truth.

Friends at this Meeting have agreed to give John Smith of Nottingham for helping to maintaine Abraham Northen in regard John Smith has promised to ease Friends of the aforesaid charge as soon as he well can.

This day Samuel Browne of Butterwick came into our Meeting & published his intention of marriage with Anne Graham of Brigg & brought a certificate signifying her consent thereto but it being first time they are desired to wait Friends answer till next Monthly Meeting.

Disburst to Thomas Brown 2s. & James Carnell 6d both 00 : 02 : 6

John Urry & Robert Coakes are desired to see that all things be clear on Samuel Brown account against next Monthly Meeting.

Next Monthly Meeting ordered at Brigg.

Signed by Joseph Richardson.

p. 229.

ATT a Monthly Meeting held at Brigg the 8th of 9th month 1700[2] :—

This day Samuel Browne of Butterwick came a second time & signified the continuance of his purpose of marriage with Anne Graham of Brigge & shee being present gave her consent & Friends finding all things clear on behalfe of both parties have left the consumation thereof to themselves with Friends advice according to Truths order.

This day Mordeca Westoby of Winteringham came a second time into our Meeting & signified the continuance of his purpose of marriage with Elizabeth Austine of Lincolne, & brought a certificate that he & shee had done the like there as alsoe Testimony was given in this Meeting that it is with parents consent, & Freinds not findeing matter of objection to hinder there proceedings on his part have left the matter to be confirmed by Lincolne Monthly Meeting on her part according to Truths order.

[1] 11th October, 1700.   [2] 8th November, 1700.

Next Monthly Meeting ordered at Brigg & a contribution brought up thither.

Signed by Joseph Richardson.

ATT a Monthly Meeting held at Brigg the 13th of 10th month 1700[1] :—

John Dent acquainted Friends at this Meeting that he is at present without a boy if Edward Gilliatt will discourse him about William Bogg.

Contributions came in as followeth :—

		£	s.	d.
Gainsbrough	.. .. ..	01	00	00
Winteringham	.. .. ..	00	15	00
Brigg	.. .. ..	00	17	00
Ile	.. .. ..	00	13	0
Garthrop	.. .. ..	00	08	0
Totall	.. .. ..	03	13	0

Disbursments :—

sent Matthew Jackson for Abraham Northen 9s. which cleares all till 9th of 10th month 1700 & 8s. more for Thomas Reckit rent.

	£	s.	d.
To Robert Colyer for shifts for John Halliwell		5	11
To Edward Gilliatt for Mary Goxhill & H. S.[2]		06	0
To the Quarterly Meeting ordered	02	00	00
Rests in Joseph Richardson hand	00	04	1
before of stock more in Joseph Richardson hand	01	12	8
Indebted to Abraham Morrice for bookes ..	01	11	10

Next Monthly Meeting ordered at Brigg.

Signed by Joseph Richardson.

p. 230.

ATT a Monthly Meeting held at the Meeting House at Brigg the 9th of the 11th month 1700[3] :—

Gainsbrough Friends acquainted this Meeting that Widdow Marshall of there town had a son which shee desired might be placed to some trade among Friends which Friends have taken notice on & will acquaint there respective Meetings with & give an account to the next Monthly Meeting.

John Urry, junior acquainted this Meeting that William Reed of Epworth had gone into the world to take a wife & was married

---

[1] 13th December, 1700.   [2] *Sic* for Hester Stephenson.   [3] 9th January, 1701.

with a preist, besides some other gross wickedness that he
comited with the weoman, soe that Friends of this Meeting
desires that they would appoint two faithfull Friends in there
Meeting to speak to him for clearing the Truth of all such
disorder & wickedness, and bring his answer to the next
Monthly Meeting.

Next Monthly Meeting ordered at Brigg.

Signed by Joseph Richardson.

ATT a Monthly Meeting held at Brigg the 14 of 12th month
1700[1] :—

The further care of Widdow Marshall son about putting out to a
  shoemaker trade is left to George Atkinson of Thorne who is
  desired to speak to a Friend in there town about takeing of
  him, & give Gainsbrough Friends notice thereof before next
  Meeting.

Thomas Wresle & Robert Coakes acquainted Friends in this Meeting
  that they had spoke to William Reed of Epworth according
  as Friends desired & that he intended to come to our next
  Meeting to answer to such matters as Friends had to object
  against him in order for there satisfaction & clearing the
  Truth which promiss they are desired to reminde him of.

This Meeting being acquainted about the disorderly practice of
  Richard Cox of Appleby by runing into the world for a wife
  & marrying with a preist. Thomas Wresle, Francis Dent &
  Joseph Richardson are disired to speak to him about it & bring
  an account to the next Meeting.

This day George Waddingham of Wintringham came into our
  Meeting & published his intention of marriage with Anne
  Marshall of the same town, & shee being present gave her
  consent but it being the first time they are desired to wait
  Friends answer till next Meeting. Thomas Wresle & George
  Frow are desired to see into the clearness of both parties.

p. 231.

Next Monthly Meeting ordered at Brigg and a contribution to be
  collected & brought thither.

Signed by Joseph Richardson.

ATT a Monthly Meeting held at the Meeting House at Brigg
the 14th of first month 1701[2] :—

The place at Thorn is not likely to be for Widdow Marshall son
  & therefore the care about him is left to Gainsbrough Friends.

[1] 14th February, 1701.   [2] 14th March, 1701.

William Reed of Epworth appearing at this Meeting some Friends was selected out & discoursed with him, & left it for him to give in his answer to the next Monthly Meeting,

The matter of Richard Cox of Appleby is still left to Francis Dent, George Frow, Thomas Wresle & John Waddingham & to bring in his answer to the next Monthly Meeting.

This day George Waddingham of Winteringham & Anne Marshall of the same signified the continuance of there purpose of marriage each with other, & all things appearing clear on behalf of both parties Friends have given consent to the same & left the consumation thereof to themselves as convenient opportunity offers.

This day John Herrison of Winteringham came into our Meeting & published his intentions of marriage with Susanna Davys of Belton & shee being present gave her consent & brought certificates signifying there parents consent but it being the first time they are both desired to wait Friends answer till next Monthly Meeting, Friends are desired in each Meeting to see into the clearness of both parties.

Contributions came in as followeth :—

	8	s,	d.
Gainsbrough	00 :	19 :	00
The Ile ..	00 :	16 :	00
Winteringham ..	00 :	17 :	6
Brigge ..	00 :	17 :	0
Garthrop	00 :	07 :	6

Disbursments :—

	£	s.	d.
To Thomas Potter for Susan Recket ..		5 :	9
To Thomas Hutchinson for Doll Pickhaver..		5 :	0
To the Quarterly Meeting	01 :	10 :	00
Rests in Joseph Richardson hand	1 :	16 :	2
Joshua Reeder paid a legacy left to Friends by his mother	00 :	10 :	00
Totall	02 :	06 :	2

Next Meeting ordered at Henry Symsons in Gainsbrough.

Signed by Joseph Richardson.

p. 232.

ATT a Monthly Meeting held at Henry Symsons in Gainsbrough the 11th day of the 2d month 1701[1] :—

This Meeting appoints both John Urry, senior & junior to speak to William Reed of Epworth about his outgoings & to give

[1] 11th April, 1701.

forth a paper of condemnation for it & give an account to the next Monthly Meeting.

This Meeting still desireth Thomas Wresle & John Waddingham to deall with Richard Cox of Appleby, that he give this Meeting better satisfaction about his outrunings.

This Meeting desireth Friends of Garthrup Meeting some reason why they appeared not at last Monthly Meeting.

This Meeting desireth that a Preparitive Meeting be kept in each Meeting upon Truths account to consider the business of the Monthly Meeting.

This Meeting orders John Urry, senior & Isaak Davis to speak to Friends of there Meeting to set up a Weekly Meeting in the Ile & give an account to the next Meeting,

This Meeting orders Thomas Wresle & John Waddingham to take care in the setling of a Weekly Meeting amongst them.

This day John Herrison & Susanna Davis came a second time into our Meeting & signified the continuance of there purpose of marraige each with other, & all things appearing clear Freinds have left the consumation to themselves with Friends advice according to Truths order.

This day Leonord Bell of Headon in the County of Nottingham came into our Meeting & published his intention of marriage with Rebecka Lambert & shee being present gave her consent it being the first time they are desired to wait Friends answer till next Monthly Meeting. Sarah Dent & Susanna Wresle are desired to see that Rebecka Lambert be clear & free from all other persons, & give an account to the next Monthly Meeting.

Next Monthly Meeting ordered to be at Winteringham.

Signed by Joseph Richardson.

ATT a Monthly Meeting held at the Meeting House at Winteringham the 9th of 3d Month 1701[1] :—

p. 233.

This Meeting desires John Urry, junior & some other Friend to speak to William Reed that he give Friends satisfaction about his outrunings & bring his answer to the next Monthly Meeting.

Thomas Wresle & Francis Dent have according to order spoke to Richard Cox of Appleby, & brought a paper to this Meeting from under his own hand owneing his condemnation for his unfaithfulness, & sorrow for his faults in runing into the world for a wife, which has given this Meeting some satisfaction for the clearing Truth & the faithfull Friends thereof.

[1] 9th May, 1701.

Robert Vesse acquainted this Meeting the reasons wherefore they could not attend the last Monthly Meeting with which Friends are satisfaied.

This Meeting has consented & agreed to have a Preparitive Meeting before each Monthly Meeting, & one Friend of each Meeting has promised to take care in it.

This Meeting still desires John Urry & Robert Coakes would acquaint Friends of there Meeting to setle a Weekly Meeting amongst them.

The further settlement of a Weekly Meeting at Winteringham is left to the care of Thomas Wresle with other Friends,

This Meeting has ordered a Meeting to be held at Francis Dents, Thornholme the 18th day of this month being the first day in the week.

This day William Vesse of Belton came into our Meeting & published his intention of marriage with Ellen Hudson of Butterwick & brought a certificate signifying her consent but it being first time they are desired to wait Friends answer till next Monthly Meeting.

John Urry & Robert Coakes are desired to see into there clearness from all other persons.

This Meeting has desired Robert Vesse to take care about some bedding for John Halliwell & give an account to the next Monthly Meeting.

This day Leonord Bell of Headon came a 2d time in our Meeting & signified the continuance of his purpose of marriage with Rebecka Lambert & shee being present gave consent & all things appearing clear on behalf of both parties ; Freinds have left the consumation thereof to themselves with Friends advice according to the good order of Truth.

Next Monthly Meeting ordered at Cotle Hall & a contribution to be collected & brought up thither.

Signed by Joseph Richardson.

Agreed to take ½ Henry Pickworth bookes.

Answer to Henry Bugg.

p. 234.

ATT a Monthly Meeting held at Cotle Hall Joshua Reeders he 13th of 4th month 1701[1] :—

John Urry, junior spoke to William Reed of Epworth & he promised to come to this Meeting but failes, it therefore desired that

---

[1] 13th June, 1701.

he speak to him againe to know the reason why & desire his appearance at our next Monthly Meeting.

Its ordered that John Urry, senior & Robert Coakes acquaint Friends in there Meeting to indeavour the settlement of a Weekly Meeting amongst them & bring an account to the next Meeting.

William Vessey came into this Meeting a second time & signified the continuance of his purpose of marriage with Ellen Hudson & shee being present gave consent & Friends finding no objection against them have left the consumation thereof according to Truths order.

Concluded that a Meeting be held at Francis Dent at Thornum the first day come a week.

& a Meeting is to be kept at David Crosby the first 4th day of 5th month.

Contributions came in as followeth :—

	£	s.	d.
Gainsbrough Meeting ..	01	00	00
Epworth Meeting	00	16	00
Winteringham Meeting ..	01	02	00
Brigg Meeting	00	12	00
Garthrop Meeting	00	12	00
Totall	4	02	00

Disbursments :—

	£	s,	d,
To Gainsbrough	01	3	7
To Isaac Davis for part of what he is to have for Marshall	01	00	00
to Epworth Meeting	00	05	00
for Dorithy Pickhaver	00	03	5
for Quarterly Meeting	01	10	00

all paid

Next Monthly Meeting ordered at John Urrys in Epworth,

Signed by Joseph Richardson.

ATT a Monthly Meeting at John Urrys in Epworth 11th of 5th month 1701[1] :—

John Urry is desired againe to speak to William Reed to come to next Monthly Meeting.

This Meeting hath concluded & agreed with Friends of the Ile Meeting that a Weekly Meeting be kept amongst them for one year at the house of Thomas Wresle in Beltoft.

[1] 11th July, 1701.

This Meeting agrees to have a Meeting kept at John Smiths house in Scotter next first day.

& that a Meeting be kept at Thornum the first day of the next month.

Next Monthly Meeting ordered at John Nainbys of Caistrop.

Signed by Joseph Richardson.

p. 235.

ATT a Monthly Meeting held at John Nainbys in Caistrop the 8th of 6th month 1701[1] :—

This day William Reed of Epworth came into the Meeting according to Friends desire & being discourst about the matter Friends have writt a few lines to John Urry, junior to desire him with William Reed to draw up a paper of condemnation, because William cannot well do it, & comunicate the same to the next Monthly Meeting where they are both to be.

Information being given to this Meeting of the disorderly walking of John Clark of Garthrop, Friends have writt a few lines to him to desire his appearance at our next Monthly Meeting.

This day Jacob Davis of Belton came into our Meeting & published his intention of marriage with Frances Herrison of Winteringham & shee being present gave her consent, but because they brought no certificate from there parents Friends of each Meeting are desired to take speciall care to see into the clearness of both parties against the next Monthly Meeting,

Next Meeting ordered at David Crosbys in Gunhouse & a contribution to be brought thither.

Signed by Joseph Richardson.

ATT a Monthly Meeting held at David Crosby in Gunhouse the 12th of 7th month 1701[2] :—

Whereas John Clark of Garthrop was desired to make his appearance at this Meeting about his disorderly walking, he being busey about getting his harvest prevented him, & therefore this Meeting desires Robert Vessy & Thomas Morley to speak to him to make his appearance at our next Monthly Meeting.

This day Jacob Davis came a second time & signified the continuance of his purpose of marriage with Frances Herrison & shee being present gave consent & all things appearing clear on behalf of both parties, Friends have left the consumation according to Truths order.

---

[1] 8th August, 1701.   [2] 12th September, 1701.

This day John Champion of Winteringham came into our Meeting and published his intention of marriage with Mary Hardy of the same & shee being present gave consent, but it being the first time they are desired to wait Friends answer till next Monthly Meeting & Friends of Winteringham Meeting are desired to see into there clearness from all other persons.

p. 236.

Contributions came in as followeth :—

	£	s.	d.
Gainsbrough	00 :	19 :	0
The Ile	00 :	18 :	6
Winteringham	00 :	17 :	0
Brigge	00 :	15 :	6
Garthrop	00 :	08 :	0
Totall	03 :	18 :	0

Disbursments :—

	£	s.	d.
To Gainsbrough for releife of Susanna Reckett & children	00 :	06 :	00
To Isaac Davis for his boy	01 :	00 :	00
To the Quarterly Meeting	01 :	10 :	00
Rests in Joseph Richardson hand	01 :	01 :	00

Next Monthly Meeting ordered to be at Brigge.

Signed by Joseph Richardson.

ATT a Monthly Meeting held at the Meeting House in Brigge the 10th of the 8th month 1701[1] :—

In regard John Clark of Garthrop came not to this Meeting according to Friends desire, its desired that Thomas Hutchinson & Thomas Morley speake to him againe to know the reason & desire his appearance at the next Monthly Meeting.

John Champion of Winteringham came this day a second time into our Monthly Meeting & signified the continuance of his purpose of marriage with Mary Harde, & shee being present gave her consent, & all things appearing clear on behalf of both parties, the consumation thereof is left to themselves wth Friends advice according to Truths order.

Inquiry being made in this Meeting about the disposall of Robert Barclays Appologies, Friends in the seaverall Meetings are desired to acquaint Friends therewith that Friends care in

[1] 10th October, 1701.

that concern be answered & give an account to the next Monthly
Meeting which is ordered to be at Brigg.

Signed by Joseph Richardson.

Next Quarterly Meeting to be the last day of the 10th month
1701[1].

Att a Monthly Meeting held at Brigge the 14 : 9 : month 1701[2] :—

Friends are desired to bring in account of there suffering for tythe
& other things to the next Monthly Meeting.

Whereas John Clark was desired to make his appearance at this
Meetinge in order to give Friends some satisfaction whom
he had offended the Truth & them, he came & some Friends
were selected out of the Meeting to discourse the matter with
him, & found that he was sorry in that he offended, & hoped
for the time to come to walk more orderly as becomes the
Truth which Friends of that Meeting are desired to take notice
of & give an account to the next Monthly Meeting.

p. 237.

John Clark ownes Friends love & care to him therein.

Richard Turner sent a letter to this Meeting which was read &
gave some satisfaction for his former miscarriages but Friends
still desires that Friends belonging the Ile Meeting take notice
whether his life & conversation be agreeable with his letter to
Friends, John Urry, junior & Robert Coakes are desired to
doe it.

Its still desired that Friends in each Meeting take care about the
disposall of Robert Barclays Apologies, & alsoe to see what
Friends in there Meeting are willing to subscribe to the takeing
of more of them against the next Monthly Meeting which is
ordered to be at Brigge & a contribution to be collected &
brought up thither.

Signed by Joseph Richardson.

Att a Monthly Meeting held at the Meeting House in Brigge
the 12 of the 10th month 1701[3] :—

The further care about Richard Turner is continued with Ile Friends,

Friends of Gainsbrough Meeting have agreed to take more of

Robert Barclayes Apollogies	07
The Ile Friends	04
Winteringham Friends	02
Garthrop Friends	02
Brigge Friends	08

[1] 31st December, 1701.　　[2] 14th November, 1701.　　[3] 12th December, 1701.

Contributions came in as followeth :—

	£	s.	d.
Gainsbrough Meeting ..		19 :	6
The Ile Meeting	00 :	15 :	0
Winteringham Friends ..	00 :	16 :	0
Brigge Friends	00 :	16 :	6
Garthrop	00 :	09 :	0
Totall	03 :	16 :	0
In Stock	00 :	19 :	0

which cleares all stock.

Disbursments :—

To Gainsbrough Friends for 26 weekes for Abraham Northen being due the 11th : 10th month which cleares all to this day ..	13 : 00
To the Ile Friends for burying Margret Snoden	12 : 00
To Garthrop for Doll Pickhaver	05 : 00
To the Quarterly Meeting	01 : 10 : 00
To Quarterly Meeting for bookes	01 : 15 : 00

Signed by Joseph Richardson.

Next Meeting ordered at Brigge.

p. 238.

ATT a Monthly Meeting held at the Meeting House at Brigge the 9th of the 11th month 1701[1] :—

The further care about Richard Turner is left to the Ile Friends

This Meeting has ordered Joseph Potter & Thomas Nayler to acquaint there Meeting, to bring an account what bookes they are willing to take of John Whiteheads about 3s. a peice, & also the Judgment of there Friends about the affirmation & bring an account to the next Monthly Meeting.

Robert Coakes & Thomas Wresle are desired to doe the same at there Meeting, George Frow & Joseph Wresle are desired for there Meeting, John Barlow & Joseph Richardson for Brigg Meeting, Thomas Hutchinson for Garthrop Meeting.

This day Josiah Spavin of Wrawby came into this Meeting & published his intention of marriage with Elizabeth Williamson of the same, but being the first time they are desired to wait Friends answer till next Monthly Meeting.

[1] 9th January, 1702.

John Barlow & Joseph Richardson are desired to see into the clearness of both parties.

Ordered that a contribution be collected & brought to the next Monthly Meeting which is to be at Brigge.

Signed by Joseph Richardson.

Att a Monthly Meeting held at Meeting House at Brigg the 13 of 12th month 1701[1] :—

Subscription came in of John Whitehead bookes as followeth :—

Gainsbrough Meeting	10
The Ile	09
Winteringham	14
Brigge Meeting	14
Garthrop	05
	—
in all	49

Contributions came in as followeth :—

	£	s.	d.
Gainsbrough		15 :	8
The Ile		12 :	6
Winteringham		16 :	0
Brigge		15 :	0
Garthrop		09 :	6
	03 :	08 :	8

Disbursments :—

	£	s.	d.
to Gainsbrough for Susan Recket rent ..		10 :	4
to Quarterly Meeting	2 :	10 :	0
In Joseph Richardson hand & for Quarterly Meeting	2 :	18 :	4

This day Josiah Spavin came a second time & signified the continuance of his purpose of marriage with Elizabeth Williamson & shee being present gave her consent & it appearing all things clear on behalf of both parties Friends have consented to there marriage according to Truths order.

Information being given to this Meeting of John Wresles evill course of life, Friends have desired Robert Colyer & Joseph Richardson to speak to him to make his appearance at our next Monthly Meeting which is to be at Brigge.

Signed by Joseph Richardson.

[1] 13th February, 1702.

p. 239.

ATT a Monthly Meeting held the 13th day of the first month 1702[1] :—

This Meeting still desireth Joseph Richardson & Robert Colyer to speak to John Wresle to appear at our next Monthly Meeting.

David Crosby acquainted Friends this day that he had it in his minde & upon his hart to vissitt Friends upon Truths account in Holland and desireth a certificate from Friends along with him, & Friends intends to give him one at the next Monthly Meeting.

Bookes came into this Meeting which was dispersed to the seaverall Meetings came to ..   ..

	£	s.	d.
	01	11	08

Ordered that a contribution be collected & brought up to the next Monthly Meeting which is to be at Francis Dents of Thornholme.

Signed by Joseph Richardson.

ATT a Monthly Meeting held at Francis Dents at Thornholme the 10th day of the 2d month 1702[2] :—

This Meeting has agreed to pay for the bookes received & disposed on, out of the stock of this Meeting at next Quarterly Meeting.

Contributions came in as followeth :—

	£	s.	d.
Gainsbrough		13	00
The Ile		15	06
Winteringham		16	00
Brigge		14	00
Garthrop		08	00
	03	07	00

Disbursments as followeth :—

	£	s.	d.
To Joseph Potter on Thomas Recket account		07	00
To Winteringham friends for assistance of Margret Martin		10	00
Rests in Joseph Richardson hand	02	10	00

Friends in this Meeting have drawn up & signed a certificate for David Crosby, & ordered another to be drawn up by Brigge Friends for Benjamine Holme of the same.

Next Monthly Meeting ordered to be at Gainsbrough.

Signed by Joseph Richardson.

[1] 13th March, 1702.   [2] 10th April, 1702.

ATT a Monthly Meeting held at the house of Henry Symsons in Gainsbrough the 8th of the 3d month 1702[1] :—

The nessesities of Hannah Whitehead was laid before this Meeting, & after some debate Brigge Friends was ordered to take care therein & consult Owstwick Meeting for her assistance & subsistence.

p. 240.

This Meeting has concluded that a Meeting for Worshipp be held at Francis Dents of Thornholme the 4th of this month 1702.

Ordered that a contribution be collected & brought into the next Monthly Meeting which is to be at Jane Morleys in Adlinfleet.

Rests in stock in Joseph Richardson hand .. .. 02 : 10 : 00

ATT a Monthly Meeting held at Jane Morleys in Adlinfleet the 12th day of the 4th month 1702[2] :—

This Meeting has inquired what care has been taken about Hannah Whitehead nessesities & finds nothing has been done soe the further care about her is left to Brigg Friends with Outswick Meeting to supply her.

Contributions came in as followeth :—

	£	s.	d.
Gainsbrough	01 :	00 :	06
The Ile	00 :	15 :	00
Winteringham	00 :	15 :	00
Brigg	00 :	14 :	00
Garthrop	00 :	08 :	06
in all	03 :	13 :	06
in old Stock	2 :	10 :	00
Totall	06 :	03 :	06

Disbursments as followeth :—

	£	s.	d.
Sent for bookes by John Barlow	01 :	11 :	08
sent by Thomas Nayler for ½ year rent for Thomas Recket house	00 :	08 :	00
sent to the Ile for releif Alice Chapman ..	00 :	05 :	00
sent to Crowle for Bridget Mosley	00 :	06 :	00
sent to Brigg for Widdow Goxhill	00 :	03 :	00
to Garthrop Meeting for Doll Pickhaver ..	00 :	03 :	00
Ordered to the Quarterly Meeting	01 :	10 :	00
	04 :	06 :	08
Rests in John Barlow hands in stock	01 :	16 :	10

Next Monthly Meeting ordered at John Urrys in Epworth.

Signed by Joseph Richardson.

[1] 8th May, 1702.   [2] 12th June, 1702.

Att a Monthly Meeting held at the house of John Urrys in Epworth the 10th of the 5th month 1702[1] :—

The further care about Hannah Whitehead is left to Brigg Friends.

Complaint being made to this Meeting by a letter from Friends at Warnsworth Monthly Meeting of the disorderly walking of John Halliwell, & of the great trouble & exercise they have (*p. 241*) had with him. This Meeting has desired John Bishopp and Thomas Foster of Crowle to speak to him to speedily repaire to the place at Luddinton Friends have provided for him & if he refuse to answer Friends request then some Friends are desired to goe to some Justice nearest to them to get a warrant to compell him to such confinement as Friends sees needfull for him & give an account to next Monthly Meeting.

Ordered that a contribution be collected & brought to the next Monthly Meeting which is to be at John Nainbys in Caistrop.

Signed by Joseph Richardson.

Att a Monthly Meeting at John Nainbys in Caistrop the 14th 6th month 1702[2] :—

Upon some discourse in this Meeting about Hannah Whitehead, Friends have agreed & disired some Friends in Brigg would meet together & write to her to putt a stop to her intentions of comeing to Brigg & alsoe to write to Owstwick Monthly Meeting by order from this Meeting, that Friends there are willing to contribute something towards her releife provided shee keep in person from us, but that we doe not think our selves chargeable with her care more than any other Monthly Meeting onely as we may extend our charity to such a poor creature for her relations sake.

Thomas Morley of Adlinfleet came into this Meeting & published his intentions of marriage with Phebe Cooke daughter of John Cooke of Hatfeild & signified by a certificate that he had done the like in Warnsworth Monthly Meeting but it being first time they are desired to wait Friends answer till next Monthly Meeting.

Complaint being made to this Meeting of the great reproach John Wresle of Brigg has given & brought upon Truth by his late drunkenness, Friends have desired Robert Colyer & Joseph Richardson to speak to him & desire his appearance at our next Monthly Meeting.

[1] 10th July, 1702.   [2] 14th August, 1702.

p. 242.

Contributions came in as followeth :—

				£	s.	d.
Gainsbrough	..	..	..	01 :	00 :	06
The Ile ..	..	..	..	00 :	17 :	00
Winteringham ..	..	..	..	00 :	15 :	06
Brigg	..	..	..	00 :	16 :	06
Garthrop	..	..	..	00 :	09 :	00
Totall	..	..	..	03 :	18 :	06
old stock	..	..	..	02 :	09 :	10

Disbursments :—

		£	s.	d.
to Gainsbrough Friends for bookes	..	01 :	13 :	8
to Edward Gilliatt for Hannah Whitehead	..	00 :	05 :	00
to William Frost for John Halliwell shoes	..	00 :	4 :	0

Remains in stock in John Barlow hands when he has received 10s. in George Frow hands the sum of .. ..   04 : 15 : 08

Next Monthly Meeting ordered to be at Brigge.

ATT a Monthly Meeting held at the Meeting House in Brigge the 11th day of the 7th Month 1702[1] :—

Edward Gilliatt of Brigg gave account to this Meeting that he had spoke to some Friends of Hull belonging Owstwick Monthly Meeting concerning Hannah Whitehead, & the matter being further considered about her present nessesities this Meeting has ordered Edward Gilliatt to pay 10s. towards her subsistence, & to acquaint Friends of there Meeting, that we doe not thinke to take her upon us as a continuall charge.

Thomas Wresle & Joseph Richardson, junior went to John Wresle to desire him to come to this Meeting but his answer was he was very sory for his faults & ashamed to appear but hoped to doe better for the future & owned Friends love & respect towards him, but Brigg Friends are still desired to watch over him & give an account to the next Monthly Meeting.

This day Thomas Morley of Adlinfleet came a second time into our Meeting & signified the continuance of his purpose of marriage with Phebe Cook daughter of John Cooke of Hatfield & upon inquiry made into his clearness (*p. 243*) from all other persons findes nothing to the contrary but they may proceed in order to marriage as conveniency offers with clearness in the Truth.

[1] 11th September, 1702.

	£	s.	d.
Ordered to the Quarterly Meeting	01	10	00

George Frow 10s. paid Thomas Richardson for
  Hannah Whitehead releife .. .. ..   00 : 10 : 00
Remaines of Stock in John Barlow hand .. ..   02 : 15 : 08

Next Monthly Meeting ordered to be at Brigge.

Signed Joseph Richardson.

ATT a Monthly Meeting held at the Meeting House the 9th of the 8th month 1702[1] :—

Information being given to this Meeting of the disorderly walking of John Clark of Garthrop & the reproach he brings upon Friends & Truth thereby, Friends desires that Thomas Morley & Thomas Hutchinson speak to him to desire his appearance at our next Monthly Meeting.

Some discourse was in this Meeting about raiseing a collection for the national stock & being but few Friends at the Meeting & the matter weighty, its concluded that the ordinary contribution be collected against the next Monthly Meeting & the further discourse & resolution of the next Monthly Meeting which is ordered to be at Brigge.

Signed by Joseph Richardson.

p. 244.

ATT a Monthly Meeting held at the Meeting House at Brigge the 13th day of the 9th month 1702[2] :—

Robert Vesse acquainted Friends in this Meeting that he had a minde to speak to John Clark of Garthrop, before Friends proceeded further with him, & that he would give an account thereof to the next Monthly Meeting.

	£	s.	d.
Contributions came in which came to	03	12	0
Disburst	02	2	0

Disbursments :—

	£	s.	d.
sent by Thomas Potter 24s. for 26 weekes which cleares for Abraham Northen to this day ..	01	04	00
To Thomas Recket by Thomas Potter	00	08	00
To Robert Coakes for Sander Chapman ..	00	05	00
To Robert Coakes for Susan Recket	00	05	00
Remains in Stock in John Barlow hand ..	04	5	8

Ordered that the Nationall Collection be collected & brought to the next Monthly Meeting which is to be at Brigge,

Signed by Joseph Richardson.

[1] 9th October, 1702.   [2] 13th November, 1702.

H

ATT a Monthly Meeting held at the Meeting House at Brigg the 12th day of the 10 Month 1702[1] :—

The suffering condition of Thomas Winder of Crowle for tythe being laid before Friends of this Meeting, thinks it best to lye it before Friends at the next Quarterly Meeting to have there advice & assistance in the matter, Robert Colyer with some Ile Friends are desired to take care in it & give account to the next Monthly Meeting.[2]

This day Richard Wresle of Thealby came into our Meeting & published his intention of marriage with Margret Martin of the same & shee being present gave her consent but it being the first time they are both desired to wait Friends answer till next Monthly Meeting. Thomas Wresle & Francis Dent are to see into the clearness of both parties.

Nationall Contributions came as followeth :—

	£	s.	d.
Gainsbrough	04 :	01 :	6
The Ile	04 :	02 :	6
Winteringham	04 :	00 :	00
Brigge	04 :	00 :	00
Garthrop	02 :	00 :	00
Totall	16 :	04 :	00

Disbursments :—

	£	s.	d.
sent Isaak Davis by William Parkinson for Stephen Marshall..	02 :	00 :	00
To John Symson, Susan Recket	00 :	03 :	03
to Edward Gilliatt for Mary Goxhill	00 :	03 :	06
to Quarterly Meeting	01 :	10 :	00
Remaines in stock	00 :	08 :	11

which was sent to Quarterly Meeting.
in Joseph Richardson hand paid .. ..   4 : 8

p. 245.

ATT a Monthly Meeting held at the Meeting House at Brigge the 8th day of the 11th month 1702[3] :—

Robert Collyer accquainted this Meeting that Friends at the Quarterly Meeting had taken some care in Thomas Winders business, & had ordered Abraham Morrice to write to the 6th day Meeting of Sufferings which he did & expected an answer in a short time, & when received would send it to John Marshall of Gainsbrough in order to give him some satisfaction.

[1] 12th December, 1702.   [2] *See* Appendix to this volume.   [3] 8th January, 1703.

Francis Dent accquainted this Meeting that he with Thomas Wresle had spoke to Elizabeth Wilkinson & she promised to come or send by writing but performing neither Francis Dent & Thomas Wresle are still desired to speak to her to know her reason & give an account to the next Monthly Meeting.

Freinds sufferings for tythe belonging Winteringham came in, but Gainsbrough : the Ile : Brigge & Garthrup Meetings are not yet comed in, & so desired to get them ready & bring them up to the next Monthly Meeting.

Its desired that Friends in each Meeting consider among themselves of keeping a Meeting for Worshipp after the Quarterly Meeting for business, & carrie up their result to the next Quarterly Meeting,

This day Richard Wressle came the second time & signified the continuance of his porpose of marriage with Margaret Martin & brought a certificate signifying the continuance of her purpose of marriage with him allsoe, & nothing appearing to hinder their intentions, Friends have left the consumation thereof to themselves, with Friends advice, according to Truth's order.

Friends at the Meeting desires Joshua Reeder to speak to Robert Vessey to appear at our next Monthly Meeting to give an account what discourse he has had with John Clark of Garthrupp which he signified to Friends.

Freinds of Addlinfleet Meeting have taken care for a settlement for John Hallywell, so that if he trouble any Friends hereafter they are to send him to the place appointed for him at Luddington.

Next Monthly Meeting is to be at Brigge.

Signed by Joseph Richardson.

	£	s.	d.
Rests in stock in Joseph Richardson hands	00 :	04 :	3
sent Mary Goxhill by John Richardson for releife	00 :	01 :	00

p. 246.

ATT a Monthly Meeting held at the Meeting House in Brigge the 12th day of the 12th month 1702[1] :—

Friends has made some progress in Thomas Winders bussiness according to his desire, which has given such satisfaction as is needfull at present.

<hr>

[1] 12th February, 1703.

Thomas Wresle & Francis Dent has spoke againe to Elizabeth Wilkinson of Wintringham & shee has confest to something of her miscarriages, & Friends in this Meeting have ordered Thomas Wresle with Francis Dent to draw up a paper of condemnation which shee has promised to signe for clearing the truth & owning Judgment & condemnation upon her selfe for her miscarriages, which they are desired to bring to the next Monthly Meeting.

Sufferings for tythe from Gainsbrough, Wintringham & the Garthrop come in but Brigge & the Ile are not.

This Meeting still desires Robert Vesse to speak to John Clark to desire his appearance at our next Monthly Meeting to answer such matters as Friends have to object against him.

Its still desired that Friends advise together in each Perticular Meeting to have there sence brought up to the next Monthly Meeting of keeping 2 dayes for the Quarterly Meeting one for bussiness the other for Worshipp.

Next Meeting ordered to be at Brigg where Friends are desired to bring some woemen Friends to it from each Meeting, & a contribution to be collected & brought up thither.

Signed by Joseph Richardson.

ATT a Monthly Meeting held the 12th day of first month 1703[1] :

Thomas Winder of Crowle being at this Meeting is satisfied with Friends advice, & desires Abraham Morice & John Marshall to goe to Faucourt to get his receipt for the charges.

Thomas Wresle & Francis Dent brought a paper of condemnation for Elizabeth Wilkinson to signe, which is returned back by them & they are desired to see it done, & bring it to the next Monthly Meeting.

p. 247.

This Meeting still desires Robert Vesse to speak to John Clark & desire his appearance at our next Monthly Meeting.

Contributions came in as followeth :—

	£	s,	d.
Gainsbrough	00 :	17 :	00
The Ile	00 :	14 :	06
Winteringham	00 :	15 :	00
Brigge	00 :	15 :	00
Garthrop	00 :	03 :	03

[1] 12th March, 1703.

Disbursments :—	£	s.	d.
Ordered to the Quarterly Meeting	01 :	10 :	00
to Thomas Potter for Abraham Northern 17 weeks at 6d. a week ending the 11th of first month 1703	00 :	08 :	06
for Susan Recket	00 :	02 :	09
to Robert Vesse on John Halliwell account ..	00 :	08 :	03
to Thomas Hutchinson for Doll Pickhaver..	00 :	02 :	06
Rests in stock in Joseph Richardson hand ..	01 :	00 :	09

Its desired that Friends in each Perticular Meeting subscribe to what number of books of John Whiteheads they are willing to take of & bring an account to the next Monthly Meeting, Thomas Potter & John Symson for Gainsbrough, William Parkinson & Thomas Winder for the Ile, Thomas Wresle & Francis Dent for Winteringham, Robert Colyer & Joseph Richardson for Brigg, Robert Vesse & Thomas Hutchinson, for Garthrop.

Next Monthly Meeting ordered at Henry Symsons in Gainsbrough.

Signed by Joseph Richardson.

ATT a Monthly Meeting held at Gainsbrough at the house of Henry Symson the 9th day of the 2d month 1703[1] :—

This Meeting desireth John Urry, senior in Epworth to speak to Friends in there Meeting & let them know that Friends are concernd in there mindes for there neglect in keeping up there week day Meeting, & give an account to the next Monthly Meeting.

Its alsoe desired that Thomas Hutchinson of Garthrop consult Friends of there Meeting in order to setle a weekly Meeting amongst them & give account thereof to the next Monthly Meeting,

Its still desired that Thomas Hutchinson & Robert Vesse speak to John Clark of Garthrop to desire his appearance at our next Monthly Meeting.

Whereas complaint has been made to this Meeting of the disorderly walking of Samuel Richardson, this Meeting orders John Barlow, Thomas Wresle & Francis Dent to deall with him for the same & bring account to our next Monthly Meeting.

p. 248.

This Meeting has appointed a Meeting for Worshipp at Francis Dent house in Thornholme the last 6th day of this month.

[1] 9th April, 1703.

This Meeting orders a contribution to be collected & brought up to the next Monthly Meeting & that some Freinds in each Meeting stirr up Friends of the same to contribute one third part more then usual, nessesities requiring it & to bring it up to the next Monthly Meeting which is ordered to be at Thealby.

Signed by Joseph Richardson.

ATT a Monthly Meeting held at the Meeting House att Thealby the 14 of 3d month 1703[1] :—

Thomas Morley & Robert Vesse gave account to this Meeting that they had setled a Meeting for Worshipp once a month at Thomas Morleys in Adlinfleet on the first 5th day in every month.

This Meeting desireth Thomas Morley & Robert Vesse to speak once more to John Clark & desire his appearance at our next Monthly Meeting.

This Meeting desireth that Robert Colyer & John Barlow deall with Samuel Richardson of Winteringham for his disorderly walking and give an account to the next Monthly Meeting.

Whereas complaint was made to this Meeting concerning Joshua Reeder disorderly walking, Richard Clark of Crowle & Robert Vesse is desired to deall with him & give an account to the next Monthly Meeting.

Contributions came in as followeth :—

		£	s.	d.
Gainsbrough	.. .. ..	01 :	04 :	10
The Ile ..	.. .. ..	01 :	02 ;	06
Winteringham ..	.. ..	01 :	03 :	06
Brigge ..	.. .. ..	01 :	05 :	00
Garthrop	.. .. ..	00 :	10 :	00
		05 :	06 :	02

Disbursments as followeth :—

	£	s.	d.
To Richard Clark for releife of Widdow Mosley		05 :	00
To Thomas Wresle for Sander Chapman releife		05 :	00
To Thomas Morley for Doll Pickhaver releife		04 :	00
To the Quarterly Meeting & other service..	02 :	10 :	00
Rests in Joseph Richardson hands	02 :	02 :	02

More in Joseph Richardson hand for stock of old the sum of .. .. 01 : 00 : 00
& to Gainsbrough 2s. 4½ Joseph paid on account 00 : 05 : 6

[1] 14th May, 1703.

This Meeting has writt to the Ile Meeting to stirr them up to a more
dilligent attending the week day Meeting & after the letter be
read & have had its service to be returned to the Monthly
Meeting.

	£	s.	d.
Disburst	00 :	7 :	10½

p. 249.

This Meeting agrees to give Jacob Davis 26s. for Robert Wilkinson
son as conveniency offers.

Lincolne Quarterly Meeting ordered the 9th & 10th day of next
month.

Next Meeting ordered at Thomas Morleys in Adlinfleet.

Signed by Joseph Richardson.

ATT a Monthly Meeting held at Thomas Morleys in Adlinfleet
the 11 of 4th month 1703[1] :—

This Meeting once more desireth Thomas Hutchison & Robert
Vesse to deall with John Clark of Garthrop about his disorderly
walking, & desires his appearance at our next Monthly Meeting,
& to give an account thereof there.

According to Friends desire Robert Colyer & John Barlow spoke
to Samuel Richardson about his disorderly walking, and
Samuel hath sent this Meeting a few lines wherein he confesseth
his faults & pretends to be sorry for them but this Meeting still
desireth Thomas Wresle & Francis Dent to have an eye over
him & give an account to this Meeting as need requires,

According to order Richard Clark & Robert Vesse has dealt with
Joshua Reeder, about his miscarriages, & he hath sent a paper
to this Meeting, wherein he seems to justify himself in hireing
of his tythes with other things Friends charges him with, this
Meeting therefore desireth Robert Vesse & Thomas Hutchinson
to deall with him for the same & give an account to the next
Monthly Meetinge.

This day Richard Alkock of Weston in the County of Nottingam
published his intention of marriage with Mary West daughter
of William West of Gate Burton in the County of Lincolne, &
brought with them certificates from parents signifying their
consents, but it being the first time they are desired to wait
Friends answer till the next Monthly Meetinge.

p. 250.

This day John Urry acquainted Friends that according to Friends
desire Friends of there Meeting has kept there week day Meeting
better than formerly.

[1] 11th June, 1703.

Next Monthly Meeting ordered at John Urrys senior in Epworth,

Signed by Joseph Richardson.

Att a Monthly Meeting held at John Urrys, senior in Epworth the 7th of 5 month 1703[1] :—

Thomas Wresle & Francis Dent are still desired to have an eye over Samuel Richardsons conversation & give an account to this Meeting as occasion will require.

According to the request of the last Monthly Meeting Robert Vesse & Thomas Hutchinson had some conference with Joshua Reeder, & he seems inclineable to take Friends advice but they are still desired to have an eye over him as to his conversation & to diswade him against the payment of tythes & to desire his appearance at next Monthly Meeting & to give an account thereof then.

John Clark appeared at this Meeting according to Friends desire & tould them that he hopes by Gods assistance to become a new man & walk more answerable to our holy proffession than formerly, but Friends desires Thomas Hutchison still to have an eye over him as to his conversation & advise him for his good & give an account to this Meeting as there may be occasion.

Next Monthly Meeting ordered at John Nainbys in Caistrop.

Signed by Joseph Richardson.

Att a Meeting held at John Nainbys in Caistrop the 13 of the 6 month 1703[2] :—

Thomas Wresle acquainted this Meeting that Samuel Richardson of there town still walks disorderly, to the reproach of Truth and greife of Friends, & alsoe that he has something in his minde further by way of advice & councell to him & his wife & intends to give Friends an account thereof to the next Monthly Meeting which Friends are satisfied in.

p. 251.

Thomas Morley acquainted this Meeting that they have had further dealing with Joshua Reeder, but findes him much out of order, & neglects comeing to Meeting, saying his wife is not willing he should because the Meeting is taken from there house, this Meeting therefore desires Thomas Morley & Robert Vesse to goe to them & inquire the truth thereof, & to give her the reasons wherefore the Meeting was removed & give an account of there answer to the next Monthly Meeting.

---

[1] 7th July, 1703.   [2] 13th August, 1703.

An account being given to this Meeting that John Clarke neglects frequenting there Meeting Thomas Morley is desired to speak to Robert Vesse & Thomas Hutchinson to speak to him and to inspect his conversation as before desird & give an account to the next Monthly Meeting.

This Meeting desires that the paper be brought into the next Monthly Meeting where both the Men & Woemen Freinds are appointed in each Meeting as Overseers that this Meeting may put them in mind of their service, & what Friends desires & expects from them, & that those Friends in each Meeting that are soe appointed attend the next Monthly Meeting as many as can conveniently & others that cannot to attend the next Monthly Meeting.

Richard Alcock of Weston came to this Meeting a second time & signified the continuance of his purpose of marriage with Mary West of Gate Burton, & shee being present gave her consent, & found by enquiry the consent of parents allsoe, & this being at the last Monthly Meeting to which he belongs obtained a certificate of his clearness from all other woemen, & this Meeting finding nothing but clearness on her part the consumation thereof is left to themselves with the advice of Friends & relations according to the good order of Truth.

Edward Gilliat & John Howell are desired to speak to John Wresle & give him an account of the sence of Friends concerning him, & they with Thomas Wresle to give an account to the next Monthly Meeting the necessities of Mary Goxhil is left to Brigge Meeting.

Next Monthly Meeting ordered at Gainsbrough and a contribution to be collected & brought up thither.

p. 252.

AT a Monthly Meeting held at Henry Simpson's house in Gainsborow; the 10th of the 7th Month 1703[1] :—

This Meeting desireth Thomas Wresle of Winteringham to speak to Samuel Richardson of the same, about his disorderly walking & give an account thereof to the next Monthly Meeting.

This Meeting desireth Thomas Hutchinson & Robert Vessey to speak to Joshua Reeder to appear at our next Monthly Meeting & answer for himself about his outgoing, & allso to accquaint Thomas Morley & him that the difference betwixt them two be speedily ended, & give an account thereof to our next Monthly Meeting.

---

[1] 10th September, 1703.

This Meeting still desires Thomas Hutchison & Robert Vessey to speak to John Clark of Garthrupp about his outgoings & bring an account to the next Monthly Meeting.

This Meeting desires Peter Nayler to have an eye over John Wresle for his preservation in the Truth & give an account to the next Monthly Meeting,

This Meeting called over the Overseers in the several weekly Meetings & Gainsborow with the Ile Overseers have appeared, the rest are desired to appear at our next Monthly Meeting.

Contributions brought in as followeth :—

	£	s.	d.
Gainsborow	00	17	06
Brigge	00	16 ;	00
Winteringham	00	17	06
Ile	00	14	06
Garthrupp	00	07	00
	03	12	06
In stock from Joseph Richard-son	02	08	04

Disbursments :—

	£	s.	d.
To Mary Goxhill		04	00
To Thomas Reckett		10	00
To Abraham Northin's Child		13	00
To Isaac Davis	01	00	00
To Bridget Mosley	00	02	06
To the Quarterly Meeting use	01	10	00

Rests in stock in Joseph Richardson hand ..   06 : 10 : 00

Next Monthly Meeting ordered to be at Thornholme at Francis Dents.

AT a Monthly Meeting held at Francis Dents in Thornholme the 8th of the 8th month 1703[1] :—

Thomas Wresle gave an account to this Meeting that he had spoke to Samuel Richardson & his wife & found things in a little better frame than formerly, which has given some satisfaction to this Meeting yet Friends still desire Thomas Wresle to have a watchfull eye over him for good & advise him as the Lord may open his heart towards him, & that David Crosby allso would discharge himself in what he feels in the love of God towards him & give an account to the next Monthly Meeting.

[1] 8th October, 1703.

Noe satisfaction being given to this Meeting about the difference between Thomas Morley & Joshua Reeder Friends desire that Thomas Hutchinson & Robert Vessey with David Crosby speak to them (*p. 253*) to make a speedy end thereto & allso to desire Joshua & his wife to appear at our next Monthly Meeting to answer to such matters & things as Friends have to charge him withal.

This Meeting still desireth Thomas Hutchinson & Robert Vessey to speak to John Clark about his disorder & get his answer & bring it up to our next Monthly Meeting.

This Meeting still desires Peter Naylor & David Crosby to speak to John Wresle about his miscarriages in drinking & other things which has brought a great greif & trouble upon Friends & bring an account thereof to the next Monthly Meeting.

This Meetting having had a long debate about the Overseers in each Meeting as allso the good advice that is recomended by such to be observed, it is agreed, that the minutes be drawn up out of the paper then received, by Brigg Friends & that Thomas Wresle & David Crosby attend that service the night before the Monthly Meeting where they are to be brought.

Friends are desired to bring an account of their suffering for tithe against next Monthly Meeting.

Next Monthly Meeting ordered to be at Brigge.

At a Monthly Meeting held at Brigge the 10th of 9th month 1703[1] :—

David Crosby gave account that he visited Samuel Richardson & found him in a somewhat hopefull or tender frame it's desired that he & Thomas Wresle continue to visit & deale with him as they find it upon them & give an account to the next Monthly Meeting,

David Crosby having visited Joshua Reeder & his wife & it appearing that things are much out of order with him its desired that David Crosby with Robert Vessey do goe to them again to make perticular enquiry & give an account to the next Monthly Meeting.

Thomas Morley accquainted Friends in this Meeting that Thomas Hutchinson has spoken to John Clark, as Friends desired, but could get little answer from him but David Crosby having something in his mind to give him a visit with Robert Vessey they are desired to deal plainly & faithfully with him & get his appearance or bring his answer to our next Monthly Meeting.

[1] 10th November, 1703.

David Crosby signified to Friends in this Meeting that he had
spoken to John Wressle about his evil conversation & that he
seemed to be sorry for it & promised amendment for the future
as he has formerly done, But Friends are desired to take notice
& see if he perform his promiss & give an account thereof at
the next Monthly Meeting or else if he continue in his evil &
wicked practices Friends will find a necessity to give forth a
Testimony against him.

Sufferings for tithe are brought into this Meeting from Gainsbrough
& Addlinfleet, The Ile, Winteringham & Brigge are to come
into the next Monthly Meeting.

p. 254.

This Meeting desires Brigg Friends to draw each Meeting a coppy
of those Minutes that Friends are carefully desired to observe
& that the Friends both men & woemen that are chosen &
appointed as Overseers in each Meeting be signified to the
next Monthly Meeting.

This Meeting appoints that a contribution be collected & brought
up to the next Monthly Meeting which is to be at Brigge.

Laid down for Mary Goxhill at twice .. .. .. 00 : 03 : 0

Signed by Joseph Richardson.

ATT a Monthly Meeting held the 10 of the 10th month att Brigge
1703[1] :—

Thomas Wresle, Francis Dent & George Frow are desired to have a
tender & watchfull eye over Samuel Richardson conversation
& if he proceed in such practices as he has been formerly guilty
of to admonish him, & alsoe to tell him that Friends desires his
appearance at our next Monthly Meeting to answer to such
matters & things as Friends have to lay to his charge.

David Crosby & Robert Vessey has been with Joshua Reeder &
taken an inspection into his state & condition, & findes things
very ill upon his account soe that they with Thomas Morley
are desired to goe to him againe to get him to give a Testimony
against himself & his wicked practices for the clearing Friends
& Truth, or else Friends will finde a nesessity to give forth a
Testimony against him at our next Monthly Meeting but they
are desired first to advise with Richard Clark about the matter.

Thomas Hutchinson has had some discourse with John Clark
Garthrup about his unfaithfullness, since the last Monthly
Meeting since which time he has come twice to our Meeting
& been better in his conversation which is some satisfaction
to Friends for their labour of love on his account but this

[1] 10th December, 1703.

Meeting still desires Robert Vessey & Thomas Hutchinson to have a watchfull & tender eye over him ; & give an account to the next Monthly Meeting.

Whereas John Wresle desires till the next Monthly Meeting to forbear giving a Testimony against his son John Wresle that he may have an oppertunity to deale with him to see if his fatherly & tender advice may work any effect upon him which Friends have granted & desires he may doe it before the next Monthly Meeting.

Friends suffering for tythe are given into this Meeting from the Ile & Winteringham & Briggs will be taken care about.

p. 255.

Friends appointed as Overseers in each Meeting as followeth :—

Gainsbrough, Henry Simpson & Peter Nayler & Sarah Nayler & Margret Simson.

The Ile, John Urry, senior & James Coakes, Mary Berrier & Ellen Vesse.

Winteringham, Thomas Wresle, Francis Dent & Wadingham John, Elizabeth Westoby & Mary Frow & Susan Wresle.

Brigg, Robert Colyer & John Barlow & Sarah Nainby, Joseph Gilliatt.

Garthrup, Thomas Hutchinson & Robert Vesse & Jane Morley & Elizabeth Cornwell.

Contributions came in as followeth :—

	£	s.	d.
Gainsbrough	00	18	00
The Ile	00	14	00
Winteringham	00	16	00
Brigge	00	16	00
Garthrop	00	06	00
	03	10	6
Stock	01	18	4
	05	08	10

Disbursments..	£	s,	d.
to John Symson for Suse Recket	00	01	00
to John Urry which he paid for Richard Turner wife house rent	00	12	06
to James Coakes for Sander Chapman releife ..	00	05	00
to Robert Vesse for Doll Pickhaver	00	04	00
to Quarterly Meeting	01	15	00
to Quarterly Meeting for bookes	00	17	00
Rests in stock in Joseph Richardson hand ..	01	14	04

Signed by Joseph Richardson.

ATT a Monthly Meeting held at the Meeting House at Brigge the 14 of the 11 Month 1703[1] :—

Thomas Wresle & George Frow are desired to have an eye over Samuel Richardson conversation, an account being given to this Meeting that he still continues as he did without any amendment of his life.

This Meeting orders Friends of Brigg to draw up a paper of condemnation against Joshua Reeder for his evill & wicked course of life haveing had long patience & used much indeavour with him for clearing themselves & Truth.

This Meeting desireth Robert Colyer & Francis Dent to give Joshua Reeder wife a vissitt, in this time of trouble & great exercise, & give an account to the next Monthly Meeting.

p. 256.

Thomas Hutchison gives an account to this Meeting that John Clark of Garthrop still comes to there Meeting, but he with Robert Vessy are desired to have a watchful eye over his conversation & give an account to the next Monthly Meeting.

Whereas John Wresle of Theaby has not had a convenient oppertunity to clear himself of his son John for his wicked & disorderly walking Friends are willing to forbear giving a Testimony against him, till he have soe cleared himself.

Joseph Stevenson of Elsham came this day into the Meeting, & published his intentions of marrigge with Jane Brown of Brigge & shee being present gave her consent but it being the first time they are desired to wait Friends answer till the next Monthly Meeting, John Barlow & Robert Colyer are desired to inspect there clearness from all other persons and give an account to the next Monthly Meeting.

The case of widdow Foster of Crowle comeing before this Meeting, & findeing her nessesities to be very great by reason of her loss by fire, this Meeting therefore orders that a collection be made in every perticular Meeting for raiseing £10 or more for her supply & brought up to the next Monthly Meeting.

This Meeting desireth John Urry, senior & Robert Coakes to use there indeavour with widdow Foster creditors to see what kindness they will be pleased to extend to the widdow now in her desolate condition & give an account to the next Monthly Meeting.

An account was given to this Meeting of George Fox bookes of Doctrinal Matters being to be reprinted as alsoe what number Friends of this Monthly Meeting are willing to take of them.

[1] 14th January, 1704.

Next Monthly Meeting ordered to be at Brigg & Friends are desired to get together by the 10th houre of the day.

Signed by Joseph Richardson.

ATT a Monthly Meeting held at the Meeting House att Brigge the 11th day of the 12th month 1703[1] :—

This Meeting orders Thomas Wresle & Francis Dent to desire Samuel Richardson appearance at our next Monthly Meeting.

This Meeting orders Brigg Friends to draw up a paper of condemnation against Joshua Reeders—to be signed by the next Monthly Meeting.

This Meeting desires Friends of Adlinfleet Meeting to have an eye over John Clark & give an account to the next Monthly Meeting.

p. 257.

Edward Gilliatt & William Williamson signifying to this Meeting that he has something in his minde to John Wresle, Friends have agreed that he clear himself & give account to the next Monthly Meeting.

Contributions about Widdows Fosters loss by fire came in as followeth :—

	£	s.	d.
Gainsbrough	02	10	0
The Ile	05	08	0
Winteringham	02	16	6
Brigg	02	10	00
Garthrop	00	17	06
Totall	14	02	06

This Meeting desires John Urry and James Coakes & Thomas Wresle to use there discretion in the disposall of it to her and give an account to the next Monthly Meeting.

Joseph Steenson of Elsham came a second time into this Meeting & signified the continuance of his purpose of marriage with Jane Brown, & shee being present signified the same & findeing nothing to object against it have left the same to them selves with Friends advice according to the good order of Truth.

This Meeting orders Brigg Friends to get a man & horse to goe with John Halliwell to Robert Vesse of Luddinton who is desired to take care about him & this Meeting is to see him indemnified.

Next Monthly Meeting ordered to be at Brigg & a contribution to be made & brought up thither.

Signed by Joseph Richardson,

[1] 11th February, 1704.

ATT a Monthly Meeting held at Brigg the 10th of the first month 1703/4[1] :—

Thomas Wresle spoke to Samuel Richardson to desire his appearance att this Meeting, but he not comeing, Thomas with Francis Dent are desired to speak to him againe & bring his positive answer to the next Monthly Meeting.

This Meeting desires Thomas Morley & Robert Vesse to have a watchfull eye over John Clark conversation & give an account to the next Monthly Meeting.

Edward Gilliatt gives account to this Meeting that he had some seasonable time with John Wresle which gave such *(p. 258)* satisfaction to this Meeting that they are willing to wait till next Monthly Meeting to see what effect it will bring forth & Brigg Friends are desired to take notice thereof & give an account to the next Monthly Meeting,

Contributions came in as followeth :—

	£	s.	d.
Gainsbrough	00 :	18 :	6
The Ile	00 :	13 :	0
Wintringham	00 :	13 :	00
Brigg	00 :	15 :	00
Adlinfleet	00 :	06 :	06
	03 :	06 :	00
Stock	01 :	14 :	04
Totall	05 :	00 :	4

Disbursments are :—

	£	s.	d.
To Abraham Northern table for 26 weeks at 6 a week till 10th day 12th month 1703/4..	00 :	13 :	0
for 2 bushels coales for Susie Recket ..	00 :	02 :	8
to Robert Colyer on John Halliwell account	00 :	12 :	6
to John Urry, senior for ½ year rent for Richard Turner wife	00 :	06 :	00
To Thomas Morley for Doll Pickhaver ..	00 :	02 :	00
Totall	01 :	16 :	2
Paid more	00 :	01 :	0

Rests in stock in Joseph Richardson hands .. 03 : 03 : 2

Robert Colyer & John Marshall are desired to acquaint the Quarterly Meeting wherefore we have sent no contribution to them at this time.

[1] 10th March, 1704.

This Meeting according to order of the last Monthly Meeting has had the paper of condemnation read amongst them concerning Joshua Reeder, & has signed it, & sent it to the Meeting to which he belongs.

This Meeting has agreed that Gainsbrough, the Ile, Winteringham & Brigg take each of them a book of George Fox workes when they come.

This Meeting being acquainted by John Urry, senior, of his son Johns disorderly proceeding with respect to his late pretended marriage the same being contrary to the good order of Truth & our practice therein, appoints Edward Gilliatt & Francis Dent to give him a vissit & desire his appearance at our next Monthly Meeting.

Next Monthly Meeting ordered to be at Francis Dents at Thornholme,

Signed by Joseph Richardson.

ATT a Monthly Meeting held at Francis Dents of Thornholme the 14 of 2 month 1704[1] :—

p. 259.

Thomas Wresle & Francis Dentt gives an account to this Meeting that Samuel Richardson still continues in his evill words & actions contrary to Truth & that they with John Nainby & his father are still inclined & feells something upon there spirits to him for clearing the Truth & alsoe for him to clear it, & give Friends some satisfaction at the next Monthly Meeting.

Thomas Morley acquaints Friends in this Meeting that John Clark has not onely left comeing to Meeting but continues in his evill course of life, & Friends haveing had long patience and forbearance with him & no amendment made to answer there love & care, have ordered Thomas Morley & Thomas Hutchinson to acquaint him that if he come not to the next Monthly Meeting to give Friends better satisfaction they doe intend to give forth a Testimony against him.

This Meeting orders Thomas Potter, John Symson and Peter Nayler to have a watchfull eye over John Wresle conversation for Truth sake & to advise & admonish him as the Lord may open there harts in love, & if he come to Brigg before that time that Edward Gilliatt & Joseph Richardson would doe the same & give an account to the next Monthly Meeting.

The matter about John Urry, junior being discoursed in this Meeting, its agreed to defer the same till further occasion offers to discourse about it.

14th April, 1704.

I

Winteringham Meeting has agreed with advice of this Meeting to
keep a Meeting at Francis Dents at Thornholme once in 6
weeks & to begin the 23d day of this month.

Whereas our Freind Anthony Westoby of Winteringham deceased
did by his last will give the sum of £10 to be disposed of at the
discretion of this Monthly Meeting, Mordeca Westoby his son
& executor brought it & paid it this day to the Meeting &
Joseph Richardson has by order given a dischargé for it, &
has it in his hand till it please the Meeting to call on him for it.

Next Monthly Meeting ordered at Gainsbrough.

Signed by Joseph Richardson.

p. 260.

ATT a Monthly Meeting held at John Symsons in Gainsbrough
the 12 of the 3d Month 1704[1] :—

Samuel Richardson sent word to Friends in this Meeting that he
intends to make his appearance at the next Monthly Meeting
& the same Friends as before are desired to have a watchfull
eye over his conversation & give an account thereof to the
next Monthly Meeting.

Thomas Hutchinson giveing no satisfactory account to this Meeting
concerning John Clark, Friends desires Thomas Hutchinson
with Thomas Morley speak to him againe in order to appear
at the next Monthly Meeting before Friends give forth a
Testimony against him.

Edward Gilliatt, John Barlow & Joseph Richardson are desired to
speak to John Wresle once more to make his appearance at
the next Monthly Meeting before Friends give forth a Testimony
against him.

John Urry, senior of Epworth brought into this Meeting £5 & paid
it which was given by Thomas Eaveratt of there Meeting to
be disposed as Friends of the Monthly Meeting saw meet, &
Peter Nayler of Gainsbrough has it in his hand till Friends
agree about the disposall of it.

This day Isaak Westoby of Gainsbrough came into the Meeting
& published his intentions of marriage with Elizabeth Richardson of Brigg, & shee being present gave her consent alsoe her
father & mother being present gave there consent alsoe, but
it being the first time they are both desired to wait Friends
answer till next Monthly Meeting.

This Meeting orders Thomas Potter & John Symson to write to
Friends of Lincolne Meeting to give a few lines for satisfaction
of Friends of this Meeting of his conversation and clearness
from all other woemen before next Monthly Meeting.

[1] 12th May, 1704.

Next Monthly Meeting ordered to be at Winteringham & a contribution to be collected & brought up thither.

Signed by Joseph Richardson.

p. 261.

ATT a Monthly Meeting held at the Meeting House at Winteringham the 9th of the 4th month 1704[1] :—

According to last Monthly Meeting order Thomas Hutchinson & Thomas Morley spoke to John Clark concerning his disorderly walking and signified Friends patience with him this long time, but he desired them to forbear a litle longer before they proceeded to give forth a Testimony against him : Thomas Hutchinson & Thomas Morley are still desired to have an eye over him for good & to desire his appearance at our next Monthly Meeting.

There comeing not a full account concerning John Wresle, Edward Gilliatt, Joseph Richardson & John Barlow are desired to speak to him once more, & to desire his appearance at the next Monthly Meeting before Friends draw up a Testimony against him.

Contributions came in as followeth :—

	£	s.	d.
Gainsbrough	00 :	18 :	6
Brigg	00 :	15 :	0
Wintringham	00 :	14 :	0
Isle	00 :	09 :	6
Adlinfleet	00 :	07 :	6
by Joseph Richardson in stock	03 :	07 :	2
	06 :	07 :	8

Disbursments :—

	£	s.	d.
To Joseph Richardson which he lade down upon a publick account	00 :	19 :	9
to Thomas Wresle, Beltoft for Isaac Davis for his apprentice	01 :	00 :	00
to Thomas Morley for John Halliwell table ..	00 :	12 :	00
to the Quarterly Meeting	01 :	10 :	00
by Thomas Potter			
Rests yet in stock in Joseph Richardson hands	02 :	05 :	11

Joseph Richardson paid of it at Lincolne since for bookes .. .. 00 : 08 : 03

Friends having had some discourse this day with Samuel Richardson & findeing upon discourse with him, that he desires a litle longer time, hopeing to better improve it & answer Friends love & care for him as by a Testimony under his own hand the same

---

[1] 9th June, 1704.

time which Freinds has granted him, a true coppy of his letter is as followeth :—

To Friends at the Meeting at Winteringham 9th of 4th month 1704.

I not being unsensible of Friends love & care they have towards me, I doe hartily desire that they may give me some time before they proceed to give out a paper against me, & if in some few months there be not some satisfaction to Truth & the Friends thereof then to proceed against me, that Truth & Friends may be cleared & I condemnd.

Samuel Richardson.

p. 262.

This day Isaac Westoby came a second time & signified the continuance of his purpose of marriage with Elizabeth Richardson & brought a certificate signifying her consent with parents alsoe & no objections proveing to hinder there proceedings Friends have left the consumation thereof to themselves with Friends advice according to the good order of Truth.

This John Beninton came a second time and signified the continuance of his purpose of marriage with Elizabeth Ward, & brought a certificate from her & her relations signifying there consent, & gave him a certificate signifying his clearness from all other persons, which after the same be found on her part have left the consumation according to Truths order.

This day John Morley came into the Meeting and published his intention of marriage with Mirriam Nainby & shee being present gave her consent, but it being the first time they are desired to wait Friends answer till next Monthly Meeting.

Next Monthly Meeting ordered at Thomas Morleys in Adlinfleet.

	£	s.	d.
Joseph Richardson account for Stock in his hand	2 :	5 :	11
paid of it since for bookes at Lincolne ..	0 :	8 :	3
paid on a publick account	0 :	1 :	6
for John Halliwell wasecoat & makeing ..	0 :	7 :	4
Rests in Joseph Richardson hands			1

ATT a Monthly Meeting held at Thomas Morleys in Adlinfleet the 14 of 5 month 1704[1] :—

Thomas Hutchinson & Thomas Morley are still desired to have an eye to John Clarks conversation & admonish him as they see occasion & give an account to the next Monthly Meeting.

There being no satisfactory account given to this Meeting about John Wresle, Edward Gilliatt, Joseph Richardson & John

[1] 14th July, 1704.

Barlow are desired to speak once again to him & if no amendment appear Friends thinks to give forth a Testimony against
him.

Thomas Wresle & Francis Dent are desired to have an eye over
Samuel Richardson conversation & give an account to the
next Monthly Meeting.

This day John Morley came a second time into our Meeting &
signified the continuance of his purpose of marriage with Mirriam
Nainby & haveing obtained consent of Friends & relations all
things being clear Friends have left the consumation according
to Truths order.

p. 263.

Friends appointed to collect the money for John Whitehead bookes
are as followeth :—

Imps. Gainsburgh, Thomas Potter for	..	..	13
The Ile, Joseph Berrier for	..	..	8
Winteringam, Stephen Wresle for		..	12
Brigg, Robert Colyer for	..	..	3
Adlinfleet, Thomas Hutchinson for		..	4

being 40 at 2s. : 8d. a peice

Next Monthly Meeting ordered at John Nainbys in Castlethorp.

Signed by Joseph Richardson.

ATT a Monthly Meeting held at John Nainbys in Caistrop the
11th of the 6th month 1704[1] :—

Thomas Hutchinson gave account to this Meeting that things were
no better with John Clark therefore he with Thomas Morley
are still desired to admonish & take notice both of his behaviour
& how he attends Meetings & give an account thereof to the
next Meeting.

John Wresle being found the same he formerly was in his evill
conversation as by an account given by Edward Gilliatt,
its still desired Edward Gilliatt, Joseph Richardson & John
Barlow have a watchfull eye over him & admonish him as
occasion offers & give an account to next Monthly Meeting.

The weomen Friends are desired to doe the like to his wife.

Thomas Wresle & Francis Dent are still desired to have an eye
over Samuel Richardson conversation & to admonish him that
if possible he may be regained & give an account to the next
Monthly Meeting.

Robert Colyer is to take care to collect the mony for John Whithead
bookes against next Monthly Meeting.

[1] 11th August, 1704.

John Halliwell is left to Brigg Friends to order as they see most convenient for a settlement.

The next Monthly Meeting ordered to be at Francis Dents att Thornholme where a contribution is to be collected & brought.

p. 264.

ATT a Monthly Meeting held at Francis Dents of Thornholme the 8th of the 7th month 1704[1] :—

Friends in the seaverall Meetings are desired to bring in there marriages to be recorded, & that for the future better care be taken to get all marriages recorded in the booke appointed for that service.

This Meeting desires that Thomas Hutchinson & Thomas Morley continue a watchfull eye over John Clarks conversation for Truth sake, as alsoe if he duly attends there Meetings and give an account to the next Monthly Meeting.

This Meeting still desires that Sarah Nainby and Mary Heptonstall speak to John Wresle wife about her miscarriages both as to Truth & to her husband, which has brought reproach on Truth and Friends & alsoe that Edward Gilliatt & John Barlow doe the same to John Wresle, & give an account to next Monthly Meeting.

Thomas Wresle gave an account to this Meeting that he went to give Samuel Richardson a vissitt, according to Friends order, but found him & his family under such great affliction as had not freedome to say any thing to him at that time, this Meeting therefore desires that he with Francis Dent would continue there care in takeing a convenient season to speak to him, & give an account to the next Monthly Meeting.

Friends are desired in there seaverall Meetings to inquire for a place of settlement with any person for John Halliwell & to agree what they will have with him, & agree with them & this Meeting will see them indemnified.

Contributions came in as followeth :—

	£	s.	d.
Gainsbrough		18 :	6
The Ile		12 :	0
Winteringham		15 :	0
Brigg		14 :	0
Garthrop		07 :	0
In stock Joseph Richardson..	1 :	08 :	0
	04 :	15 :	4

[1] 8th September, 1704.

Disbursments :—   £   s.   d.
> To John Marshall for Abraham Northern table
> from the 10th of first month 1704 till the
> 8 of the 7 month   ..   ..   ..   13 : 00
> To Joseph Berrier for widdow Mosley releife   02 : 6
> To Thomas Wresle for releife widdow Oyle   02 : 0
> To Robert Colyer for bookes   ..   ..   ..   03 : 5
> To Robert Colyer for Mary Goxhill   ..   ..   05 : 0
> To Doll Pickhaver by Thomas Morley   ..   04 : 00
> To the Quarterly Meeting   ..   ..   .. 01 : 05 : 00

Rests in stock in Joseph Richardson hand ..   02 : 00 : 5

This Meeting orders Francis Dent, Edward Gilliatt & Thomas
Potter to attend the service of the Quarterly Meeting.

Next Monthly Meeting ordered to be at Brigg.

Quarterly Meeting ordered the 4th day before the time cald Michael-
mas.[1]

> Signed by Joseph Richardson.

p. 265.

ATT a Monthly Meeting held at Brigg the 13th of the 8th month
1704[2] :—

Its ordered by Friends of this Meeting that Freinds bring an account
of there marriages with there births & buryls as they may
happen amongst them.

Thomas Morley gives Friends an account at this Meeting that
John Clark does more duly attend there Meeting then formerly,
& is in hopes he is better in his conversation, but they are
still desired to continue there care over him in love, & give
account thereof to the next Monthly Meeting.

Friends desires Edward Gilliatt & John Barlow to give John
Wresle of Brigg the sence of this Meeting concerning him, &
of the long continuance of there care & tenderness for him if
bye any means he might be reclaimed, & give an account of
there Judgment concerning him to the next Monthly Meeting.

This Meeting still desires that Thomas Wresle & Francis Dent
would give Samuel Richardson family a vissitt & see how things
are with them & give an account thereof to the next Monthly
Meeting.

Friends upon consultation in this Meeting about John Halliwell
have advised & agreed where he comes to Friends houses that
they make application to the next Justice of the Peace to get
him sent to the House of Correction & this Meeting will see
them indemnified.

[1] 25th September, 1704.   [2] 13th October, 1704.

An epistle was read in this Meeting & ordered to be coppied out & given to the seaverall Meetings to be considered of, & a Meeting to be appointed to answer Friends desire.

Whereas some difference has been between Thomas Credforth[1] of Epworth & his son in law Henry Clark, Friends have advised them to putt & they have agreed to reffer the matter to some Friends to end the same upon forfeture of forty pounds.

Edward Gilliatt & Thomas Morley are desired to speak to John Urry, junior to appear at our next Monthly Meeting & those dissatisfied Friends in there Meeting appear alsoe.

Friends are ordered to bring an account of there suffering for tythe to the next Monthly Meeting fairly drawn over.

The bookes divided in this Meeting came to 10 : 8.

Next Monthly Meeting ordered to be at Brigge.

Signed by Joseph Richardson.

p. 266.

A coppy of John Urry, junior, his Letter of Condemnation.
Dear Friends,

I am really sorry that I have given soe just an occation of offence, both to the Truth & Friends, as I have done in my disorderly proceedings in marriage ; & that which adds weight to my exercise herein is, that I did not doe it for want of understanding ; but want of a due & early care, & watchfullness ; for which I doe feell I am judged & condemned in my self : Therefore doe I the more freely offer this as a Testimony against my soe untruthlike practices ; esteeming all but too little to make satisfaction to the Truth for that I have unwarrantably done : And withall can doe no less than accknowledge your love & tenderness towards me ; still desiring your prayers for my restoration againe ; that if happily it may please the Lord that I may find peace with him : And that we may all of us be in unity & fellowshipp one with another ; is the earnest desire of him ; who once was, and still desires to be your Friend in the Truth.

John Urry, junior.

Att a Monthly Meeting held at the Meeting House at Brigg the 9th of the 9th month 1704[2] :—

Thomas Hutchinson gives Friends an account at this Meeting that they are in hopes John Clark is better in conversation then formerly, however they are desired still to have an eye over him in love, & give further account to the next Monthly Meeting.

---

[1] *Sic* for Cutsforth.   [2] 9th November, 1704.

Edward Gilliatt being not here to give an account what he has done about John Wresle, Brigg Friends are desired to speak to him, to clear himself that if there be no amendment Friends may draw a paper of condemnation against him to be ready against next Monthly Meetinge.

Thomas Wresle & Francis Dent are still desired to give Samuel Richardson family a vissitt & see how things are with them & give an account to the next Monthly Meetinge.

p. 267.

Some debate being in this Meeting about John Halliwell have agreed that he shall have notice of a paper of condemnation drawn up against him before next Monthly Meeting.

Thomas Wresle & James Coakes are desired to speak to Thomas Cutsforth of Epworth that he stand to Friends arbitration or appear at next Monthly Meeting to shew his reasons.

Gainsbrough & Winteringam have brought in there suffering for tythe but the Ile, Adlinfleet & Brigg are to bring theres into the next Monthly Meeting.

James Coakes & Edward Gilliatt are desired to speak to John Urry, junior in Epworth & desire his appearance at our next Monthly Meeting.

James Coakes of Butterwick came into this Meeting & published his intention of marriage with Penellopy Wollus of Crowle & shee being present gave her consent but it being the first time they are both desired to wait Friends answer till next Monthly Meeting,

Thomas Wresle & Isaac Davis are desired to see into the clearness of both parties & give account thereof to the next Monthly Meeting.

Next Monthly Meeting ordered at Brigge & that a contribution be collected & brought up thither.

> Signed by Joseph Richardson.

ATT a Monthly Meeting held at Brigg the 8 day of the 10th month 1704[1] :—

Thomas Morley gives Friends account at this Meeting that John Clark is more orderly in his conversation as far as they knew ; but they are still desired to have an eye to him & give an account to next Monthly Meeting,

Its still desired that Thomas Wresle & George Frow have an eye over Samuel Richardson conversation and gave account to the next Monthly Meeting.

[1] 8th December, 1704.

p. 268.

Whereas the difference depending betwixt Thomas Cutsforth of Epworth & his son in law Henry Clark & his sister was by them reffered to the award of Richard Clark, Edward Gilliatt & Thomas Morley, who after a consideration of matters betwixt them delivered there award, & the said Thomas Cutsforth being dissatisfied, charges the said arbitrators with unjust dealing therefore upon complaint of Edward Gilliatt & Thomas Morley doe order Thomas Wresle to give him notice to appear at the next Monthly Meeting to make good his charges.

Whereas Edward Gilliatt was desired to speak to John Wresle who personally appeared in this Meeting & gave Friends some satisfaction, being in hopes of his returne from his former ungodly conversation, Edward Gilliatt is desired to have an eye over him & his conversation, & incourage him in his good resolution as he may see meet, & give an account to the next Monthly Meeting John Sharpe, Edward Gilliatt & John Barlow are desired to speak to John Halliwell to appear at our next Monthly Meeting to give answer to the charges that Friends have against him as to his wicked & ungodly conversation.

Sufferings for tythe & other things that came not into last Monthly Meeting are brought into this Meeting.

According to the request of last Monthly Meeting Edward Gilliatt had an oppertunity with conferring John Urry, junior & he gave some hopes that things would be better with them for the future, & Thomas Wresle is desired to give an account if John attend there Meeting.

Contributions came in as followeth :—

	£	s.	d.
Gainsbrough	17	:	6
Brigg	14	:	6
Ile	13	:	0
Wintringham	15	:	6
Adlinfleet	07	:	6
	3 : 8 : 0		
in stock	2 : 0 : 5		

	£	s.	d.
to Joseph Richardson which he paid	00	: 5	: 0
to John Urry for Anne Browne	01	: 00	: 00
to Robert Colyer for bookes	00	: 10	: 08
to Robert Colyer for the use of the Quarterly Meeting	01	: 10	: 00
Totall	03	: 5	: 8
Rests in stock in Joseph Richardson hand..	02	: 02	: 09

Robert Colyer, John Barlow & Thomas Morley is appointed to attend the service of the Quarterly Meeting.

Robert Colyer acquainted Friends in this Meeting that it was in his minde to vissit Friends Meetings in the north cuntry, & desires this Meeting assent, & Friends gave there consent to it.

Next Monthly Meeting ordered to be at Brigge.

Signed by Joseph Richardson.

p. 269.

ATT a Monthly Meeting held at Brigg the 12th day of the 11th month 1704[1] :—

Robert Vesse gives account to this Meeting that John Clark continues more orderly in his conversation than formerly & diligent in frequenting there Meetings both first day & week day, & that he beleives he is better in himself, which Friends are glad of, & is some satisfaction for all there labour of love towards him, but they are still desired to have a watchfull eye over him for Truth sake.

John Halliwell appearing at this Meeting ; & after some discourse with him, Friends have unanimously agreed that if he continue at Brigg, or whereever he may come & be troublesome, that some Friend goe to the next Justice of Peace & make complaint against him in order to get a Warrant to have him sent to the House of Correction or last place of settlement at Crowle, & this Meeting will see the charge indemnified.

Friends have sent a few lines to Samuel Richardson to make his appearance at our next Monthly Meeting in order to answer the charge that Friends have against him, Joseph Wresle and John Waddingham are desired to take care therein.

Edward Gilliatt has sent an answer to Thomas Cutsforth letter & Friends have ordered Thomas Wresle to give Thomas Cutsforth notice to appear at our next Monthly Meeting, And alsoe to desire John Urry, junior, to appear at our next Monthly Meeting.

John Massie of Holbitch Marsh came into this meeting, & published his intention of marriage with Katherine Barlow of Brigg & shee being present gave her consent as alsoe her father & mother but it being first time they are both desired to wait Friends answer till next Monthly Meeting.

Thomas Winder of Ealand in the parish of Crowle came into this meeting & published his intention of marriage with Mary Morfitt of the same, & shee being present gave her consent, but it being first time they are both desired to wait Friends answer till next Monthly Meeting,

[1] 12th January, 1705.

Andrew Annon of Lee came into this Meeting & published his intention of marriage with Rachell Standley of Waddingham[1] & brought a certificate signifying her consent, but it being first time they are desired to wait Friends answer till next Monthly Meeting.

Next Monthly Meeting ordered at Brigge.

Signed by Joseph Richardson.

p. 270.

ATT a Monthly Meeting held at the Meeting House at Brigge the 9th of 12 month 1704[2] :—

Thomas Hutchinson gives account to this Meeting that John Clark is as disorderly in his conversation as formerly notwithstanding the patience & tenderness of Friends towards him for Truth sake & therefore he is desired by Thomas Hutchinson to make his appearance at our next Monthly Meeting to answer such charges as Friends have against him, else Friends will finde a nessesity to disown him.

Samuel Richardson appeared at this Meeting & made some acknowledgment of his faults & miscarriages before Friends & we hope in some good sence has promised for the future to amend his conversation, else he is willing that Friends should disown him for the clearing themselves & the Truth ; Joseph Wresle & John Waddingham are desired notice of his conversation & report same to the Meeting.

Whereas Thomas Cutsforth was desired by Friends at the last Monthly Meeting to make his appearance at this Meeting to answer to such matters & things as Edward Gilliatt, Richard Clark & Thomas Morley has to lay to his charge. Thomas Wresle of Beltoft gave him notice thereof but he has not appeared according to Friends desire, Isaac Davis & Isaac Brown are desired to speak to him once more to make his appearance at our next Monthly Meeting & alsoe to know the reasons wherefore he does not frequent Friends Meetings.

Its desired by Friends in this Meeting that some Friends from each Meeting take care to the sence of Friends of each Monthly Meeting concerning the prisson room at Lincolne, whether any Friends as debtors shall have the privilidge thereof.

John Massy of Holebitch Marsh came into this Meeting & signified the continuance of his purpose of marriage with Katherine Barlow of Brigg & shee being present signified the same as alsoe her father & mother, & nothing of impediment appearing to hinder there proceedings have left the consumation thereof to themselves with Friends advice according to Truths order.

---

[1] *Sic : recte* Waddington.   [2] 9th February, 1705.

Thomas Winder of Ealand came a second time & signified the continuance of his purpose of marrage with Mary Morfitt & shee being present signified the same, & Friends upon inquiry findeing nothing to hinder there proceedings have left the consumation thereof to themselves with Friends advice according to Truths order.

p. 271.

Andrew Annon of Lee came into this Meeting & signified the continuance of his purpose of marriage with Rachell Standley of Waddinton & Friends finding nothing to hinder there proceedings have left the consumation thereof to themselves, & the Meeting to which shee belongs to accomplish as may be seen meet.

Next Monthly Meeting ordered at Brigge & a contribution to be collected & brought up thither.

Signed by Joseph Richardson.

ATT a Monthly Meeting held at Brigg the 9th of the first month 1705[1] :—

Thomas Morley gives some account to this Meeting that he thinks John Clark somewhat better than formerly, & hopes his indeavours for an amendment but Friends being not well satisfied concerning him have desired Joseph Richardson to write to him & give him Friends sence & Judgment & signe it as by order of this Meeting.

David Crosby & Edward Gilliatt thinks to give Samuell Richardson a vissitt before next Meeting, & give an account of there service with him to the next Monthly Meeting.

There is a paper drawn up of Friends sence & Judgment about the prison room, which is ordered to the Quarterly Meeting.

Thomas Cutsforth not appearing this Meeting disires Thomas Wresle & Samuel Browne take notice whether Thomas Cutsforth proceed to prosecute the suite with his son & daughter, & give an account to the next Monthly Meeting.

This day James Coakes of Butterwick came a second time & signified the continuance of his purpose of marriage with Penelope Woolley[2] & shee being present gave her consent & nothing appearing to hinder there proceedings have left the consumation thereof to themselves with Friends advice according to Truths order.

This Meeting orders Thomas Potter & Thomas Morley to attend the service of the Quarterly Meetinge.

[1] 9th March, 1705.   [2] *Sic : recte* Wallace.

p. 272.

Contributions came in as followeth :—

	£	s.	d.
Gainsbrough		18 :	06
The Ile		11 :	00
Winteringham		16 :	06
Brigge		14 :	00
Adlinfleet		07 :	06
In stock..	2 :	00 :	05
Totall	5 :	07 :	11

Disbursments :—

	£	s.	d.
To Thomas Potter for Susie Recket	00 :	01 :	8
To Thomas Potter for Abraham Northen from the 8 of 7th month to the 9th of the first month 1705	00 :	13 :	0
To Joseph Richardson which he paid	00 :	12 :	08
To Thomas Morley for Doll Pickhaver ..	00 :	02 :	6
ordered to the Quarter Meeting	01 :	10 :	0
Rests in stock in Joseph Richardson hand	02 :	08 :	01

James Coakes gives account to this Meeting that whereas William Parkinson has run out to Mary his wife with a preist & other miscarriages that he spoke to him about it, & findes him much ashamed of his actions, & leaves it to Friends to doe with him as they see meet but he is ashamed to appear among Friends, soe Friends orders James Coakes & Isaac Brown to speak to him to give forth a Testimony under his own hand for his evill practice for clearing Truth & the Friends of it.

Sara Colyer gave Friends account in this Meeting that shee had it upon her minde to vissitt Friends Meetings norward & in Scotland with her companion Ellen Midleton, and Friends having unity with the same have given her a certificate on that behalf which shee is to return to this Meeting after shee comes back againe.

Next Monthly Meeting ordered to be at Thealby.

Signed by Joseph Richardson.

ATT a Monthly Meeting held at Thealby the 13th of the 2d Month 1705[1] :—

Joseph Richardson writt to John Clark according to the last Monthly Meeting order, but no account coming to this Meeting how he resented it, Thomas Morley & Robert Vesse are desired to speak to him, & bring his answer to the next Monthly Meetinge.

[1] 13th April, 1705.

p. 273.

Samuel Browne is desired to speak to William Parkinson to draw up something as a Testimony against his evill practices for the clearing Truth & Freinds & send or give it to Robert Colyer at Gainsbrough for Friends to peruse, that if they see meet may inlarge it, & get it ready against next Monthly Meetinge.

Samuel Richardson appearing at this Meeting and Friends haveing had much discourse with him, his father & he desires another months time in hopes of amendment which if it doe not appear, that Friends give forth a Testimony against him, for clearing the Truth & Friends, John Waddingham & Joseph Wresle are desired to take notice thereof & give an account to the next Monthly Meeting.

Freinds of Winteringham Meeting has nominated & chosen Richard Wresle & John Waddingham overseers in there Meeting in the places of Thomas Wresle & Francis Dent.

Next Monthly Meeting ordered at Gainsbrough.

ATT a Monthly Meeting held at Gainsbrough 11th of 3d month 1705[1] :—

Thomas Hutchinson gave account that Thomas Morley & Robert Vesse had spoke to John Clark but can obtaine no satisfaction from him onely hopes to prevaile with him to appear at next Monthly Meeting, & Thomas Morley & Thomas Hutchinson are desired to speak to him about it.

John Dent gives this Meeting an account that there appears no amendment in Samuel Richardson, its therefore agreed by Friends unanimously, that a Testimony or paper of condemnation be drawn up against him & his wicked practices for the clearing the Truth & Friends & that Robert Colyer, John Barlow & John Dent draw it up & bring it to the next Monthly Meeting.

William Parkinson of West Butterwick sent a paper to this Meeting acknowledging his outrunings, but it being judged too short, is sent back to be amended for the more full clearing of the Truth, & giveing Friends better sattisfaction. Thomas Wresle, James & Robert Coakes are ordered to give him this & bring the other up to the next Monthly Meeting.

p. 274.

This Meeting haveing under there consideration the appointing a generall Meeting for Worshipp at Gainsbrough refers the further consideration to the next Monthly Meeting.

[1] 11th May, 1705.

Thomas Huchison haveing proposed to have a Meeting at his house, the same is agreed to and Meeting appointed next first day come a week being the 20 instant & soe to continue in course.

This Meeting haveing under consideration a legacy given by Anthony Westoby deceased to this Meeting refers the further consideration till the next Monthly Meeting.

This Meeting orders a contribution to be collected and brought up to the next Monthly Meeting which is ordered to be at Thomas Morleys in Adlinfleet.

Signed by Joseph Richardson.

ATT a Monthly Meeting held at Thomas Morleys in Adlinfleet the 8th day of the 4th month 1705[1] :—

John Clark of Garthrop not appearing at this Meeting according to the last Meetings order, Thomas Hutchinson & Thomas Morley are desired to see if they can prevaile with him to come to the next Monthly Meeting.

Robert Colyer & John Barlow according to the last Meetings order brought a paper of condemnation against Samuel Richardsons evill life & conversation, which was read and approved of, but his father desireing Friends further forbearance doth agree to forbear signing of it till next Monthly Meeting & if by that time there appear no amendment that then the said writeing or Testimony be signed & made publick. Joseph Wresle & George Frow are desired to have a watchfull eye over him for good, & to give there sence & account of him to the next Monthly Meeting.

Thomas Wresle gave this Meeting an account that there had not been a convenient oppertunity to get William Parkinson to draw up Testimony more fully & signe it, this Meeting desires James Coakes & Thomas Wresle to indeavour to get it done & brought up to the next Monthly Meeting.

This Meeting agrees that a generall Meeting for Worshipp be held at Gainsbrough the 15th Instant.[2]

Joseph Richardson by letter desiring that the further consideration of Anthony Westobys legacy be deffered till the next Monthly Meeting this Meeting consents to it.

p. 275.

Thomas Huntsman of Elloughton in the County of York, came into this Meeting & published his intention of marriage with Jane

[1] 8th June, 1705.
[2] The first recorded use of the present Gainsborough Meeting House; licensed 16th April, 1705.

Nainby of Brigge, & shee being present gave her consent & they are desired to bring certificates from there parents to the next Meeting of there clearness from all other persons, but it being the first time are alsoe desired to wait Friends answer till next Monthly Meeting.

Stephen Wresle of Thealby came into this Meeting and published his intention of marriage with Mary Morley of Adlinfleet & shee being present gave her consent but it being the first time they are desired to wait Friends answer till next Monthly Meeting. They are alsoe desired to bring certificates for Freinds satisfaction, that they are both clear from all other persons,

Contributions came in as followeth :—

				£	s.	d.
Gainsbrough	..	..	..	00 :	19 :	0
The Ile ..	..	..	..	00 :	08 :	0
Winteringham ..	..	..	..	00 :	14 :	0
Brigge ..	..	..	..	00 :	14 :	6
Adlinfleet	..	..	..	00 :	07 :	6
stock brought up	..	..	..	02 :	08 :	01
				05 :	11 :	07

Disbursments :—

	£	s.	d.
to Joseph Richardson which he paid	00 :	14 :	01
To John Simson for coales for S. R.[1]		01 :	09
To Thomas Wresle for Isaac Davis upon his prentice account Marshall	01 :	00 :	00
for Mary Goxhill releife	00 :	05 :	00
for Doll Pickhaver by Robert Vesse	00 :	03 :	00
for Quarterly Meeting	01 :	10 :	00
Rests in stock in Joseph Richardson hands..	01 :	17 :	09

Whereas there appears a slackness in the Ile Friends both as to there contributions & comeing up to the Monthly Meeting, this Meeting appoints Joseph Richardson & Robert Colyer to write to them about it.

Next Monthly Meeting ordered at Winteringham.

Signed by Joseph Richardson.

ATT a Monthly Meeting held at the Meeting House in Winteringham the 13 of the 5th month 1705[2] :—

John Clark not appearing at this Meeting nowithstanding he has been soe often desired by Friends that have had long patience

[1] *Sic* for Susanna Reckitt.   [2] 13th July, 1705.

& forbearance towards him, Friends desires Thomas Hutchison would once more acquaint that Friends desireth his appearranc at the next Monthly Meeting to give Friends some satisfaction or else a Testimony will be given forth against him for the clearing of Friends & the Truth,

William Parkinson sent a writeing under his own hand to this Meeting wherein he condemns his disorderly practice, in takeing a wife not of our society & marry her with a preist, which is ordered to be recorded, & this Meeting orders James Coakes & Thomas Wresle to inspect his conversation & admonish him as they see meet, & give an account to the next Monthly Meeting.

p. 276.

This day the Testimony against Samuel Richardson & his wicked practices was read, he being present Freinds asked him what he had further to say he answered them that he would have them signe it for the clearing themselves & the Truth, which was accordingly done & ordered to be recorded & alsoe to be made publick.

Its agreed upon that the legacy of £10 left by Anthony Westoby deceased, this Meeting orders it to be given to the use of Brigg Meeting house with a provisoe, that they adjust the difference among themselves about the charge of there Meeting House or else bring the money to the next Monthly Meeting to be disposed of.

Stephen Wresle came a second time into our Meeting & signified the continuance of his purpose of marriage with Mary Morley shee being present gave consent & upon inquiry all things proveing clear on behalf of both parties, the consumation thereof was left to themselves at there own conveniency according to the good order of Truth.

A contribution is agreed upon to be collected in each Meeting, for the reliefe of William Birket who has suffered loss by fire, & to be brought up to the next Monthly Meeting.

The five pounds in Peter Naylers hand, given by Thomas Earott which was to be disposed of by this Meeting, this Meeting gives it to the service of the Ile Meeting towards there charge of building a new Meeting House.

A Meeting is appointed at Robert Vesses in Luddinton the first first day of the next month, which falls to be on the 5th day of the month.

Next Monthly Meeting ordered to be at John Nainbys in Castle-thorp.

Signed by Joseph Richardson.

Here followes William Parkinson letter of condemnation for his disobedience & outrunings.

To Friends of Gainsbrough Meetinge the 13 of the 5th month 1705[1] & to others whome it may concern.

These may let you know that I am very sorry that I have been soe far prevaild upon, by the enemy of my soules peace to be drawn to take a woeman which was not of our society (*p. 277*) to wife, & marry her with an hireling preist contrary to the practice of the primitive Christians who was carefull not to joyn themselves in that relation with unbeleivers, neither can it be found in all scriptures, that any man whatsoever was authorised by God or Christ Jesus to joyne people together in marriage & haveing found trouble of conscience for my outrunings and takeing such undew liberty as aforesaid to the dishonour of Truth & trouble & sorrow to the professers of it I doe hereby condemn that & all other practices & things in which I have been found that are inconsistant with the spotless Truth & judge that spirit that led me into the evill, takeing the shame wholy to my self & desires the prayers of the faithfull for my recovery, & return to the stock of the Lords companions, from whome I have strayed for want of takeing heed to the light of Christ Jesus.

William Parkinson,

A coppy of Samuel Richardson paper of condemnation.

To all people to whome this writeing shall come.

Know yee that whereas Samuel Richardson of Winteringham haveing been convinced of the blessed truth, which we the people of God in scorn cald Quakers make proffession of, but not takeing heed to the grace of God in his own hart, which teacheth to live soberly, righteously & godly in this world, hath been led away, by the temptations of the wicked one the Devill & Sathan into viz. drunkenness which is the root of many evills, being debauched in his conversation & beating his wife from time to time, for which we have dealt with him reproveing & admonishing him often with long patience & forbearance, that he might be led to repentance & amendment of life, much indeavours have been used to reclaime him out of evill, all which hath hitherto been in vaine, he continuing in that gross sin of drunkenness & many other evills. Therefore we finde a nessesity upon us for the Lords sake his Truth and people, who make proffession of his holy name to clear ourselves of him & the blessed Truth, that we

---

[1] 13th July, 1705.

have no fellowshipp with him not his unfruitfull workes of darkness, but doe disown him & all his wicked practices which hath greatly greived us, & much dishonoured that worthy name of the holy God whereby the heathen hath had occasion given, to open there mouthes against the Truth, & blaspheme God & his tabernacle & those that dwell therein therefore we testify & declare to the world that he is unto us as an heathen man, untill he come to repentance & acknowledgment of the Truth from which he hath departed.

Signed by the appointment of the Monthly Meeting held at Winteringham the 13 of the 5th month 1705 by

> Robert Colyer
> & Thomas Morley.

p. 278.

ATT a Monthly Meeting held at the house of John Nainbys in Castlethorp the 10th of the 6 month 1705[1] :—

John Clark not appearing at this Meeting as requested, Thomas Morley & Thomas Hutchinson are againe ordered to speak to him, & give him a paper which Friends have sent him from this Meeting for the further clearing of themselves and the Truth that if he appear not at the next Monthly Meeting to give Friends some satisfaction Friends may proceed to give forth a Testimony against him.

James Coakes & Thomas Wresle not meeting with a convenient oppertunity to speak to William Parkinson, but are desired to doe it before next Monthly Meeting, and give Friends an account thereof.

Brigg Friends met together & adjusted the charges & accounts of there new Meeting House according to the order of the last Monthly Meeting soe that this Meeting with the last, that the £10 Legacy left by Anthony Westoby be given them to the assistance of there aforesaid charge.

Money collected for the supply of William Birkets loss by fire as followeth & put into John Barlows hands :—

			£	s.	d.
Imps. Gainsbrough	..	..	01	00	00
Brigg	..	..	02	01	00
Winteringam	..	..	01	02	00
Adlinfleet	..	..	00	10	00
			4	13	00

Ile not yet come in.

[1] 10th August, 1705.

Thomas Huntsman came a second time into this Meeting & signified
the continuance of his purpose of marriage with Jane Nainby
& shee being present signified the same, & all things appearing
clear on behalf of both parties upon inquiry the consumation
thereof is left to themselves with Friends & relations advice
according to the good order of Truth.

p. 279.

Our Friend Susanna Richardson haveing had a concern upon her
minde, to vissit Friends in the south parts of England & Wales,
laid the matter before this Monthly Meeting the 11th of the
6th month last 1704 & Friends haveing unity with her gave her
a certificate, which shee has returnd into the Meeting againe
this day, & given us such an account of her service among
Friends as was both comfortable & to our satisfaction.

Our Friend Sarah Collier alsoe had a concern upon her minde to
vissitt Friends Meetings in Scotland & some counties in the
north west of England laid the same before Friends of this
Meeting the 9th of the first month last 1704/5 & Friends
haveing unity with her gave her a certificate which this day
shee returned into the Meeting, & gave such an account of
her service, as was greatly comfortable & to Friends satisfaction ; blessed be the Lord.

Our Friend Thomas Robinson sent a paper which was read in this
Meeting requesting a contribution towards the assistance of a
Friend that has been at much charge in building a new Meeting
House at Bourn, which was considered on but left further to
the consideration of the next Monthly Meeting.

Next Monthly Meeting ordered at Gainsbrough & a contribution
to be collected & brought up thither.

Signed by Joseph Richardson,

ATT a Monthly Meeting held at the Meeting House at Gainsbrough the 14 of the 7 Month 1705[1] :—

John Clark not appearing at this Meeting, Thomas Morley & Thomas
Hutcheson are desired to speak to him to appear at the next
Monthly Meeting before a paper of condemnation be drawn
up against him.

Thomas Robinson paper is still referd to the consideration of next
Monthly Meeting.

Ordered that a generall Meeting for Worship be held at Gainsbrough
14 of 6 Instant.

[1] 14th September, 1705.

p. 280.

The case of John Wresle of Brigg being laid before this Meeting
its ordered that Edward Gilliatt, Joseph Richardson & John
Nainby speak to him to appear at our next Monthly Meeting
before a paper of condemnation be drawn up against him.

Contributions came in as followeth :—

	£	s.	d.
Gainsbrough		17 :	00
Brigg		16 :	06
Ile		12 :	00
Winteringham		16 :	06
Adlinfleet		07 :	06
	3 :	09 :	06

Disbursments :—

	£	s.	d.
to Joseph Potter for Susan Recket		01 :	0
for Doll Pickhaver		05 :	0
To Quarterly Meeting	01 :	00 :	00
Rests in stock in Joseph Richardson hand ..	01 :	17 :	0
& stock in Robert Colyer hand	02 :	03 :	6

Ordered that Thomas Potter & Edward Gilliat attend the service
of the Quarterly Meeting.

Next Monthly Meeting ordered at Brigg.

Signed by Joseph Richardson,

ATT a Monthly Meeting held at the Meeting House at Brigg
the 13th of the 8th Month 1705[1] :—

Thomas Robinson paper is still refered to the next Monthly Meeting.

John Clark appeared at this Meeting & upon some discourse with
him Friends have agreed to forbear & wait, another month, to
see what further satisfaction they may obtaine thereby it being
his desire, before a paper of condemnation goe forth against
him.

John Wresle appeared at this Meeting & upon some discourse with
him, Friends have agreed to forbear another month to see what
satisfaction they may receive thereby he alledging his wife
to be the occasion.

p. 281.

This Meeting has agreed with Gainsbrough Friends to hold a
Meeting for Worshipp at Gainsbrough the 6 day of this month,
& that Friends of each Meeting give notice to the Friends
thereof.

[1] 13th October, 1705.

Its desired that Friends in each Meeting collect there sufferings for tythe & bring an account thereof to the next Monthly Meeting.

Whereas some Friends are lately deceased that was chosen Overseers in Winteringham & Gainsbrough Meeting its desired that Friends take into consideration what Friends they thinke most fitt to supply there places & bring account to next Monthly Meeting.

Friends in this Meeting haveing debated the sallary of a Friend that come among us to teach Friends children, have consented & agreed to pay the Friend ten pound, & alsoe his table for one year for his encouragement, & the children that are not Friends there wages are to help to pay towards the agreement.

Next Monthly Meeting ordered at Brigg.

Signed by Joseph Richardson.

ATT a Monthly Meeting held at Brigg the 16 of the 9th Month 1705[1] :—

Thomas Robinson paper of request being debated in this Meeting the further consideration thereof is referd to the next Monthly Meeting.

Whereas John Clark has frequented Meeting since the last Monthly Meeting & Thomas Morley gave an account that they knew nothing but well to his conversation its therefore desired that Thomas Morley & Robert Vesse have still an eye over him for good, & give an account to the next Monthly Meeting.

p. 282.

Edward Gilliatt & Robert Colyer gave account to this Meeting that the conversation of John Wresle as farr as they knew was pretty well since last Monthly Meeting therefore Robert Colyer & John Barlow are desired to have an eye to his conversation & give account to the next Monthly Meeting.

Sufferings for tythe came into this Meeting from Gainsborough, Winteringham & Adlinfleet, but Brigg & the Ile are desired to bring theres into the next Monthly Meeting.

Richard Wresle & George Frow are chosen Overseers for Winteringham Meeting.

Thomas Potter & John Symson are chosen Overseers to assist Peter Nayler for Gainsbrough Meeting.

Whereas at the last Monthly Meeting it was agreed & a covenant made with our Friend Seth Walker in Lancashire to come

---

[1] 16th November, 1705.

& teach schooll here its requested by his brother that he may not come till spring it being a more convenient time to begin that undertaking to which this Meeting consents.

Whereas after some debate in the Quarterly Meeting about the prisson room in the castle yard, whether it should be continued or not, the conclussion of the Meeting was that it should be given up, but since that thro the dissatisfaction of some, the said Meeting orders a rehearing of the matter for the more generall satisfaction of Friends in the county therefore this Meeting desires the representatives of each Meeting belonging the Monthly Meeting to give a report thereof & bring there sence & Judgment to the next Monthly Meeting.

An account being given to this Meeting that our Friend Thomas Winder is carried prissoner to Lincolne upon account of tythe, this Meeting orders Edward Gilliat to write to the goaler to let him have a convenient room in the castle, & this Meeting will see the rent paid.

Ordered that a contribution be collected & brought to the next Monthly Meeting which is to be at Brigg.

Signed by Joseph Richardson.

p. 283.

ATT a Monthly Meeting held at the Meeting House at Brigg the 14 of the 10th Month 1705[1] :—

The further consideration of Thomas Robinson letter was read & haveing much charge upon us at present cannot answer his request yet.

Thomas Hutchinson gives this Meeting account that John Clark frequents there Meetings & is somewhat orderly in his conversation therefore still desires Thomas Morley & Thomas Hutchinson may watch over him for good & give an account to next Monthly Meeting.

Robert Colyer gives an account to this Meeting that he does not know but John Wresle is orderly in his conversation, therefore Robert Colyer & John Barlow are desired still to watch over him & give account to next Monthly Meeting.

The Ile & Brigg sufferings for tythe came into this Meeting, & all was sent to the Quarterly Meeting.

The consideration of the castle room was fully debated in this Meeting & Friends from the seaverall or the most part of them have agreed for the continuance thereof as formerly, for a comfort & refreshment of poor Friends that may be cast into prisson for Truths Testimony.

[1] 14th December, 1705.

Contributions came in as followeth :—

	£	s.	d.
Gainsbrough		18 :	0
Brigg		15 :	0
Winteringham		14 :	0
Ile		12 :	6
Adlinfleet		07 :	6
	3 :	07 :	0

Stock not come in
  in Joseph Richardson hand
    37s. all
  in Robert Colyer hand 43 : 6.

Disbursments :—	£	s.	d.
to Thomas Potter for Abraham Northen for			
20 weeks	01 :	00 :	00
for Susie Recket	00 :	02 :	6
for Bridget Mosley	00 :	02 :	00
to George Frow for Ellen Walker	00 :	02 :	06
to John Barlow for bookes	00 :	10 :	00
To the Quarterly Meeting	01 :	00 :	00

Rests in stock in Joseph Richardsons hand   10 : 00
    which makes up 37s.

Thomas Potter, Thomas Nainby, Thomas Wresle & Stephen Wresle
  are appointed for the Quarterly Meeting service.

Next Monthly Meeting ordered at Brigg.

Signed by Joseph Richardson.

p. 284.

ATT a Monthly Meeting held at Brigge the 11 of the 11th month
1705[1] :—

The further consideration of Thomas Robinson letter of request
  is left to the next Monthly Meeting to answer what Friends
  sees meet against next Quarterly Meeting.

Its desired that Thomas Hutchinson & Thomas Morley have an
  eye over John Clarks conversation for Truths sake & give
  account thereof to the next Monthly Meeting.

Robert Collier & John Barlow being from home they are still desired
  to take notice of John Wressles conversation & give account
  thereof to the next Monthly Meeting.

There was pretty much debate at the Quarterly Meeting about
  the prison room for Friends & it was by the major part to
  continue the same as formerly.

[1] 11th January, 1706.

The nessesitous condition of Mary Goxhill was laid before this Meeting & Friends have left it to Brigg Friends to supply her wants & give account to the Monthly Meeting who will see them indemnified.

Next Monthly Meeting ordered to be at Brigg.

ATT a Monthly Meeting held at the Meeting House in Brigge the 8 day of 12th month 1706[1] :—

The further consideration of Thomas Robinson request is left to the next Monthly Meeting to answer.

Its still desired that Thomas Hutchison & Thomas Morley have an eye over John Clark conversation for Truth sake & give an account to the next Monthly Meeting.

Robert Colyer & John Barlow are still desired to have an eye over John Wresle & give an account to the next Monthly Meeting.

The consideration of Mary Goxhill condition is left to Brigg Friends, to give her some releife & give an account to the next Monthly Meeting.

p. 285.

This Meeting desires Edward Gilliatt to indeavour that Thomas Winder may have liberty to vissit his wife now she lyes in.

This Meeting having under consideration the affaire of schooll for Freinds children at Brigg, Brigg Friends are desired to consider what they can raise among themselves towards the sallary agreed for with the Monthly Meeting & give an account to the next Monthly Meeting.

This Meeting thinks fitt that for the future the names of those Friends that comes from each Meeting be recorded & that Friends take care to send such as are duely quallified.

Some Friends from the Ile Meeting signifies there dissatisfaction in Meeting with Friends at there new Meeting House at Beltoft, on account of some contributer to the said Meeting House they judge unworthy, & has left there complaint to be satisfied by the next Monthly Meeting, this Meeting desires that Friends in each Meeting consider of the matter & bring there Judgment to the next Monthly Meeting.

George Atkinson of Thorne in the county of Yorke came into this Meeting & published his intention of marriage with Sarah Dent of Thealby, she being present gave her consent, but it being the first time they are desired to wait Friends answer till next Monthly Meeting.

[1] 8th February, 1706.

Francis Seaton of Belton came into this Meeting & published his intention of marriage with Sarah Browne of West Butterwick & shee being present gave her consent but it being first time they are desired to wait Friends answer till next Monthly Meeting.

John Berrier of Ealand came into this Meeting and published his intention of marriage with Sarah Seaton of Belton shee being present gave her consent, but it being first time they are desired to wait Friends answer till next Monthly Meeting.

p. 286.

This Meeting being acquainted that Elizabeth Smith of Scotter is desirous to put out two of her sons apprentices, Thomas Nainby signifies that he thinkes of a master for one of them, & is desired to write to the Friend about it & bring in his answer to the next Monthly Meeting.

A contribution is ordered to be collected & brought up to the next Monthly Meeting, & its alsoe desired that as many men & woemen Friends come up thereto from each Meeting & the Overseers of each Meeting come to give an account of the state of there Meeting.

Next Meeting ordered to be at Brigg.

Signed on behalf of the Meeting by Joseph Richardson.

ATT a Monthly Meeting held at the Meeting House at Brigg the 8 of the first month 1706[1] :—

Its still desired that Thomas Morley & Robert Vesse have an eye over John Clark & speak to him about his neglect in frequenting there Meetings & give an account to next Monthly Meeting.

Its desired that Robert Colyer & John Barlow have an eye over John Wresles conversation, & speak to him as way may open and bring an account to the next Monthly Meeting.

This Meeting desires Brigg Friends further consideration about a sallary to be raised, for the master that teaches Friends children in there town & give account to the next Monthly Meeting.

The Representatives for every Meeting are as followeth :—
Gainsbrough, Peter Nayler & Thomas Potter.
Brigg, Robert Colyer & John Barlow.
Ile, Thomas Wresle & James Coakes.
Winteringham, John Dent & Stephen Wresle.
Adlinfleet, Robert Vesse.

[1] 8th March, 1706.

The further consideration of putting out two of Widdow Smith children apprentices is left to the next Monthly Meeting & John Barlow & Edward Gilliatt are desired to advise with her about it & bring account to the next Monthly Meeting.

Contributions came in as followeth :—

	£	s.	d.
Gainsbrough	00 :	18 :	0
Brigg	00 :	15 :	6
Ile	00 :	10 :	6
Adlinfleet	00 :	07 :	6
Winteringham .. .. .:	00 :	14 :	0
Stock in Joseph Richardson hand	00 :	17 :	00
in Robert Colyer hand ..	02 :	03 :	06

Disbursments as followeth :—

	£	s.	d.
To Brigg Meeting	00 :	16 :	01
To John Bishop for Bridgett Mosley	00 :	02 ·	00
to Robert Colyer for Quarterly Meeting ..	01 :	00 :	00
To Robert Colyer for Burn Meeting house ..	02 :	10 :	00
Remaines in stock in Joseph Richardson hands	02 :	18 :	11

p. 287.

Thomas Potter & Robert Colyer appointed to attend the Quarterly Meeting Service.

Whereas complaint is made to this Meeting by some Friends of the Ile, against Richard Clark for payment of tythes which being inconsistant with the Truth, & dissatisfaction to Friends, its therefore agreed that Edward Gilliatt, Robert Colyer & Thomas Potter, goe over to deall with him & admonish him about it & bring his answer to the next Monthly Meeting.

George Atkinson of Thorne came a second time into our Meeting & signified the continuance of his purpose of marriage with Sarah Dent of Thealby & shee being present consented thereunto, & Friends not findeing objections to hinder the intentions have left the consumation thereof to themselves according to the good order of Truth.

Francis Seaton of Belton came a second time into this Meeting & signified the continuance of his purpose of marriage & shee being present gave consent & Friends findeing nothing but clearness on behalf of both parties, have left the consumation thereof according to Truths order.

John Berrier of Ealand came a second time into this Meeting & signified the continuance of his purpose of marriage with Sarah Seaton of Belton & shee being present gave her consent

& Friends findeing no objections to hinder there said intentions have left the consumation thereof to themselves according to Truths order.

A Meeting for Worshipp is appointed by this Meeting to be held at Gainsbrough the 15th Instant.

Next Monthly Meeting ordered to be at Gainsbrough.

Signed by Joseph Richardson.

ATT a Monthly Meeting held at the Meeting House att Gainsbrough the 12 of the 2 month 1706[1] :—

Representatives, Gainsbrough, Peter Nayler, Thomas Potter, John Symson.
Brigg, William Williamson, Robert Colyer.
The Ile, Isaac Davis & John Urry.
Winteringham, Stephen Wresle & Mordeca Westoby.
Adlinfleet, Thomas Hutchison.

p. 288.

Its still desired that Thomas Morley & Robert Vessy have an eye over John Clark & speak to him for his neglecting Meetings & give account to the next Monthly Meeting.

Robert Colyer gives an account to this Meeting that John Wresle is more orderly & frequents Meetings more diligently, its still desired that Joseph Richardson & Thomas Nainby watch over him & give an account to the next Monthly Meeting.

This Meeting desires Brigg Friends speedy consideration & result about the sallary to be raised for a master that teaches Friends children with them, & not faile of giveing an account to the next Monthly Meeting.

This Meeting haveing an account that Widdow Smith has an offer of a master for one of her sons, and is inclined for some time to keep the other at home leaves it to Gainsbrough Friends to advise & assist her as they may see meet & give an account to the next Monthly Meeting.

The advice of the Meeting for Sufferings at London relateing the preventing the inconveniences of Friends marriages being cald in question, & alsoe the advice from the 2d dayes Morning Meeting at London with respect to a register of all the Meeting Houses & certificates for the same being seaverally read, Brigg Friends are appointed to write out coppyes of the same for every Perticuler Meeting, soe as they may be distributed att next Monthly Meeting & further considered of.

[1] 12th April, 1706.

This Meeting appoints a Meeting for Worshipp to be held at Gainsbrough the last 6th day of this Month.

Next Monthly Meeting ordered at Thealby.

Signed by Joseph Richardson.

ATT a Monthly Meeting held at Thealby the 10th of the 3d
month 1706[1] :—

Representatives: John Symson, Joseph Potter from Gainsbrough.
Thomas Nainby & William Frost from Brigg.
Thomas Wresle from the Ile Meeting.
George Frow, Richard Wresle & John Wresle from Wintering-
ham.
Robert Vesse & Thomas Morley from Adlinfleett.

p. 289.

According to request of the last Monthly Meeting Thomas Morley
had an eye to John Clarks conversation, & findes it to the dishonour of Truth & likewise spoke to him signifying Friends
long indeavours with him for his return & amendment but
all there tender care & love has been to no effect, soe that to
clear the Truth Friends must disown any fellowship with him
which he desired might be delayed till next Monthly Meeting
to which this Meeting assents, Robert Vesse is desired to
acquaint him to appear at next Monthly Meeting.

Thomas Nainby gives an account that John Wresle comes pretty
dilligently to Meetings & is prity orderly soe farr as he knows,
but Joseph Richardson & Thomas Nainby are still desired to
have a tender eye over him & give account to next Monthly
Meeting.

Brigg Friends not yet comeing to a result to raise a sallary what
they can for the schoolmaster teaching there children are
desired to effect it, & bring an account to the next Monthly
Meeting, & alsoe a coppy of the minnite that was drawn at
the Meeting when the schoolmaster was agreed with for the
satisfaction of some concernd.

This Meeting condescends that Gainsbrough Freinds indeavour
to make a bargaine with the Friend that offers to take Elizabeth
Smith son an apprentice to the taylor trade & bring an account
to the next Monthly Meeting.

Its desired that Friends in every Meeting that have Meetings kept
at there houses or publick Meeting Houses, bring a coppy of
the certificate, & in whose hands they lodge to the next Monthly
Meeting to the end that a record be kept as by advice from
London.

[1] 10th May, 1706.

Next Monthly Meeting ordered to be at Adlinfleet & a contribution collected & brought up thither.

p. 290.

ATT a Monthly Meeting at Thomas Morleys in Adlinfleet the 7th of 4 Month 1706[1] :—

Representatives as followeth :—

Gainsbrough, John Sympson & John Marshall.
Brigge, Robert Colyer & William Frost.
Winteringham, George Frow & Stephen Wright.
The Ile, Isaac Davis & James Coakes.
Adlinfleet, Thomas Morley & Thomas Hutchinson.

William Frost gives account to this Meeting from Joseph Richardson that John Wresle continues to come pretty orderly to Meetings. Joseph Richardson and Thomas Nainby are still desired to have an eye over him & admonish him as way may open, & give an account to the next Monthly Meeting.

Friends of Gainsborough Meeting give account that they have made an agreement with John Craine, a taylor to take Elizabeth Smith son apprentice for 8 year for £7 : 10 : 0 to be paid in manner following viz. £3 at his binding £2 in one year after that & the rest in 2 equall payment in one year & half after that his time to begin the first of 3d month 1706.

According to order of last Monthly Meeting the following account of publick Meeting Houses within the compass of this Meeting is brought in viz. :

Gainsbrough Meeting House recorded or allowed according to law, the attested originall certifficate is lodged with Gainsbrough in John Marshall hands.

Winteringham Meeting House allowed according to law the 20 of 8 month 1698 & the attested certifficate lodged with Mordeca Westoby of Winteringham.

The Meeting House of John Wresle of Thealby according to law attested & the certificate in John Wresles hands.

p. 291.

The Meeting House at Brigg licensed according to law : & the licence is in Edward Gilliatts hands & the deeds in Joseph Richardsons hand.

The Meeting House at Beltoft licensed according to law & the certificate lodged with Thomas Wresle same place.

The house of Thomas Hutchisson of Fockerby & Robert Vessys of Luddinton licensed according to law & the certificates lodged with each of them.

[1] 7th June, 1706.

Robert Vesse haveing failed to give this Meeting account of message from last Monthly Meeting to John Clarke, Thomas Morley is appointed to stirr up Robert Vessy in the matter & assist him alsoe therein, & give account to the next Monthly Meeting.

Brigg Friends are desired to give an account how the £10 legacy of Anthony Westoby was disposed and give account to the next Monthly Meeting.

Complaint being made that John Urry, senior & junior absents the Meeting at Beltoft, this Meeting appoints Robert Colyer & Thomas Potter to goe to speak to them about it, & bring there answer to the next Monthly Meeting.

Robert Colyer & John Marshall are appointed to attend the service of the Quarterly Meeting.

Contributions came in as followeth :—

	£	s.	d.
Gainsbrough		18 :	0
Brigg		15 :	0
Ile		08 :	6
Winteringham		15 :	0
Adlinfleet		07 :	6
Stock from Joseph Richardson	2 :	18 :	11
Totall	06 :	2 :	11

Disbursments :—

	£	s.	d.
To John Marshall for John Crane	03 :	00 :	00
To Joseph[1] for Mary Goxhill	00 :	05 :	00
to George Frow for Ellin Walker	00 :	02 :	06
to Thomas Morly for Doll Pickhaver	00 :	03 :	00
to Robert Colyer for Quarter Meeting	01 :	10 :	00
to Joseph Richardson being the remaining Stock	01 :	02 :	05

Next Monthly Meeting appointed at Beltoft.

p. 292.

ATT a Monthly Meeting held at the Meeting House in Beltoft the 12 of the 5th month 1706[2] :—

Representatives : Gainsbrough, Peter Naylor & Joseph Morley.
Brigg, Robert Colyer, Joseph Richardson & Edward Gilliatt.
The Ile, Jacob Davis & Isaac Davis.
Winteringham, Joseph Wresle & John Dent.
Adlinfleet, Thomas Hutchison & Thomas Morley.

Thomas Hutchison & Thomas Morley are desired to inspect John Clarks conversation & reminde him of his shortness in not

[1] *Sic* for Joseph Richardson.   [2] 12th July, 1706.

performing his promiss in comeing to this Meeting they alsoe
are desired to acquaint him that Friends desires his appearance
at the next Monthly Meeting.

After much debate in this Meeting with the Isle Friends about the
settlement of there first day Meeting they agreed that if John
Urry, senior, came next first day to the Meeting at Beltoft,
& no further occasion of offence was given that they would
condescend to keep a Meeting at his house once in 6 weeks time.

Joseph Richardson gives an account that he has nothing to offer
against John Wresles conversation at present therefore he
is desired with John Barlow to have an eye to him & give
an account to the next Monthly Meeting.

The case of Hannah Reeder, wife to Joshua, came before this Meeting,
& its left to Freinds of Adlinfleet to inspect into it & give an
account to the next Monthly Meeting.

The money for George Fox Doctrinall Epistles is to be collected
& brought to the next Monthly Meeting which is to be at
Caistrop or Castlethorp.

Signed in behalf of the said Meeting.

By Joseph Richardson.

p. 293.

ATT a Monthly Meeting held at John Nainbys in Castlethorp
the 9th of the 6 : month 1706[1] :—

Representatives : Gainsbrough, Thomas Potter & Thomas Nayler.
Brigg, Robert Colyer & Joseph Richardson.
Winteringham, George Frow & Joseph Wresle.
The Ile, Thomas Wresle.
Adlinfleet, Robert Vesse, junior.

Friends desires Thomas Morley to stirr up John Clark to make his
appearance at our next Monthly Meeting, before Friends doe
proceed to give forth a Testimony against him.

This Meeting desires Thomas Wresle & David Crosby to goe to John
Urrys & speak to John Urry, junior for his neglect in comeing
to Meetings on the first dayes at Beltoft, & advise him as the
Lord may put it into there harts, & bring his answer to the
next Monthly Meeting.

This Meeting desires Joseph Richardson and Thomas Nainby to
continue there care over John Wresle & give account to the
next Monthly Meeting.

The money collected for George Fox doctrinall bookes & epistles
is done by Gainsbrough & Brigg friends but Wintringham &
the Ile are not yet brought in.

[1] 9th August, 1706.

L

This Meeting has left the matter of Joshua Reeders wifes children to Thomas Morley, Robert Vesse & Thomas Hutchinson to discourse Amcoates people & bring an account to the next Monthly Meeting.

This Meeting desires David Crosby & John Bishopp to goe to Crowle preist, & get his answer to Thomas Robinson letter & to give Thomas Winder wife a vissitt in the love of God, and to advise her in her affaires & give account to the next Monthly Meeting.

Next Monthly Meeting ordered at Gainsbrough & a contribution to be collected & brought thither & notice to be given to the Overseers in each Meeting to attend there service there in giveing account of the state of there Meeting.

Signed in behalf of the Meeting by

Joseph Richardson.

p. 294.

ATT a Monthly Meeting held at Gainsbrough 13th 7 month 1706[1] :—

Representatives as followeth :—

Gainsbrough, Peter Nayler & John Marshall.
Brigg, Joseph Richardson & Robert Colyer.
Winteringham, Stephen Wresle & Mordeca Westoby.
The Ile, John Bishop & James Coakes.
Adlinfleet, Thomas Morley.

Thomas Morley is still desired to indeavour to prevaile with John Clark to appear at our next Monthly Meeting or else to let him know that Friends will give forth a paper of condemnation against him.

This Meeting haveing an account that John Urry, senior & junior, have of late attended there Meeting at Beltoft in the Ile, thinkes fitt to appoint a Meeting to be held at John Urry on the first day seavenight being the 22 instant, & desires that notice thereof be given next first day Meeting at Beltoft & alsoe some Friends from every Meeting to attend the same.

This Meeting still desires Joseph Richardson & Thomas Nainby to continue there care over John Wresle & give an account to the next Monthly Meeting.

This Meeting still leaves the care of Joshua Readers wifes children to Thomas Morley, Robert Vesse & Thomas Hutchinson.

[1] 13th September, 1706.

Contributions came in as followeth :—

	£	s.	d.
Gainsbrough	00	17	00
Brigg	00	15	00
Winteringham		13	00
Ile	00	07	00
Adlinfleet	00	07	06
Stock	01	01	00
in Joseph Richardson hand ..	04	06	00

Disbursments :—

	£	s.	d.
To John Marshall for bookes & carridge ..		06	11
To John Symson for Widdow Recket coales..		01	08
To Thomas Potter for 39 weekes for Abraham Northern		19	06
To Peter Nayler for Quarterly Meeting ..	01	00	0
Stock left with Joseph Richardson	01	07	5

p. 295.

James Hobson of Maxfield in the County of Chester came into this Meeting & published his intention of marriage with Susanna Richardson, Joseph Richardson daughter, of Brigg & shee being present gave her consent he brought a certificate that he had done the same at the Monthly Meeting to which he belongs but it being the first time they are both desired to wait Freinds answer till next Monthly Meeting.

Brigg Friends haveing received a letter from Friends at Leeds about John Halliwell, its desired that Friends in each Perticular Meeting take the matter into consideration soe as he may be some where setled or taken care of, & that a conclusion be come to about him at next Monthly Meeting.

Peter Nayler & Thomas Potter ordered to attend the service of the Quarterly Meeting.

Next Monthly Meeting ordered at Wintringham.

Signed in behalf of the Meeting by

Joseph Richardson.

Att a Monthly Meeting held at Wintringham the 11th of 8th month 1706[1] :—

Representatives as followeth :—

Gainsbrough, Isaac Westoby & Thomas Morley.
Brigg, Robert Colyer & William Williamson.
Winteringham, George Frow & Richard Wresle.
The Isle, Isaac Westoby[2] & John Harrison.
Adlinfleet, Thomas Morley & Thomas Hutchisson.

[1] 11th October, 1706.   [2] *Sic :* recte of Gainsborough.

Thomas Morley acquaints Friends that he signified the sence of
the last Monthly Meeting to John Clark & he gave him expecta-
tion of his appearance here which proves to the contrary
therefore Thomas Morley & Thomas Hutchinson are desired
to tell him that he has wearied Friends patience in dealing with
him soe long for his good, & no amendment appearing, they disire
his appearance at next Monthly Meeting to give some satisfaction
before a paper of condemnation be given forth against him.

p. 296.

This Meeting desires the Isle Meeting to setle a Meeting once a
month or six weeks at John Urrys in Epworth & give account
to the next Monthly Meeting.

Joseph Richardson gives account that he heares no ill of John
Wresles conversation therefore he with Thomas Nainby are
still disired to have a watchfull eye over him & give account
to the next Monthly Meeting.

The care of Hannah Reeder children is left to Friends of Adlinfleet
Meeting.

Gainsbrough Friends are desired to bring up the minnits of the Meeting bussiness & the paper of generall directions for collecting a
generall history of Truth progress to the next Monthly Meeting.

Sufferings for tythe & other matter are desired to be brought up
to the next Monthly Meeting.

James Hobson of Maxfeild came a second time into this Meeting
& signified the continuance of his purpose of marriage with
Susanna Richardson, & shee being present gave her consent,
& all things appearing clear on behalf of relations & touching
any other persons as by certificate was seen, Friends left the
consumation thereof to themselves with Friends advice according to the good order of Truth.

Next Monthly Meeting to be held next first sixt day of next month
at Brigg.

> Signed in behalf of the Meeting by
>
> > Joseph Richardson.

p. 297.

ATT a Monthly Meeting held at Brigg Meeting House the first
day of the 9th month 1706[1] :—

Representatives as followeth :—

Gainsbrough, John Marshall & Thomas Nayler.
Brigg, Joseph Richardson & Robert Colyer.
Winteringham, John Dent & Leanord Bell.
The Isle, James Coakes & Samuel Brown.
Adlinfleet, Thomas Hutchisson.

[1] 1st November, 1706.

John Clark not appearing at this Meeting as often desired & expected, Friends findeing themselves pretty clear of him, have once more desired Thomas Hutchinson & James Coakes to signify to him Friends sence & judgment & if he doe not make his appearance at our next Monthly Meeting intends then to give forth a paper of condemnation against him.

Friends in the Isle Meeting have debated the matter about setling a Meeting at John Urrys house, senior in Epworth & have agreed to keep a Meeting at his house the first first day in every month for the future.

Joseph Richardson & Thomas Nainby are still desired to continue there care over John Wresle & give account to next Monthly Meeting.

Friends desire Thomas Morley, Thomas Hutchinson & Robert Vesse to advise with the overseers of Amcoats about Hannah Reeders children how what & where they are desirous to put them forth, & Friends are alsoe desired to inquire in there respective Meetings if there be any Friends that are willing take & treat with Friends about them.

Friends are disired to bring up there sufferings for tythe to next Monthly Meeting.

Ordered next Monthly Meeting be held at Brigg the first sixt day of the 10th month next & that a contribution be collected & brought thither.

Signed by Joseph Richardson.

p. 298.

ATT a Monthly Meeting held at Brigg the 6th day of the 10th Month 1706[1] :—

Representatives as followeth :—
Gainsbrough, Joseph Potter & John Jackson.
Brigg, Robert Colyer & Joseph Richardson.
Winteringham, Joseph Wresle.
The Ile, Thomas Wresle & Isaac Davis.
Adlinfleet, Thomas Morley & Robert Vesse.

John Clark not appearing at this Meeting notwithstandinge James Coakes & Thomas Hutchinson were ordered by the last Monthly Meeting were ordered to acquaint him that if he did not appear to give Friends some satisfaction they thought themselves clear & intended to give forth a Testimony against him, but Robert Vesse not understanding the minnite desires that he may speak once more to him about it, which he together with Thomas Morley are desired to doe, & give him the sence of Friends & bring in his answer to the next Monthly Meeting.

[1] 6th December, 1706.

Friends still desires Thomas Morley & Robert Vesse & Thomas
Hutchinson to take care as they see meet, by advising with
Amcoates overseers about Hannah Reeders children & give
account to the next Monthly Meeting.

Friends suffering for tythe came into this Monthly Meeting from
Gainsbrough, Winteringham & Adlinfleet, but the Isle & Brigg
Meeting are not yet perfected soe are desired to get them ready
to send to the Quarterly Meeting.

Contributions came in as followeth :—

	£	s.	d.
Gainsbrough	00 :	18 :	0
Brigge	00 :	17 :	0
Winteringham	00 :	17 :	00
The Ile	00 :	10 :	00
Adlinfleet	00 :	08 :	06
In stock J.R.[1]	01 :	07 :	05
	04 :	17 :	11

Disbursments :—

	£	s.	d.
To Joseph Potter for Susie Recket	00 :	05 :	4
To Thomas Wresle for Bridget Mosley & bookes	00 :	01 :	00
To Joseph Richardson for Mary Goxhill ..	00 :	02 :	06
To Robert Vesse for Julian West	00 :	01 :	00
To Joseph Wresle for Widdow Walker ..	00 :	02 :	06
To John Sharp for John Halliwell	00 :	10 :	00
To Quarterly Meeting by R. C.[2]	01 :	05 :	00
for releife of Thomas Winder	01 :	00 :	00

Rests in stock in Joseph Richardson hands ..   01 : 10 : 06

Thomas Morley & Robert Vesse are ordered to attend the service
of the Quarterly Meeting.

Ordered the next Monthly Meeting be held at Brigg the first 6th
day of the next Month.

Signed by Joseph Richardson.

p. 299.

ATT a Monthly Meeting held the 3d day of the 11th Month
1706[3] :—

Representatives as followeth :—

Thomas Nayler & Joseph Morley from Gainsbrough.
John Sharp & Thomas Nainby for Brigge.
George Frow & John Dent from Winteringham.
None from the Ile nor Adlinfleet.

---

[1] *Sic* for Joseph Richardson.   [2] *Sic* for Robert Collier.   [3] 3rd **January, 1707.**

Its desired by Friends at the Quarterly Meeting that an account be given of the progress of Truth & the first Friends that preacht the Gospell among us, and the execise they met withall for there Testimony.

Suffering for tythe not yet come from the Ile & Brigge Meeting.

No bussiness further appearing (by reason that Friends could not come out of the Ile nor Marshland) have ordered the next Monthly Meeting to be the first 6th day of the next Month at Brigge.

Signed by Joseph Richardson.

ATT a Monthly Meeting held at Brigg the 7th day of the 12th month 1706[1] :—

Representatives as followeth :—

Gainsbrough, Thomas Potter & Isaac Westoby
Brigg, Robert Colyer, Joseph Richardson.
Winteringham, Joseph Wresle & Stephen Wresle.
The Ile, James Coakes & Joseph Berrier.
Adlinfleet, Thomas Morley & Robert Vesse, junior.

John Clark not apearing as desired by Friends from time to time to give Friends any satisfaction, notwithstanding all there indeavours and patient waiting for many years for his recovery, Friends have wightily considered, & made examination if there be any Friend not clear in themselves concerning him, & finding nothing by Friends of there own Meeting nor by any Friends among the Monthly Meeting, but they have cleared themselves & the Truth as much as in them lyes concerning him have unanimously agreed upon serious & weighty consideration to give forth a Testimony against him for clearing of themselves & the Truth of such disorderly persons & practices, & have left to some Friends of Brigg Meeting to draw up the paper to be ready at next Monthly Meeting and Thomas Morley is desired to acquaint him with it, that if he have any thing to object against it to make his appearance at next Monthly Meeting.

p. 300.

Thomas Morley gives account to this Meeting that theres litle more done with them about Hannah Reeders children, soe that the care thereof is still continued with Friends of there Meeting & give an account to the Monthly Meeting as they see cause.

Sufferings for tythe from the Ile Meeting came in & whats from Brigg will be ready to send with the rest to our Friend Thomas Robinson.

[1] 7th February, 1707.

Friends haveing under there consideration of the takeing an account of the first Friends that came to preach the gospell among us, & of the progress of Truth since according to Friends desire in a printed paper its desired that Friends in each Meeting doe well consider the matter & bring what account they can from the most antient & faithfull friends among them to the next Monthly Meeting & that Friends read the paper in there Meeting relateing to that affaire that they may know how the better proceed therein. Its alsoe desired that Thomas Wresle & John Bishopp take the paper & goe to Robert Reeder & read it to him, & bring in writing what information he can give them therein.

Friends haveing an account at this Meeting of John Wresles great disorder in drunkenness, have ordered Robert Colyer & Joseph Richardson to speak to him as they finde it with them & bring his answer to the next Monthly Meeting.

Robert Coakes of West Butterwick came into this Meeting & published his intention of marriage with Hannah Tuke of the same & shee being present gave her consent but it being the first time they are both desired to wait Friends answer till next Monthly Meeting.

John Bishopp, junior, of Crowle came into this Meeting and published his intention of marriage with Jane Wilson of Ealand shee being present gave her consent, but being the first time they are desired to wait Friends answer till next Monthly Meeting.

James Coakes & Joseph Berrier to inspect into the clearness of these persons from all others & of there conversation as becomes the Truth & give account to the next Monthly Meeting.

Ordered that a contribution be collected & inlarged by reason of the nessesities that are upon us & to be brought up to the next Monthly Meeting which is to be at Brigg, & that as many of our weomen Friends come thither as can possibly come that Friends may be comforted one with another.

Signed by Joseph Richardson.

p. 301.

ATT a Monthly Meeting held at Brigg the 7th of the first month 1706/7[1] :—

Representatives for Gainsbrough, Peter Nayler & Thomas Potter.
Brigg, Robert Colyer & Joseph Richardson.
The Ile, Thomas Wresle & John Berrier.
Winteringham, George Frow & Mordeca Westoby.
Adlinfleet, Thomas Hutchisson.

Robert Vesse has signified by letter to this Meeting that he has had some discourse further with John Clark, & by his letter

---

[1] 7th March, 1707.

has ingaged himself & John Clark, if life & health be to both, appear at our next Monthly Meeting.

The care of Hannah Reeders children is continued with Adlinfleet Freinds.

Friends are desired to get what account they can of the first spreading of Truth & by whome & send it to Thomas Robinson in order to be sent to London.

Robert Colyer & Joseph Richardson went to John Wresle as Friends desired & has soe farr prevailed with him as he has given forth against himself & was read in this Meeting, which was approved on & ordered to be recorded.

Robert Coakes of Butterwick came a second time & signified the continuance of his purpose of marriage with Hannah Tuke, & shee being present gave her consent & no objection appearing to hinder there proceedings have left the consumation thereof to themselves with Friends advice according to Truths order.

John Bishopp of Crowle came into this Meeting & signified the continuance of his purpose of marriage with Jane Wilson, & shee being present gave her consent, and alsoe brought certificates from Friends & relations signifying clearness on both parties from all other persons, soe have left the consumation thereof to themselves with Friends & relations advice according to the good order of Truth.

p. 302.

John Wresles letter to the Monthly Meeting for Friends satisfaction, wherein he condemns himself for his evill course of life for the clearing of Truth & Freinds.

Loving Freinds,

After my kind love to you, I have here sent you a few lines, to clear Freinds & the Truth, as concerning me in the first place I doe acknowledge your love & kindness has been very great towards mee and your long forbearance wating for my retorn but I have not answered your kindness towards mee; but has given the Lord just occasion of late to withdraw his love from mee therefore in a few words, I have nothing against Frends at all but the falt is in my self likewise I must own it has been this wicked sin of drunkeness that has been my ruin and distruction all a long and allways was the occasion of my disorder in any kinde and likewise must owne the great good will of the Lord has had towards mee for in steade of judgement he has showed mercy many a time and in divers manners for his striving has been long with me whereby he might have cut me of in the hight of my transgression and still been just and true likewise he has many times laide my condittion very plane before me. Likewise I have taken notis when I have kept my selfe for sometime from the wicked sin before named that I have been brought into a very good frame of minde and I have taken notis in that condittion that the grand enemy of my poor soule has lade severall temptations of divers kinds before mee and while I kept my selfe in that frame I have had strenth to resist and as it weare a feare placed before mine eyes but then after a time of falling into excess of drink againe then did I bring the temptation which before was lade even with greedyeness being lost and feare cast behind my back that afterwards I have said within my selfe to the ruing that this drink brings mee unto. Likewise I cannot ommit but one time which I cannot forget I pray you bear with me it was a time in which I did leade a very wicked & profaine life in which I did not known what course to take but after a little time I fell into worke some miles of and I was glad of it therefore I made a vow unto the Lorde that I would not drinke no strong drinke (*p. 303*) while I was in that place so the Lord gave me strength to perform it so that I cannot say that ever I had in my life so much peace and satisfaction as I had in that little time so I must confes it is nothing but drink that hinders all my good. One thing more has been lade to my charge which I am clear of that I should a been the occasion of some going into excess with my selfe, which was not so, but on the contrary truly dessiers that none by no meanes should take liberty by my evill example but rather take warning by me that they come not in the same condittion so shall conclude and commit my selfe to him with whome I have to doe.

from John Wressell.

Contributions came in as followeth :—

	£	s.	d.
Gainsbrough	1 :	2 :	6
The Ile	0 :	13 :	0
Winteringham	0 :	17 :	0
Brigg	0 :	18 :	0
Adlinfleet	0 :	07 :	06
In stock in Joseph Richardson hand	00 :	06 :	10½
	04 :	04 :	10½

Disbursments :—

	£	s.	d.
To Thomas Potter for 25 weekes at 6d. a week for Abraham Northern & Susie Recket	00 :	15 :	8
To Seth Walker scoolmaster	01 :	00 :	00
to George Frow for Ellin Walker	00 :	01 :	08½
To Thomas Morly for Joshua Reeder children	03 :	07 :	06

soe that nothing in stock remaines.

Thomas Potter, Robert Colyer & Edward Gilliatt are ordered to attend the service of the Quarterly Meeting.

Next Monthly Meeting ordered to be the 2d 6th day of the next month at Gainsbrough.

Signed by Joseph Richardson.

Att a monthly Meeting held at Gainsbrough the 11th of the 2d month 1707[1] :—

p. 304.

Representatives as followeth :—

From Gainsborough, Peter Nayler & Thomas Potter.
Brigg, Robert Colyer & John Sharp.
Winteringham, Stephen Wresle.
The Ile, James Coakes & Isaac Davis.
Adlinfleet, Thomas Morley & Robert Vesse.

Its ordered by this Meeting that James Coakes & Isaac Davis take care that John Bishop & Robert Coakes marriages be recorded in the Meeting booke.

Robert Vesse gives account to this Meeting that John Clark is under some weakness of body soe that he could not possibly come, therefore if he be restored to health he is desired to come to the next Monthly Meeting, & Robert Vessy is desired to put him in minde thereof.

Friends are desired in each Meeting to make inquiry if they can finde a suitable master for Hannah Reeder eldest son to a tayler trade or any other that may be thought suitable, & give account to the next Monthly Meeting.

The care of Hannah Reeder children are left to Friends of that Meeting.

Hannah Brown of Brigg findeing it convenient to remove to Spalding or elswhere desires a certificate from Friends. Brigg Friends are desired to doe it in behalf of this Meeting.

Thomas Watson of Holme belonging Elloughton Meeting published his intention of marriage with Elizabeth Tranmore of Fockerby, it being the first time they are desired to wait Friends answer till next Monthly Meeting.

Next Monthly Meeting ordered to be at Winteringham & a contribution to be collected & brought up thither.

Signed by Joseph Richardson.

[1] 11th April, 1707.

p. 305.

ATT a Monthly Meeting held at the Meeting House att Winteringham the 9th of 3d month 1707[1] :—

Representatives as followeth :—

from Gainsbrough, Thomas Nayler & Joseph Morley.
    Brigg, Robert Colyer & John Nainby.
    Winteringham, Richard Wresle & George Frow.
    Ile, Thomas Wresle & John Bishopp.
    Adlinfleet, Thomas Morley & Thomas Hutchison.

John Clark not appearing at this Meeting as was expected, Friends for the more fully clearing themselves & the Truth have defered the signeing the paper of condemnation against him till the next Monthly Meeting to see if he will then appear to give Friends satisfaction before it be done.

Whereas no master presents to take Hannah Reeders eldest son its still desired that Friends make further inquiry & give account to the next Monthly Meeting.

Thomas Watson of Holme came a 2d time into our Meeting & signified the continuance of his purpose of marriage with Elizabeth Tranmore of Fockerby & shee being present gave her consent, & all things appearing clear on behalf of both parties the consumation thereof is left to themselves with Friends advice to perfect the same as they see meet.

Its agreed upon at this Meeting that a Meeting in generall for Worshipp be held at Brigg the last 4th day of this month.

Contributions came in as followeth :—

	£	s.	d.
Gainsbrough	00 :	15 :	0
Brigg	00 :	15 :	0
The Isle	00 :	10 :	6
Winteringham	00 :	14 :	0
Adlinfleet	00 :	07 :	06
	03 :	02 :	0

Disbursments :—

To Joseph Richardson upon account of scoolmaster   ..   ..   00 : 18 : 00
more which he laid out ..   ..   00 : 01 : 00
To Thomas Morley for & upon account of
    Hannah Reeder Children ..   ..   ..   02 : 3 : 00

Next Monthly Meeting ordered to be at Adlinfleet & a contribution to be brought up thither.

[1] 9th May, 1707.

p. 306.

ATT a Monthly Meeting held att Thomas Morleys in Adlinfleet the 13th of the 4th month 1707[1] :—

Representatives as followeth :—

Gainsbrough, Peter Nayler, Thomas Potter.
Brigg, Robert Colyer & John Sharp.
Winteringham, Stephen Wresle.
Ile, James Coakes, Isaac Davis.
Adlinfleet, Robert Vesse, Thomas Morley.

Its ordered by this Meeting that James Coakes & Isaac Davis take care that John Bishop & Robert Coakes marriages be recorded att next Monthly Meeting.

Robert Vessy gives account to this Meeting that John Clark is under some weakness of body prevents his being at the Meeting.

Its agreed at this Meeting that a Meeting for Worshipp be held at Robert Vesse house next 6th day.

Isaac Davis agrees with Friends at this Meeting to take Hannah Reeder son an apprentice till he accomplish the age of twenty one yeares, & to have 3 pound the first year & forty shillings a year for 3 yeares next following & Isaac is to finde him all nessesary apparell.

John Clark not appear as desired but absented himself before Friends could get an oppertunity with him have desired Robert Vesse to speak to him once more, to appear att next Meeting before the paper be signed against him.

Contributions came in as followeth :—

Gainsbrough	..	..	..	00 : 16 :	6
Brigg	..	..	..	..	00 : 15 :	00
Winteringham ..		..	..	00 : 11 :	6
Ile	..	..	..	..	00 : 11 :	6
Adlinfleet		..	..	..	00 : 07 :	6

Disbursments :—		£	s.	d.
to Joseph Berrier for Bridget Mosley	..	..	00 : 02 :	6
to Robert Colyer for bookes ..		..	..	00 : 02 :	5
to Thomas Morly for Hannah Reeder ..		..	00 : 06 :	09
to Thomas Hutchinson for Doll Pickhaver		..	00 : 03 :	00
to John Marshall for Quarterly Meeting		..	01 : 00 :	0

Rests in Robert Colyer hands ..   ..   ..   00 : 17 : 04

Robert Colyer & Stephen Wresle ordered to attend the Quarterly Meeting Service.

[1] 13th June, 1707.

Next Monthly Meeting ordered at Thealby & a contribution to be collected & brought up thither.

Signed by Joseph Richardson.

p. 307.

ATT a Monthly Meeting held at the house of John Wresles in Thealby 11th of the 5th month 1707[1] :—

Representatives as followeth :—

Gainsbrough, John Symson, Thomas Nayler.
Brigge, John Nainby, Robert Colyer.
Winteringham, George Frow, John Wresle.
The Isle, Thomas Wresle.
Adlinfleet, Thomas Morley.

The care of binding Hannah Reeder son an apprentice is put to Thomas Hutchisson & Thomas Morley.

Robert Vesse giveing satisfaction to Friends in this Meeting concerning John Clark according to the last Meeting request, he is disired by Friends at this Meeting to clear himself thereof before the next Meeting & give an account thereof.

Its desired by Friends at this Meeting that an account be brought to the next Monthly Meeting what is collected in each Meeting upon the account of breifs for fire in order to be sent to London.

Friends in the Ile Meeting has altered the Meeting and fixed it to be held at John Urrys in Epworth the last first day in every Month.

This Meeting leaves the care of Widdow Smith son to Brigg Friends to see if they can provide him a master & give an account to the next Monthly Meeting.

Contributions came in as followeth :—

	£	s.	d.
Gainsbrough	00	16	00
Brigg	00	15	00
Winteringham	00	14	06
The Ile	00	09	00
Adlinfleet	00	08	06
Stock in Robert Colyer hand	00	17	04
Totall	04	00	4

Disbursments :—

	£	s.	d.
To Thomas Nayler for John Crane upon Samuel Smith account	02	00	00
To Robert Colyer in stock	02	00	04

[1] 11th July, 1707.

Next Monthly Meeting to be at Beltoft where Thomas Winders
bussiness is to be further considered.

Signed by Joseph Richardson.

ATT a Monthly Meeting held at Beltoft the 8th 6th month
1707[1] :—

Representatives as followeth :—
Gainsbrough, Peter Naylor, Isaac Westoby.
Brigg, Robert Colyer, Joseph Stephenson.
Winteringam, Joseph Wresle.
Ile, John Urry senior & Isaac Davis.
Adlinfleet, Robert Vessey.

p. 308.

Thomas Morley gives account to this Meeting that Widdow Reeders
son of Amcoates is bound an apprentice to Isaac Davis of
Belton shoemaker & that his indentures does not take place
till 1711 as appears by the indenture, & the said Isaac promises
to give a note under his hand to finde him with meat, drink,
washin & lodging with all nessesary wearing apparell suitable
& requisit till then.

Robert Vessey acknowledges his shortness in not discharging his
self to John Clark, & desires this Meeting to give another
months time to deliver his minde before the paper of condemnation go forth against him—to which the Meeting
consents.

Brigg Meeting onely has brought an account of what they have
collected upon breifs for fires, & the rest of the Meeting are
desired to bring theres to the next Monthly Meeting.

Brigg Friends are desired to give an account to the next Monthly
Meeting in putting Widdow Smith son apprentice to a suitable
master.

This Meeting desires John Urry, junior & Thomas Wresle to vissit
Thomas Winder wife, & advise with her about her bussiness
as need requires & give account to the next Monthly
Meeting.

This day Richard Sayner of Selby & Rachell Webster of Brigg came
into this Meeting & published there intention of marriage
each with other but it being the first time they are both desired
to wait Friends answer till the next Monthly Meeting. Isabell
Gilliatt & Elizabeth Colyer are to inquire into her clearness
from all other persons.

[1] 8th August, 1707.

This Meeting appoints a Meeting to be held here next fourth day come a week in order to put an end to some difference among Friends in this Meeting.

Ordered that a contribution be collected & brought up to the next Monthly Meeting which is to be at Castlethorp at John Nainbys house.

Signed by Joseph Richardson.

p. 309.

ATT a Monthly Meeting held at John Nainbys house in Castlethorp the 12 of the 7th month 1707[1] :—

Representatives as followeth :—

Gainsbrough, Thomas Potter & John Marshall.
Brigge, Robert Colyer & Joseph Richardson.
Ile, Isaac Davis, John Berrier.
Winteringam, David Crosby, Stephen Wresle.
Adlinfleet, Thomas Morley, Robert Vessey.

Whereas Isaac Davis promises to finde the Widdow Reeder son (his apprentice) with meat, drinke, washing, lodging, wearing apparell & all other nessesaries suitable to the full end and expiration of his apprentishipp, he hath now given a note under his hand for the performance thereof.

Robert Vessey gives some reasons for John Clark not appearing at this Meeting, its thought fitt that he be forborn another month, & Robert Vessy is desired to acquaint him therewith.

Joseph Richardson & Robert Colyer are desired to discourse with Thomas Williamson about Widdow Smith son, & give an account to the next Monthly Meeting.

Those who have not brought up there collections for breifes are desired to carry them to the Quarterly Meeting.

This Meeting appoints a Generall Meeting for Worshipp to be held at Brigg next fourth day.

The case of John Wresle of Brigg being laid before this Meeting & Joseph Richardson haveing something in his minde to him is desired to clear himself and give an account to the next Monthly Meeting.

This Meeting desires John Barlow & Abraham Kent to inquire for a suitable place for Widdow Reeders daughter, & bring an account thereof to next Monthly Meeting.

[1] 12th September, 1707.

p. 310.

Contributions came in as followeth :—

				£	s.	d.
Gainsbrough	..	..	..		17 :	6
Brigg	..	..	..		16 :	6
Winteringham	..	..	..		14 :	0
Ile	..	..	..		10 :	6
Adlinfleet	..	..	..		08 :	6
In stock	..	..	..	02 :	00 :	00
Totall	..	..	..	05 :	07 :	0

Disbursments :—

	£	s.	d.
To Isaac Davis for Joshua Reeders son put apprentice by this Meeting	03 :	00 :	00
To Thomas Potter for 26 weekes for Abraham Northern	00 :	13 :	00
To Robert Colyer for Quarterly Meeting ..	01 :	00 :	00
Rests in stock in Robert Colyer hands ..	00 :	14 :	00

to be given to Thomas Winder at the Quarterly Meeting if he soe meet.

This Meeting desires that Friends of every Perticular Meeting be put in minde to take an account of there sufferings for tythe in order to have them recorded & sent up to London.

This day Richard Sayner of Selby came a second time & signified the continuance of his purpose of marriage with Rachel Webster of Brigg, & shee being present gave her consent, & all things appearing clear on behalf of both parties both by inquiry & certificates Friends have consented to the purpose aforesaid & left the consumation thereof to themselves at there own conveniency.

Robert Colyer & Thomas Potter are appointed to attend the service of the Quarterly Meeting.

Signed by Joseph Richardson.

ATT a Monthly Meeting held at Brigg the 10th : 8 month 1707[1] :—

Representatives as followeth :—

Gainsbrough, William West & Abraham Kent.
Brigg, Robert Colyer & Joseph Stephenson.
Winteringham, John Dent.
The Ile, John Bishopp.
Adlinfleet, Thomas Hutchison, Robert Vesse.

[1] 10th October, 1707.

M

The care of Widdow Smith son to a suitable master is left to Joseph Richardson & Robert Colyer.

John Clark appearing at this Meeting & not giveing such satisfaction to Friends as desired, yet he desired the paper of condemnation might be suspended for a while, hopeing to give better satisfaction, which Friends assented too.

Account being given by Brigg Friends that they have weightily considered John Wresles conversation, & thinks themselves clear of him, Therefore this Meeting orders Brigg Friends to draw up a paper of condemnation against him before the next Monthly Meeting, & acquaint him therewith & John Dent is likewise desired to acquaint his relations to see if they have any thing to object why it may not goe forth against him.

p. 311.

Widdow Reeder daughter is ordered to be brought to the next Monthly Meeting in order to goe to a master.

This Meeting desires the trustees of the Ile Meeting to collect the moneys lately subscribed to for dischargeing the debt that rests upon the Meeting House account.

Sufferings for tythe are to be brought into the next Monthly Meeting which is to be at Brigg the 3d 6th day of next Month.

Subscribed by Joseph Richardson.

ATT a Monthly Meeting held at Brigg Meeting House the 20th of the 9th month 1707[1] :—

Representatives as followeth :—
Gainsbrough, Thomas Potter & Thomas Nayler.
Brigg, Thomas Nainby & Robert Colyer.
The Ile, James Coakes & Jacob Davis.
Winteringham, Joseph Wresle & Stephen Wresle.
Adlinfleet, Thomas Hutchisson.

Thomas Morley & Thomas Hutchinson are desired to inspect into John Clarks conversation if it be better then formerly & give an account to the next Monthly Meeting for Friends satisfaction.

The paper of condemnation concerning John Wresle was read in this Meeting & generally consented unto, & Robert Colyer & Thomas Nainby are desired to read it to him, & desire him to goe to his fathers who desires to see him before the next Monthly Meeting that if satisfaction be not given the paper then to be signed & goe forth against him.

[1] 20th November, 1707.

Sufferings for tythe came in from Adlinfleet but Gainsbrough, Brigg, the Ile & Winteringham are desired to get theres ready & bring into the next Monthly Meeting.

Our Friend Robert Colyer laid before this Meeting that it was upon his minde to vissitt some Friends Meetings northward in Yorkshire, which Friends in this Meeting assents to & desires the Lord may be with him & assist him in his service.

Inquiry being made in this Meeting whether Friends keep up there week day meetings & findeing some remisness have ordered Brigg Friends to draw up a paper for the stirring Friends up to there duty therein as alsoe to dilligence in there first day Meetings, & bring it to the next Monthly Meeting to be sent to the seaverall Meetings.

p. 312.

Ordered that a contribution be collected & brought up to the next Monthly Meeting which is ordered to be at Brigg the 3d 6th day of the next Month.

Inquiry being made in this Meeting whether Friends dilligently keep up there week day Meetings and findeing some remisnes in some Meetings therein have desired some Friends of Brigg Meeting to draw up a paper for the stirring Friends up to there duty as alsoe to dilligently attend there first day Meetings & to comunicate the same to the Monthly Meeting in order to be coppied out & sent to the seaverall Meetings.

Signed by Joseph Richardson.

ATT a Monthly Meeting held at Brigg the 19 day of the 10th month 1707[1] :—

Representatives as followeth :—
Gainsbrough, Peter Nayler, Abraham Kent & William Martin.
Brigg, Joseph Richardson & Seth Walker.
The Ile, Samuel Brown & Robert Coakes.
Winteringham, John Dent & Mordeca Westoby.
Adlinfleet, Robert Vesse.

Inquiry being made in this Meeting about John Clarks conversation, Robert Vesse relates to Friends that there is hopes of an amendment which Friends will be glad of, if it continue, but its desired that Robert Vesse & Thomas Morley have an eye towards him for good & give a further account to the next Monthly Meeting.

According to the last Monthly Meeting order Robert Colyer & Thomas Nainby gave John Wresle a vissit & read the paper

---

[1] 19th December, 1707.

to him, which brought such a concern upon his minde as he went to his father, who upon discourse with him, hoped of an amendment of his son, and therefore desired that Friends would defer signing the paper till another Monthly Meeting (*p. 313*) was over which Friends have agreed to, onely desires Brigg Friends continue there tender care over him & give an account to the next Monthly Meeting.

Friends suffering for tythe came into this Meeting from Winteringham & part from Gainsbrough & the rest of theres & the Ile Meeting will be taken care on to be carried to the Quarterly Meeting.

Brigg Friends drew up paper according to order & was read in this Meeting, & ordered to be coppied out & sent to the seaverall Meetings belonging this Monthly Meeting.

Contributions came in as followeth :—

	£	s.	d.
Gainsbrough	00	18	6
Brigg	00	16	0
The Ile	00	12	0
Winteringham	00	14	6
Adlinfleet	0	09	04
	03	10	04

Disbursments as followeth :—

	£	s.	d.
to Robert Vesse for Doll Pickhaver		2	6
to Quarter Meeting	01	0	00
Rests in stock in Joseph Richardson hand	02	07	10

Representatives for the Quarterly Meeting are Edward Gilliatt, John Barlow, Stephen Wresle & Abraham Kent or any two of them.

Next Monthly Meeting ordered at Brigg the 3d 6th day of the next Month.

Signed by Joseph Richardson.

Att a Meeting held at the Meeting House att Brigge the 16th of the 11th month 1707[1] :—

Representatives as followeth :—

Gainsbrough, Thomas Potter & John Jackson.
The Ile, Thomas Wresle.
Brigg, Joseph Richardson & John Barlow.
Winteringham, Stephen Wresle & John Beninton.
Adlinfleet, Thomas Morley.

Thomas Morley & Thomas Hutchinson are desired to have an eye over John Clark conversation & give an account thereof to the next Monthly Meeting.

[1] 16th January, 1708.

p. 314.

Joseph Richardson gives account to this Meeting that they have heard nothing against John Wresles conversation since the last Monthly Meeting therefore Joseph Richardson & John Barlow are desired by this Meeting to have an eye over him & give account to the next Monthly Meeting.

The papers of sufferings belonging the Ile Meeting being a wanting at this Meeting Thomas Wresle is to inquire of John Urry concerning them, & Joseph Richardson of Edward Gilliatt, & give account to the next Monthly Meeting.

It is desired that John Wresle of Thealby see to the setling of the burying place at Winteringham as he & the Meeting approves of & that account be brought thereof to the next Monthly Meeting.

Ordered that the next Monthly Meeting be held the 3d 6th day of the next month.   Signed by Joseph Richardson.

ATT a Monthly Meeting held at Brigg Meeting house the 20 day of the 12 month 1707[1] :—

Representatives as followeth :—

Gainsbrough, Joseph Potter, Isaac Westoby.
Winteringham, John Dent, Leanord Bell.
Brigg, Joseph Richardson, Thomas Nainby.
The Ile, James Coakes, Isaac Brown.
Adlinfleet, Thomas Morley.

Thomas Hutchisson and Thomas Morley are desired to have an eye into John Clarks conversation & advise him as they see meet & give account to the next Monthly Meeting.

Joseph Richardson gives account that John Wresle has fallen into some disorder with drinke since the last Monthly Meeting, yet he still desires Friends further forbearance signifying his indeavours of giveing better satisfaction of his amendment therefore this Meeting desires Robert Colyer & Joseph Richardson to take notice of his conversation & give account to the next Monthly Meeting.

Sufferings for tythe belonging the Isle Meeting being a wanting this meeting desires James Coakes & John Urry, junior make a new collection of them & bring them to the next Monthly Meeting.

p. 315.

John Dent gives account that John Wresle of Thealby has given directions, for the conveyances of the burying place at Winteringham to such trustees as this Meeting approves of.

[1] 20th February, 1708.

John Sharp expects 18d a week for Hannah Reeders daughter from the time shee has been with him, & from this time eight pound if shee continue with him till eighteen years old, but leaves the conclusion of the matter till next Monthly Meeting.

Its disired that such Friends as are Overseers in each Meeting come up to the next Monthly Meeting & give an account how things are amongst them in order that the Monthly Meeting may give account to the Quarterly Meeting. And alsoe what breife are collected be brought in.

Ordered that a contribution be collected & brought to the next Monthly Meeting which is to be at Brigg the first 6th day of the next month.

Signed by Joseph Richardson.

ATT a Monthly Meeting held at the Meeting House in Brigg the 5th of the first month 1707[1] :—

Representatives as followeth :—

Gainsbrough, Peter Nayler, Thomas Potter.
Winteringham, George Frow, Stephen Wresle.
Brigg, Joseph Richardson, Robert Colyer.
Isle, John Urry, Isaac Davis.
Adlinfleet, Robert Vessy, Thomas Morley.

Thomas Morley & Robert Vesy are still desired to have an eye over John Clarks conversation, & alsoe to admonish him as they see meet & give account to the next Monthly Meeting.

Joseph Richardson acquaints Friends at this Meeting that they have heard nothing against John Wresle conversation since last Monthly Meeting therefore Friends desires that Joseph Richardson would have there eye towards him, & speak to him as they see meet.

John Wresle of Thealby is desired to execute the conveyances about the buryingard at Winteringham (which are now ready) to such trustees as are already agreed upon & give account to the next Monthly Meeting.

John Jackson gives account to this Meeting that his father & he has a minde to take Hannah Reeder daughter to learn to spin Jersy, this Meeting offers to give them 40s. per annum for 3 year next, & shee to serve ten yeares, & expects there answer next 3d day, & they are to finde her all nessesaries, meat, drink, clothing & all other things.

p. 316.

The Overseers of the seaverall Meetings gives account to this Meeting that there first day Meetings are dilligently attended

———————
[1] 5th March, 1708.

and there week day Meetings indeferently save in the Isle,
where the week day Meeting is not kept up, but they are
desired to come up in the practice thereof. The Testimonys
of Truth is pretty well kept up, & there is a tender care in
faithfull Freinds to admonish such as they see a shortness in.

Contributions came in as followeth :—

	£	s.	d.
Gainsbrough		17 : 00	
Brigg		14 : 06	
Winteringham		14 : 00	
The Ile		12 : 06	
Adlinfleet		09 : 06	
Stock in Joseph Richardson hand		47 : 00	
	05 : 15 : 04		

Disbursments as followeth :—

	£	s.	d.
to Thomas Potter for Abraham Northen which is due this day	00 : 13 : 00		
To the same for Susie Recket	00 : 03 : 00		
to John Sharp for Hannah Reeder table	01 : 02 : 6		
to Thomas Potter to pay for books	00 : 10 : 00		
for the Quarterly Meeting	01 : 00 : 00		
Stock left in Joseph Richardson hand	02 : 06 : 10		
	05 : 15 : 04		

The writeings belonging Crowle burying place lodges in Joseph
Berrier hand of Ealand.

John Barlow, Thomas Potter, Robert Colyer & Thomas Morley or
any two of them are to attend the service of the Quarterly
Meeting.

Next Monthly Meeting ordered the 2d 6th day of the next month.

Signed by Joseph Richardson.

ATT a Monthly Meeting held at Gainsbrough 9th of 2 month
1708[1] :—

Representatives as followeth :—

Gainsbrough, Peter Nayler, Thomas Potter.
Brigg, John Barlow, John Sharpe.
Winteringham, Stephen Wresle.
The Isle, John Urry.
Adlinfleet, Thomas Morley.

[1] 9th April, 1708.

Thomas Hutchisson & Thomas Morley are still desired to have an
   eye over John Clark conversation & give account to next
   Monthly Meeting.

John Barlow & John Sharp gives account to this Meeting of the
   disorderly conversation of John Wresle, & feares his wife
   is much in blame, therefore Friends at this Meeting desires
   Joseph Richardson and Robert Colyer to deall with them
   both & alsoe the woemen Friends of there Meeting & give
   account thereof to the next Monthly Meeting.

John Sharp of Brigg has agreed with this Meeting to take Hannah
   Reeder daughter which is now with him, for tenn yeares next,
   from the date of the last Monthly Meeting, & provide for her
   meat, drinke, washing & lodging & all nessesaries of apparell
   what ever, and this Meeting promises to pay him six pounds
   at three times by equall proportions, Viz (*p. 317*) 40s. at next
   Monthly Meeting & 40s. at year end, & 40s. at year end after
   that, and John Sharp is to give a note under his hand to
   confirme the agreement till the indentures be drawn sealed &
   take place.

Whereas a letter came to this Meeting from the Monthly Meeting
   at Mansfield in Nottinghamshire, requesting by certificate
   whether or no, we were in unity with him William Birket who
   lately resident in Brigg Meeting, & is now removed in order
   to setle with his family in Nottinghamshire, this Meeting
   thinkes Brigg Friends most fitt to answer the letter, & orders
   them to write to Friends an answer, for there better satisfaction.

The next Monthly Meeting ordered to be at Thealby & a contribution
   to be collected & brought up thither.

                          Signed by Joseph Richardson.

ATT a Monthly Meeting held at Thealby 14th 3d month 1708[1]:—

Representatives as followeth :—
   from Gainsbrough, William West & Joseph Morley.
      Winteringham, Stephen Wresle & John Dent.
      Brigg, Robert Colyer, John Sharp.
      The Isle, Thomas Wresle & John Urry.
      Adlinfleet, Thomas Hutchisson.

Thomas Hutchisson & Thomas Morley are still desired to have a
   watchfull eye over John Clark conversation & give account
   to the next Monthly Meeting.

Its agreed that David Crosby goe to speak with John Wresle and
   his wife as its in his minde, & give an account how he finds
   them to the next Monthly Meeting.

                  [1] 14th May, 1708.

Whereas the Meeting has under consideration the bargaine between John Sharp of Brigg & Hannah Reeder, its agreed that indentures be drawn, & haveing at this Meeting given him 40s. on the account he is to give a note under his hand of the receipt of it, and the indentures are to take place at the time cald Candlemas 1708.

An answer being drawn by this Meeting to the letter from Mansfeild Friends about William Burket, the same is ordered to be signed by Robert Colyer, & sent to Mansfeild first oppertunity.

Contributions as followeth :—	£	s.	d.
Gainsbrough	00	18	00
Brigge	00	15	06
Winteringham	00	15	06
The Ile	00	14	00
Adlinfleet	00	09	06
Stock	00	02	06
in all	05	18	06

Disbursments :—	£	s.	d.
to Mathew Jackson	00	02	06
To Sander Chapman, Isle	00	07	08
To Bridget Mosley	00	03	03
To John Sharp	02	00	00
To Thomas Hutchison for Hannah Reeder children	03	05	1
Rests still due to Reeders	00	06	04½

p. 318.

The matter relateing to the Widdow Smith is left to the next Monthly Meeting.

Next Monthly Meeting ordered to be the first 6th day of the next month at Adlinfleet & a contribution to be collected & brought up thither.   Signed by Joseph Richardson.

ATT a Monthly Meeting held at Thomas Morleys house in Adlinfleet the 4th of the 4st month 1708[1] :—

Representatives as followeth :—
Gainsbrough, John Simson & John Marshall.
Brigg, Robert Colyer, Joseph Richardson, junior, John Oxley.
Winteringham, George Frow, Stephen Wresle.
Isle, Joseph Berrier, Isaac Davis.
Adlinfleet, Thomas Hutchinson, Thomas Morley.

Thomas Hutchison & Thomas Morley are still desired to have an eye towards John Clark conversation & give account to next Meeting.

[1] 4th June, 1708.

David Crosby gives account at this Meeting that he has had an oppertunity with John Wresle & his wife, & they both acknowledge there outrunings & Friends tender love towards them, & hoped they should manifest there amendments in there conversation, however this Meeting desires Robert Colyer & David Crosby to have an inspection into there conversation & give account to the next Meeting.

This Meeting desires those Friends of each Meeting that goes up to the Quarterly Meeting to carry an account of what collected upon the account of breifs.

Contributions came in as followeth :—

	£	s.	d.
Gainsbrough	00	18	00
Brigg	00	14	00
Winteringham	00	12	0
The Isle	00	13	00
Adlinfleet	00	09	00

Disbursments :—

	£	s.	d.
To John Marshall for John Parker for Widdow Smith son	02	00	00
To Isaac Davis for Hannah Reeder son	01	00	00
To the same laid out for	00	01	0
To Thomas Morley for Hannah Reeder account	00	05	00

This Meeting thinkes it convenient that each Meeting keep a Preparitive Meeting & alsoe a book for that service & give an account to the next Monthly Meeting which is to be at Beltoft & a contribution to be collected & brought up thither.

Joseph Richardson, senior, John Marshall, Stephen Wresle, John Bishopp & Thomas Hutchisson attend the service of the Quarterly Meeting or any two of them.

Signed by Joseph Richardson.

p. 319.

ATT a Monthly Meeting held at the Meeting House at Beltoft the 9th of 5th month 1708[1] :—

Representatives as followeth :—

Gainsbrough, Thomas Nayler, Matthew Jackson.
Brigg, Robert Colyer, Joseph Richardson.
Winteringham, Richard Wresle, Mordeca Westoby.
The Isle, John Urry senior, James Coakes.
Adlinfleet, Thomas Morly, Robert Vesse.

Thomas Hutchison & Thomas Morly still desired to have an eye to John Clark conversation.

[1] 9th July, 1708.

Robert Colyer gives account to this Meeting that they have not
heard any thing against John Wresles conversation since the
last Monthly Meeting, he with Joseph Richardson is desired
to have a tender eye towards them & give an account to the
next Monthly Meeting.

Complaint being made against his wife for her disorderly walking,
its desired some woemen Friends of there Meeting goe &
admonish her to an amendment.

This Meeting haveing inquired of the seaverall representatives
of each Meeting, whether they have a Preparitive Meeting
according to former advice, Gainsbrough, Brigg & the Isle
are in the practice thereof but Winteringham & Adlinfleet
are still a wanting therein, its desired they alsoe may come into
that good order & give account to the next Monthly Meeting.

Contributions came in as followeth :—

	£	s.	d.
Gainsbrough	00	17	06
Brigg	00	16	00
Winteringham	00	12	06
The Isle	00	11	09
Adlingfleet	00	09	06
	03	07	03

Disbursments :—

	£	s.	d.
To Isaac Davis being in full for the 2d payment for Hannah Reeders son	01	00	00
to Robert Colyer for close for Hannah Reeder daughter with John Sharp	01	10	05
to John Urry, senior for Sander Chapman	00	05	00
to Thomas Morley for Doll Pickhaver	00	02	06
	02	07	10
In stock in Joseph Richardson hand	00	09	04

Next Monthly Meeting ordered to be at John Nainbys house in
Castlethorp.   Signed by Joseph Richardson.

p. 320.

ATT a Monthly Meeting held at John Nainbys in Castlethorp
the 13 of the 6 month 1708[1] :—

Representatives as followeth :—

Gainsbrough, John Simson, John Marshall.
Brigg, Joseph Richardson, Robert Colyer.
Winteringham, John Dent & Leonard Bell.
The Isle, Thomas Wresle, James Coakes.
Adlinfleet, Thomas Hutchison.

[1] 13th August, 1708.

Thomas Morley & Thomas Hutchinson are still desired to have a watchfull eye over John Clark & give account to next Meeting.

The matter touching John Wresle & his wife, haveing been debated in this Meeting, and it appearing shee has been some cause of his outrunings William Williamson and Gervas Cornwell are desired to let them know that if they both doe not speedily indeavour an amendment a paper for disowning of them will be signed by Friends & given forth against them.

Enquiry being made further about the generall settlement of Preparative Meetings & the keeping a booke for matters recording therein, some further account thereof is desired at the next Meeting.

Robert Colyer having laid before this Meeting his intentions of vissiting Friends Meetings at London &c. this Meeting has approved thereof.

Rachell Browne of Brigg imparts to this Meeting her intentions of goeing to London to live. Friends desires that Brigg Friends may draw a certificate for her as they shall see meet to give on her behalf.

Whereas complaint has been made against seaverall Freinds that has subscribed towards the charge of Beltoft Meeting house, on account of there delaying in a kind of refuseing the payment of there subscriptions, this Meeting appoints Thomas Wresle & James Coakes tenderly to forward there complyance with the payment of it, or otherwise those who shall refuse the same to appear at the next Monthly Meeting to give there reason for there not paying of it.

Ordered that a contribution be collected & brought up to the next Monthly Meeting which is to be at Gainsbrough.

Signed by Joseph Richardson.

p. 321.

ATT a Monthly Meeting held at Gainsbrough 10th of 7 month 1708[1]:—

Representatives as followeth :—

Gainsbrough, Peter Nayler, Thomas Potter.
Brigg, John Nainby, John Oxley.
Isle, John Urry, junior.
Winteringham, John Raines.
Adlinfleet, Thomas Morley.

John Urry is desired to send what births & burialls is in there Meeting to Joseph Richardson in order to be recorded.

[1] 10th September, 1708.

Thomas Morley & Thomas Hutchinson is desired still to have an
  eye over John Clarks conversation & give account to the next
  Meeting.
Inquiry being made about keeping a booke for the Preparative
  Meeting service, the Friends that comes from each Meeting are
  desired to bring Friends answer to the next Monthly Meeting.
William Williamson & Gervis Cornwell are still desired to speak
  to John Wresle about his disorderliness, & 2 weomen friends
  of Brigg Meeting to speak to her : shee appearing to be a
  great cause of his disorder & to give an account to the next
  Monthly Meeting.
Thomas Wresle & James Coakes are desired to speak to Friends
  of there Meeting that have subscribed towards the Meeting
  House charge, to acquaint such as absolutely refuse to pay,
  that this Meeting expects there appearance at the next Monthly
  Meeting to give reasons for there refusall.
William Birket case is left to the Quarterly Meeting advice.
Contributions brought in as followeth :—

				£	s.	d.
Gainsbrough	..	..	..	00 : 18 :	6	
Brigg	..	..	..	00 : 13 :	6	
The Isle	..	..	..	00 : 12 :	0	
Winteringam	..	..	..	00 : 13 :	0	
Adlinfleet	..	..	..	00 : 09 :	0	
				03 : 06 : 00		

Disbursments as followeth :—

			£	s.	d.
To John Craine on Samuel Smith account	..		01 : 05 : 00		
To Thomas Potter for bookes ..	..	..	00 : 01 : 00		
To Thomas Morley for Doll Pickhaver ..	..	..	00 : 02 : 06		
To Thomas Potter for Quarter Meeting	..	..	01 : 00 : 00		
Totall	..	..	2 : 8 : 6		
In stock in Joseph Richardson hand	..	..	00 : 17 : 6		

Thomas Potter, Thomas Nainby & John Barlow are appointed to
  attend the Quarterly Meeting service or any two of them.
The next Monthly Meeting to be kept at John Urrys in Epworth.
                    Signed by Joseph Richardson.

p. 322.
    ATT a Monthly Meeting held the house of John Urrys in Epworth
the 8th of the 8th Month 1708[1] :—

The representatives are as followeth :—
Gainsbrough, Peter Nayler & Thomas Potter.
Brigg, Robert Colyer & Thomas Burton.

            [1] 8th October, 1708.

Winteringham, John Beninton.
The Isle, John Urry & Isaac Davis.
Garthrop, Thomas Hutchisson.

Thomas Hutchisson gives account of John Clarks remissness in
seaverall matters therefore Thomas Morley & Thomas Hutchisson is still desired to have a watchfull eye over him, & give
account of his conversation to the next Monthly Meeting.

Inquiry being made about keeping a booke in the Preparative
Meetings for the recording of matter that offer therein, the
further consideration thereof is left to the severall Meetings
who are desired to send there sence thereof to the next Monthly
Meeting.

Robert Colyer & Thomas Burton gives account to this Meeting of
the disorderly walking of John Wresle & his wife since the last
Monthly Meeting, therefore Robert Colyer & Thomas Nainby
are desired to speak to them, & if there be no amendment
to bring an account to the next Monthly Meeting, that
Friends may proceed in giveing forth a paper of condemnation
against them.

The case of William Birket being discoursed in this Meeting it is
consented unto by Friends that wee should contribute towards
his releife, where he is, & that Brigg Friends are desired to
write to Friends at Mansfield Monthly Meeting concerning it.

Next Monthly Meeting ordered to be at Brigg and that a contribution
be collected for William Birket releife & brought up to the
next Monthly Meeting.

Signed by Joseph Richardson.

ATT a Monthly Meeting held at Brigg the 12 of the 9th month
1708[1] :—

Representatives as followeth :—

Gainsbrough, John Marshall, Thomas Potter.
Brigg, Robert Colyer, Joseph Richardson.
Isle, James Coakes, Paull Dixon.
Winteringham, no body.
Adlinfleet, Thomas Morley.

p. 323.

Freinds in this Meeting being dissatisfied that no body appeared
from Winteringham Meeting to attend Truths service, have
ordered some of Brigg Friends to write to them to ster them
up to more deligence & give an account to the next Monthly
Meeting. Robert Colyer, Thomas Nainby & Joseph Richardson
are orderd to write to them.

[1] 12th November, 1708.

Thomas Morley giveing account of John Clarkes continued remissness in comeing to Meetings, is with Thomas Hutchson desierd to ster him to & encourage him in more deligence & to give a account of their success therein to next Monthly Meeting.

Further enquiery being made about keeping a booke in the Preparitive Meetings for recording maters that ofer therein & Friends of the severall Particular Meeting except Brigg not haveing yett come into the practis theareof are desiered to doe it ore bring there reasons for the contrary to the next Monthly Meeting.

Robert Colyer give an account of John Wresles contiuening disorderleness & that thear is no hopes of amendmente, the sence of this Meeting is that a paper of condemnation be given forth against him att the next Monthly Meeting if Freinds from the seaverall Meetings then have not any thing to object against it : & the care of John Wresels is lefte to the consideration of Freinds of Brigg Meeting who are desiered to give their sensce therein to the next Monthley Meeting.

John Urry, junior, of Epworth came to this Meeting & desiered his intention of marrage with Elizabeth Crispin of Lainham & brought her letter to this Monthly Meeting to signifie her consente therein allso a certificate from Clarbrough Monthly Meeting signifieing their they haveing appeared theare to declear thear said intention of it being the first time he desiered to waite Friends answer till the next Monthly Meeting & James Coakes & Isaac Davis are desierd to enquire into his clearness & to give an account theareof.

p. 324.

Conteributions brought in on the account of William Burkett viz. :—

				£	s.	d.
Gainsbrough	..	..	..	00 :	10 :	6
Brigg	..	..	..	00 :	10 :	0
The Isle	..	..	..	00 :	10 :	0
Winteringham	..	..	..	00 :	11 :	0
Adlingfleet	..	..	..	00 :	08 :	6
				02 :	10 :	0

This Meeting apoints that an account of Friends Suferings for tythes be brot up to the next Monthly Meeting a contribution is appointed to be colected & brott up to the next Monthly Meeting which is orderd to be att Brigg.

ATT a Monthely Meeting holden att Brigg the 10th of the 10th 1708[1] :—

Repersentatives as followeth :—

Gainsbrough, Thomas Nalyer, Joseph Morley.
Brigg, Thomas Nainby, John Barlow.

[1] 10th December, 1708.

The Isle, Isaac Davis, Robte Coakes.
Winteringham, Stephen Wresell, John Dente.
Adlingfleet, Robert Vessey, Thomas Morley.

Thomas Morlye & Robert Vessye are desiered to have an eye to
John Clarkes conversation & to his attending Meetings &
advice as they se meet & give an account to the Next Monthly
Meeting.

Brigg Meeting & Adlingflett are comd into the practiss of haveing
a book of record in thear Prepartive, Gainsbrough, the Isle,
Winteringham Meetings are desierd to come in to the practis
thear of & give an account to the next Monthly Meeting.

Thear appeared nothing against John Wresells conversation since
laste Monthly Meeting thearfore it is the sence of this Meeting
that Freinds waite till the next Monthly Meeting to see if
anye reformation be found in him Thomas Nainby & Robert
Colyer are desiered to have a cercumspect eye over him & give
an account to the next Monthly Meeting & likewise that they
speak to his wife & give an account of the sence of this
Meeting if no womens Freinds take it upon them to deale
with her.

p. 325.

Suferings came in upon account of tyhes from Gainsbrough, Brigg,
Winteringham & Adlingfleete, the Isle are desiered to take
care to bring thears in.

John Urry, junior, published his intention of marrage the 2th time
with Elizabeth Crispin of Lanham & Friends appointed to
enquir into his clearness from others have certificate to the
same thearfore have nothing to object against it their further
procedings but leaves the further consideration thearof to
Friends of Clarbrough Monthly Meeting according to the good
order of Truth.

Signed by Joseph Richardson.

Conterbutions as followeth :—

				£	s.	d.
Gainsbrough	..	..	..	0 :	18 :	0
Brigg	..	..	..	0 :	14 :	10
The Isle	..	..	..	0 :	12 :	6
Winteringham	..	..	..	0 :	12 :	6
Adlingfleet	..	..	..	0 :	09 :	0
				3 :	4 :	10
Stock came in ..	..	..		0 :	17 :	6
in all	..	..		4 :	4 :	4

Disbursments :—	£	s.	d.
To Thomas Nayler to pay Susannah Wreckett rentt	0 :	2 :	6
To William Frost foar pare shoues for Hannah Reader	0 :	3 :	0
To Isaac Davis was lade down for severall Freinds	0 :	12 :	6
To Thomas Morley for Dorathy Pickhaver ..	0 :	2 :	6
To Thomas Nayler for the use of the Quartly Meeting	1 :	0 :	0
To the same for Thomas Windr prisner att Lincon	0 :	10 :	0
For the Testamony of Truth	2 :	10 :	6
Stock in Joseph Richardsons hand	1 :	13 :	10

Thomas Potter, Thomas Nainby, Stephn Wresell, Thomas Morley or any three of them are apoynted to attend the servis of the Quarterlye Meeting.

Next Monthly Meeting to be at Brigg.

p. 326.

AT a Monthly Meeting held att Brigg the 14th 11 month 1708/9[1] :—

Representatives :—

Gainsbrough, John Jackson & Isaac Westoby.
Brigg, Thomas Nainby & Robert Collyer.
The Isle, Thomas Wressell.
Winteringham, Stephn Wressell & John Benington.
Adlingfleet, none.

Thear being none from Adlingfleet, Thomas Morley & Robert Vessey continued as before are desiered to have an eye to John Clarkes conversation & to his attending Meetings & advice as they see meett & give an account to the nextt Monthly Meeting.

Gainsbrough Freinds are comed into the practice to keep a Preparative Meeting booke as was desiered the last Monthly Meeting butt Winteringham & the Isle are yett wanting.

The Isle not bringing in thear account of sufferings for tythes the last Monthly Meeting & none from thence now they are to be enquiered for the next Monthly Meeting in order to be carred up to the next Quarterly Meeting.

[1] 14th January, 1709.

N

John Wresle appeared att this Meeting & gave Friends a paper concerning his presente condition with hopes of amendment which gave some satisfaction to the Meeting to have further patience to wate for return.

The repersantatevs to the Quarterly Meeting gives an account that the next Quarterly Meeting is appointed to be in the 4th day in the Size week or else on the 4th day before the time called Lady day.

The next Monthly Meeting is appointed to be att Brigg.

(p. 327 contains an exact copy of the letter from John Wresle previously given on pp. 302 and 303.)

p. 328.

Here followes another of John Wresles letters of condemnation of himself to Friends at there Monthly Meeting 14th of 11 month 1708[1]:—

Loving Friends, after my kind love to you I desire you once more to hear these few lines with patience. In the first place I do let you understand I have been a man inclined to drink from my very childhood & as I grew up I fell more & more in love with it, so that I would have it either by lawfull means or unlawfull which was a very sad thing so that I ran so farr that I was very near to destruction both of soul & body had not the Lord in his infinite mercy looked down upon me & plainly laid my condition before me & through the Lords mercies I have known in some measure a forsaking, likewise I think I never was unwilling to hear you at any time neither publick or private & not only so but I have made my confession in some measure before you, & this I am bold to say because I know it to be truth, that I have in a greater measure forsaken than ever I made confession, in consideration I best know how my condition has been, so that Friends do you not think that it is a very hard thing that I should be disowned by you & likewise by my relations because they know that I am under condemnation & likewise you know or at least may know that I am despised & disowned by my own family for which I give them no just occasion for so doing but can truly say I have nothing but love & goodwill towards them & can truly labour both night & day for the good of my self & them, & I am glad with all my heart that the Lord hath inclined me so to doe, & if you all say nay, I know it is through the Lord's mercy I am as I am so Friends if you doe condemn me to the world I neither can nor will justifie my self to them, so shall conclude your friend. Brigge the 14th of 11th month 1708/9.

John Wresle.

[1] 14th January, 1709.

ATT a Monthly Meeting held at Brigg the 11th of the 12 month 1708/9[1] :—

Representatives as followeth :—
Gainsbrough, Thomas Potter & Thomas Nayler.
Brigge, Robert Colyer & John Nainby.
The Isle, no body because of bad way & weather.
Winteringham, John Dent.
Adlinfleet, Thomas Morley.

p. 329.

Thomas Morley & Robert Vessy are still desired to have an eye to John Clarks conversation & give account to next Monthly Meeting.

All the Meetings belonging this Monthly Meeting are come into the practice of haveing a book of record in there Preparative Meetings except Winteringham Meeting who are desired to come into the practice thereof.

Nobody being here from the Isle Meeting, therefore Thomas Nayler is desired to put the Friends of that Meeting in mind that they take care to bring their sufferings to the next Monthly Meeting.

Notwithstanding John Wresle appeared at our last Monthly Meeting & gave some satisfaction to the Meeting to have further patience to wait for his return yet since that has fallen into open drunkenness to the great dishonour of Truth & Joseph Richardson having something in his mind to impart to him the paper of condemnation is deferred signing till the next Monthly Meeting ; The Isle Meeting being allso wanting.

Joseph Richardson, junior, acquainted this Meeting that he has a concern upon his mind to visit Friends Meetings in London & desires our unity & concurrence therewith, to which we have assented & given him our certificate & does desire him at his return to give this Meeting an account of his service in the work of the Lord.

Sarah Collyer allso gave account to this Meeting that she has a concern upon her mind to visit Friends in the west parts of England & desired she might have this Meetings concurrence therewith having unity therewith have given her our certificate desiring at her return that she may give account to this Meeting of her service in the Truth.

John Jackson likewise signified to this Meeting the concern that was upon his mind to visit Friends in Holderness, & desired Friends unity therewith, this Meeting consenting thereto have

[1] 11th February, 1709.

given their certificate desiring at his return to give account of his service therein.

The representatives here present are desired to acquaint the several Meetings of the reprinting George Fox's Journals & give account what Friends has a mind to subscribe to the next Monthly Meeting.

This Meeting desires that a contribution be collected & brought to the next Monthly Meeting which is appointed to be here the 1st 6th day of the next Month & that the Overseers of every Meeting come to the next Monthly Meeting in order to give account of the state of their Meetings.

p. 330.

At a Monthly Meeting held at Brigge the 11th of the 1st month 1709[1] :—

Representatives as followeth :—

From Gainsbrough, Thomas Naylor & Thomas Potter.
Brigge, Robert Collyer & John Barlow.
The Isle, Jacob Davis & James Coakes.
Winteringham, Robert Knight & Stephen Wresle.
Addlingfleet, none.

Winteringham Friends are agreed to get a book for recording matters at the Preparative Meeting, but not having got one, enquiery is to be made of it next Monthly Meeting.

This Meeting hath signed a paper of condemnation against John Wresle, junior of Brigge after long forbearance thereof.

Addlingfleet Meeting being wanting John Clarks conversation is to be enquired into at the next Monthly Meeting.

Contributions came in as followeth :—

	£	s.	d.
from Gainsbrough	00	17	6
from Brigge	00	14	6
from the Isle	00	11	0
from Winteringham	00	11	0
Addlingfleet not come in			
the Stock before was	01	13	10
all	04	07	10
Take off	02	09	00
Rests in Joseph Richardsons hand	01	18	10

[1] 11th March, 1709.

Disbursments :—	£	s.	d.

To Susan Wrecket at Gainsbrough .. ..   2 : 6
To Brigge Friends .. ..   3 : 6
To Bridget Mosley in the Isle .. .. ..   3 : 0
To be carried to the Quarterly Meeting .. 1 : 0 : 0
Paid for books which is given into Thomas
  Potter hand which he is to give account of
  the next Monthly Meeting .. .. 01 : 00 : 0

It is left to Gainsbrough Friends to give Peter Poe a certificate to take with him to London.

The Overseers of each Particular Meeting being enquired of concerning the state of their several Meetings the substance of the account given was that there remained a concern upon Friends for the regulation of what is amiss though no particular complaint was made.

Thomas Potter, James Coakes & Robert Collyer, or any two of them are ordered to attend the Quarterly Meetings service.

The next Monthly Meeting is ordered to be at Gainsbrough.

Signed by Joseph Richardson.

Here followes the paper of condemnation given forth in this Meeting against John Wresle, after all the patience, labour & forbeance of Friends with & towards him.

p. 331.

To all people to whom this present writing shall come. Know ye that whereas John Wressle of Brigge having from a child been educated in the holy profession of the blessed Truth which we the people in scorn called Quakers make profession of, but he not taking heed to that blessed principle of God in his own heart, viz. the grace of God that brings salvation (according to the holy scriptures) teaching us (as the antient christians) that denying ungodlyness & worldly lusts we should live soberly righteously & godlyly in this present evil world he hath been led aside & captivated with that gross sin of drunkenness whereby he hath dishonoured the name of God & our holy profession notwithstanding we have laboured with him, reproving & admonishing him with great patience & long-suffering that if possible we might reclaim him but all our labours & endeavours have been ineffectual, save that he hath often been brought to an acknowledgement & confession of his sin owning our care & love towards him often testifieing against himself both in word & writing in much seeming tenderness, especially one writing which much clears Friends & Truth, notwithstanding he still continues in the said sinn of drunkenness to the great dishonour of God his Truth & poeple. Wherefore we have found a necessity upon us to testifie against him shewing unto the world we have no fellowship with him, nor his unfruitful works of darkness he being unto us as a heathen man untill it shall please the Lord to give him a fresh visitation & repentance not to be repented of which we earnestly pray for.

Signed in this our Monthly Meeting held at Brigge the 11th of the 1st month 1709 by us.

Joseph Richardson, senior.
Robert Colyer.
Thomas Potter.
Thomas Nayler.
Thomas Nainby.
John Barlow.
James Coakes.
Thomas Burton.
Jacob Davis.
Robert Knight.

(p. 332 and the upper part of p. 333 contain an exact copy of the Minutes of the Meeting of 11 : 1 : 1709 already given on p. 330.)

p. 333.

ATT a Monthly Meeting held at Gainsbrough the 8 of 2d month 1709[1] :—

Representatives as followeth :—

Gainsbrough, Peter Naylor & Thomas Potter.
Brigg, Robert Colyer & John Nainby.
The Ile, Thomas Wresle & Francis Seaton.
Winteringham, Stephen Wresle.
Adlinfleet, Thomas Hutchisson.

Winteringham Meeting hath gott a Preparative Meeting booke according to there agreement.

Ordered that the paper of condemnation against John Wresle be read and published at Brigg Meeting on the first day.

Adlinfleet contribution not yet come in.

Thomas Morley & Thomas Hutchisson are desired to inspect into John Clark conversation & give account to next Monthly Meeting.

A contribution ordered to be made for the releife of Samuel Trouton & to be had up to the Quarterly Meeting.

[1] 8th April, 1709.

A contribution proposed to be made for releife of poor Friends of Mumby Meeting, & is refered to our next Monthly Meeting.

This Meeting apppoints Stephen Wresle to demand a legacy of George Atkinson, left to the use of this Meeting by Francis Dent & bring it up to the next Monthly Meeting or else the reason why he refuses to pay it.

John Jackson having given this Meeting an account of his jorney & travills in vissitting Friends in there Meetings, & alsoe of his service & satisfaction therein returnd his certificate according to Friends advice & desire.

Ordered that the money for releife of William Birket be lodged with Thomas Potter, & to be paid quarterly for that service.

A contribution ordered to be collected & brought up to the next Monthly Meeting, which is appointed to be at Winteringham.

p. 334.

    ATT a Monthly Meeting held at Winteringham the 13th of the 3d month 1709[1] :—

Representatives as followeth :—

    Gainsbrough, John Marshall & Thomas Nayler.
    Brigg, Thomas Nainby & John Sharp.
    Winteringham, Richard Wresle, George Frow.
    The Ile, Thomas Wresle, John Harrison.
    Adlinfleet, Robert Vessy, Thomas Morley.

Thomas Morley & Thomas Hutchisson are still desired to have an eye to John Clark conversation & give account to next Monthly Meeting.

Report being made to this Meeting that Stephen Wresle had spoke to George Atkinson touching a legacy left to this Meeting by Francis Dent, & the said George is willing to pay it, & Stephen is desired to receive the money of George Atkinson, & this Meeting will give him a discharge.

This day Thomas Nainby of Brigg, junior, published his intention of marriage with Elizabeth Barlow of the same shee being present gave her consent, but it being the first time they are desired to wait Friends answer till next Monthly Meeting. Ann Richardson & Elizabeth Colyer are to enquire into her clearness and alsoe Thomas is desired to procure a certificate from Warnsworth Monthly Meeting touching his conversation & clearness from all others.

The contribution for releife of Samuel Trouton is referd to the next Monthly Meeting.

        [1] 13th May, 1709.

Contributions as followeth :—

				£	s.	d.
Gainsbrough	..	..	..	01	00	06
Brigg	..	..	..	00	15	06
Winteringham	..	..	..	00	12	00
The Ile	..	..	..	00	10	00
Adlinfleet two	..	..	..	00	18	00
				05	14	10

Disbursments as followeth :—

	£	s.	d.
To John Marshall for Susan Recket	00	03	8
To Thomas Wresle for William Wreet rent ..	00	09	0
To John Sharp for a year pay due now upon account of Hannah Reeder	02	00	0
To Thomas Morley upon Widdow Reeder account	03	02	02
	05	14	10

Ordered that a contribution be collected for the service of Mumby
Meeting & brought up to the next Monthly Meeting which is
to be at Adlinfleet.

Signed by Joseph Richardson.

ATT a Monthly Meeting held at Thomas Morleys in Adlinfleet
the 10 of 4th month 1709[1] :—

Representatives as followeth :—

Gainsbrough, John Symson, Isaac Westoby.
Brigg, Robert Colyer, John Barlow.
Winteringham, George Frow, Mordeca Westoby.
Ile, Isaac Davis, John Bishopp, Adlingfleet, Thomas
    Hutchisson.

p. 335.

Stephen Wresle not giveing account to this Meeting concerning
the legacy left by Francis Dent, he is desired to speak to
George Atkinson & receive it of him & give account thereof
to the next Monthly Meeting.

Thomas Nainby of Brigg, junior, came into this Meeting and
signified the continuance of his purpose of marriage with
Elizabeth Barlow of the same, shee being present gave consent &
all things appearing clear on behalf of both parties, Friends has
left the accomplishment thereof to themselves with advice of
there Friends according to the good order of Truth.

[1] 10th June, 1709.

Contributions came in as followeth :—

	£	s.	d.
Gainsbrough	00 :	18 :	00
Brigg	00 :	13 :	06
Winteringham	00 :	11 :	06
The Ile	00 :	09 :	6
Adlingfleet	00 :	09 :	0
	03 :	01 :	06

Disbursments :— £ s. d.

To Robert Colyer for releife of the nessesities
of Mumby Monthly Meeting .. .. 03 : 01 : 06

A contribution to be made for releife of Samuel Trouton & brought
to the next Monthly Meeting which is to be at John Urrys in
Epworth. John Barlow is desired to lye down three pounds
for the use of Samuel Trouton & this meeting will repay him.

Signed by Joseph Richardson.

ATT our Monthly Meeting held at John Urrys in Epworth 8th
of 5th month 1709[1] :—

Representatives as followeth :—

Gainsbrough, Peter Nayler & Joseph Potter.
Brigg, William Williamson & Gervis Cornwell.
Winteringam, Robert Knight and William Marshland.
The Ile, John Urry, senior & James Coakes.
Adlinfleet, Thomas Hutchinson & Thomas Morley.

Stephen Wresle not haveing oppertunity to speak to George Atkinson
about the legacy left this Meeting by Francis Dent, is desired
still to get it of him againe next Monthly Meeting.

Contributions as followeth :—

	£	s.	d.
Gainsbrough	00 :	18 :	00
Brigg	00 :	14 :	06
Winteringham	00 :	12 :	00
The Isle	00 :	11 :	00
Adlinfleet	00 :	09 :	06
	3 :	05 :	00

Disbursments as followeth :— £ s. d.

To Robert Colyer for John Barlow upon account			
of Samuel Trouton	03 :	00 :	00
to Isaac Davis on Hannah Reeder account ..	00 :	05 :	00
Totall	03 :	05 :	00

[1] 8th July, 1709.

A contribution ordered to be collected & brought to the next Monthly Meeting which is to be at Gainsbrough.

Signed by Joseph Richardson.

p. 336.

ATT our Monthly Meeting held at Gainsbrough the 12 of 6th month 1709[1] :—

Representatives as followeth :—

Gainsbrough, John Marshall, John Symson.
Brigg, John Barlow, John Oxley.
Winteringham, William Marshland.
Isle, John Urry, junior, Isaac Davis.
Adlinfleet, Thomas Morley, Robert Vessy.

This Meeting still desires Stephen Wresle to get the legacy of Francis Dent & bring or send it to the next Monthly Meeting.

Contributions came in as followeth :—

				£	s.	d.
Gainsbrough	..	..	..	00 :	18 :	0
Brigg	..	..	..	00 :	17 :	6
Winteringham	..	..	..	00 :	12 :	0
The Isle	..	..	..	00 :	12 :	00
Adlingfleet	..	..	..	00 :	09 :	0
Totall	..	..	..	03 :	08 :	6

Disbursments as followeth :—

	£	s.	d.
To Isaac Davis on account of Hannah Reeder son which was due the foreend of last 3d Month..	01 :	15 :	00
To John Urry for Sander Chapman	00 :	05 :	00
	02 :	00 :	00

Rests in stock with Thomas Potter .. .. 01 : 08 : 6

Theres alsoe a small stock in Thomas Potter hand which he is desired to give account of at next Monthly Meeting.

A contribution ordered to be collected & brought up to the next Monthly Meeting which is to be at Gainsbrough.

Signed by Joseph Richardson.

ATT our Monthly Meeting held at Gainsbrough 9th of 7th month 1709[2] :—

Gainsbrough, Peter Nayler, Thomas Potter. Brigg, Thomas Nainby, Robert Colyer.

---

[1] 12th August, 1709.			[2] 9th September, 1709.

Winteringham, Mordeca Westoby, William Marshland. The Isle. Thomas Wresle. Henry Clark. Adlingfleet, Thomas Morley.

Stephen Wresle & John Dent are desired to take care to get the legacy (left by Francis Dent) of George Atkinson, & bring or send it to the next Monthly Meeting.

Contributions came in as followeth :—

	£	s.	d.
Gainsbrough		18 :	6
Brigg		17 :	6
Winteringham		11 :	6
The Isle		12 :	00
Adlingfleet		09 :	00
In stock..	01 :	19 :	08
Totall	05 :	08 :	02

Disbursments as followes :—

	£	s.	d.
To Thomas Morley which he laid down upon Hannah Reeder account	00 :	07 :	00
to Thomas Wresle for releife of Bridget Mosley & Thomas Wright	00 :	02 :	00
Thomas Potter for Quarterly Meeting ..	01 :	00 :	00
Rests in stock in Thomas Potter hand ..	03 :	09 :	02

This day Joseph Richardson, junior, & Sarah Colyer gave account to Friends in this Meeting of there seaverall services in the ministry among Friends where they traviled as alsoe he at London & shee at Bristoll to the satisfaction of Friends in this Meeting & alsoe brought in there certificates & left them with Friends.

Next Monthly Meeting ordered at Brigg.

Signed by Joseph Richardson.

p. 337.

ATT a Monthly Meeting held at Brigg the 14th of the 8th month 1709[1] :—

Representatives as followeth :—

Gainsbrough, Abraham Kent, Seth Walker.
Brigg, Robert Colyer, Joseph Richardson.
The Isle, Robert Coakes.
Winteringham, George Frow, John Dent.
Adlinfleet, Thomas Hutchisson.

---

[1] 14th October, 1709.

Friends desires George Atkinson if his occasions will give him leave to come to our next Monthly Meeting, or send such part of the legacy left by Francis Dent as he thinks convenient, John Dent and George Frow are desired to acquaint him with it.

The collection for the nationall stock was discoursed by Friends in this Meeting, & its refered to the next Monthly Meeting what sum shall be raised.

Friends are desired to bring there sufferings upon account of tythe or steeplehouse rates to the next Monthly Meeting.

Whereas John Jackson of Gainsbrough has laid before Friends of this Meeting that he has a concern upon him to vissitt Friends Meetings in & about Norfolk & has laid the same before Friends at there Preparative Meeting to which he belongs as alsoe the consent of Friends therein, Friends alsoe at this Meeting have given there consent alsoe desireing the Lord may be with him, & attend him in that weighty service, & when he returnes to give Friends account of his service as alsoe to bring in his certificate to the Monthly Meeting.

Francis Seaton of Butterwick came into this Meeting & published his intention of marriage with Rebecca Gibbons of Beltoft & shee being present gave her consent but, haveing brought no certificate from her mother & father in law who are not Friends, of there willingness & consent, this Meeting desires Robert Coakes & Thomas Wresle, see that all things be done & made clear in that matter & all other matters in there own Meeting that no objections may arise to hinder there proceedings at our next Monthly Meeting.

Next Monthly Meeting ordered to be the first 6th day of the next month at Brigge.

Signed by Joseph Richardson.

p. 338.

ATT a Monthly Meeting held at Brigg the 4th of 9th month 1709[1] :—

Representatives Thomas Potter, Isaac Westoby.
Brigg, Joseph Richardson, Robert Colyer.
Winteringham, Stephen Wresle, Robert Knight.
Isle, no body.
Adlinfleet, Thomas Morley.

There appearing no body to represent the Isle Meeting therefore Friends have written to them to give satisfaction for soe great a neglect.

[1] 4th November, 1709.

George Atkinson has signified by letter to Robert Colyer that he is willing to pay three pounds in lieu of a legacy left by Francis Dent to this Meeting.

Its ordered that sufferings upon account of tythes be brought into the next Monthly Meeting.

Francis Seaton of Butterwick came a second tyme into this Meeting & signified the continuance of his purpose of marriage with Rebecca Gibbons of Beltoft & shee being present gave her consent as alsoe the consent of parents but Friends of there Meeting having omited giveing satisfaction of there clearness from all others, Friends have writt to them about it, that some of them come over to Joseph Richardson, Robert Colyer, John Barlow & William Williamson or any two of them of there clearness, before they accomplish there said intentions.

This Meeting orders a contribution to be collected for raiseing a nationall stock & brought to the next Monthly Meeting.

Next Monthly Meeting ordered to be the first 6th day of the next month at Brigge.

Signed by Joseph Richardson.

ATT a Monthly Meeting held at Brigg the 2d of X month 1709[1] :—

Representatives as followeth :—
Gainsbrough, Seth Walker, Abraham Kent.
Brigg, John Barlow & Joseph Richardson.
The Isle, James Coakes & William Parkinson.
Winteringham, Stephen Wresle, Mordeca Westoby.
Adlinfleet, Robert Vessy.

Thomas Crook of Pontefract came into this Meeting & published his intention of marriage with Hannah Colyer of Brigg & shee & her parents being present gave there consent, but it being the first time they are desired to wait Friends answer till next Monthly Meeting.

p. 339.

John Dent is still desired to receive the legacy of George Atkinson & bring it to the next Monthly Meeting.

John Urry gives account to this Meeting that Thomas Wresle has spoke to Josiah Chesman, & he took it kindly that Friends care was over him, & promised to be more dilligent in frequenting Meetings with them, however John Urry & Thomas Wresle are still desired to have a watchfull eye for good, & speak to him as occasion offers, & give account to the next Monthly Meeting.

[1] 2nd December, 1709.

Whereas David Crosby writt a letter to Joseph Richardson in
answer to one which he sent him, concerning a legacy, but
Friends not being satisfied with his letter have appointed
John Urry, junior, goe to speak to him about it & acquaint
him that Friends desires his appearance at our next Monthly
Meeting.

Contributions came in as followeth :—

	£	s.	d.
Gainsbrough	00	19	00
Brigg	00	16	00
Isle	00	12	00
Winteringham	00	10	06
Adlinfleet	00	09	00
	£03	06	6

Disbursments as followeth :—

	£	s.	d.
To Susan Recket, Gainsbrough	00	03	06
To Joseph Richardson for Alice Hiblin ..	00	05	00
To John Urry for William Wreet	00	12	02
To Thomas Hutchinson for Doll Pickhaver	00	03	00
To John Barlow for Quarterly Meeting he laid down	01	00	00
To Robert Colyer for Quarterly Meeting ..	01	00	00
Remains in Joseph Richardson hands ..	00	02	10

John Jackson returnd his certificate into this Meeting & gave
Freinds an account of that service & satisfaction he had in
the places where he traviled as in Norfolk & elswhere.

This Meeting desires that the Overseers in each Meeting attend
the service of the next Monthly to give an account of the
state of there Meeting, that soe an account may be given to
the Quarterly Meeting according to former advice.

Thomas Burton acquainted Friends in this Meeting that he hath a
concern upon his minde to vissit Friends meetings in the east
parts of Yorkshire, this Meeting hath given him a certificate
of there unity with him therein & desires he may return it to
the Meeting againe after he has performed his service.

Next Monthly Meeting at Brig.

Signed by Joseph Richardson.

p. 340.

George Atkinson haveing not paid the legacy of three pound which
he promised to give this Meeting some Freinds of Winteringham are desired to speak to him about it, as oppertunity
presents.

Satisfaction being given to this Meeting by the Isle Friends as
    desired the consumation of the marriage was left to them
    according to the good order of Truth.

Sufferings upon the account of came up to this Meeting from
    Winteringham Meeting onely the rest of the Meetings are
    desired to make theres ready & carry them up to the Quarterly
    Meeting.

Contributions for the nationall stock as followeth :—

				£	s.	d.	
Gainsbrough	..	..	..	04 :	01 :	06	
Brigg	..	..	..	04 :	00 :	00	
The Isle	..	..	..	00 :	00 :	00	there's to be brought to the Quarterly Meeting.
Winteringham	..	..	..	03 :	00 :	00	
Adlinfleet	..	..	..	01 :	17 :	06	
Totall	..	..	..	12 :	19 :	00	

Ordered that Abraham Kent, John Barlow, Gervis Cornwell,
    Stephen Wresle or any two of them attend the service of the
    Quarterly Meeting.

The next Monthly Meeting appointed to be the 13th day of the
    next month.

                    Signed by Joseph Richardson.

APPENDIX

Although an Act passed in 1696 (7 & 8 Will : III, cap. 6) and made perpetual by 3 & 4 Ann, cap. 18, enabled two Justices to ascertain what was due in respect of tithe, &c., and levy the amount by distress, and most tithe owners took advantage of this, yet they were not compelled so to do, and a few still used the older, and more oppressive, procedure of the Exchequer & Ecclesiastical Courts. The matter came before Parliament and it was shown that in ten selected cases £800 had been taken in respect of original demands totalling £15 ; Walpole passed a bill through the Commons to make the simpler procedure compulsory, but it was thrown out by the Lords owing to the opposition of the Bishops.

The case of Thomas Winder (pp. 114, 115–6, 152, 154, 162, 175) is referred to in a memorial to both Houses of Parliament thus :

" THOMAS WINDER, was Prosecuted in the Exchequer, in the Year 1701, by Solomon Ashburn, Vicar of Crowle, for Forty Shillings Tythe, of three Acres of Flax, and 3s. 6d. for three Years Easter-Reckonings, to a Decree of 33£ for Non-payment of which, he was Committed to Lincoln-Castle, in 1705, and there remaines close Prisoner ; notwithstanding Five Shillings per Acre was paid by the Party that Sold him the Flax ; and also half the value of the 40s. was proffer'd him in kind, by one who was Partner in Purchasing the abovesaid Flax. He is a Poor Man, and hath beat Hemp, &c., to Earn Bread for his Family."[1]

---

[1] The Suffering-Case of Several of the PEOPLE Commonly Called QUAKERS, On Suits mostly Commenced for Tythes, in the COURT of EXCHEQUER. (J. Sowle, London, 1709.)

INDEX OF PERSONS AND PLACES

Adlingfleet, co. York, 5 (2), 23 (3)–5, 27, 44–5 (2)–8 (3), 56, 68, 72, 76–7 (2), 89, 90, 94 (3), 110 (2)–112, 115, 118–9 (2), 124, 127–8, 131–2 (2)–3, 137–8, 142, 144 (2)–5 (2), 148, 150–1, 153, 155–9 (3)–60 (2)–61 (2)–63 (2)–64 (2)–66 (3)–72 (3)–73 (3)–74 (2)–77 (2)–79 (2)–80 (2)–83 (2)–85 (4)–86 (2)–87 (3)–92 (4)–93 (2), 195–96 (3), 198 (2)–200 (4)–1 (3)–2 (2)–3 (3)–7.
Alcock, Richard, 119, 121
Amcotts, co. Linc., 162, 165, 166, 175
Annon, Andrew, 140, 141
Appleby, co. Linc., 99, 100, 101 (2)
Ascogh, Edward, 41
Atherton, Hannah, 21
Atkinson, George, 33–4, 36 (3)–8, 99, 154, 156, 199 (4), 200–1, 203–5 (2)–6
Austin, Elizabeth, senior, 23, 24
......, ..., junior, 96, 97
Axholme, Isle of, co. Linc., 3 (2), 17–9, 21–2, 25 (2)–6 (2)–9, 31 (2), 35 (3)–6, 40, 43–4 (2)–5 (2)–6 (2), 49, 51, 53–4, 57–8, 60, 63–4, 66, 68 (2)–9 (2), 70 (2)–1 (2)–2 (2)–3 (2)–5, 79 (2), 80 (2), 82 (3), 84–94, 95 (3), 98, 101–3, 105–6 (3)–7 (3)–8 (2)–10 (2)–111, 114 (2)–6 (2)–9, 122 (2), 124–5 (3), 127–9, 131, 133–4, 137–8, 142, 145 (2)–6, 148, 150–6 (2)–9, 160 (2)–1 (3)–2 (2)–3 (2)–4 (2)–5 (2)–6 (3)–7 (4)–8, 170–3 (2)–4 (3)–7 (2)–8 (2)–9 (2), 180 (3)–1 (3)–3 (3)–5 (3)–6 (2)–7 (3)–9, 190 (2)–2 (4)–3 (3), 195 (3)–6 (2)–199, 200 (2)–1 (3)–2 (2)–3 (3)–4 (2)–7 (2).

Bainton, Gervase, 79, 80
Barclay, Robert, 93, 94
Barlow, Elizabeth, 199, 200
......, John, 95, 107–8, 110 (2), 112–3 (2), 117–9, 125–6, 130–1, 133 (2)–5, 138–9, 143–4, 148, 151–3 (2)–5 (2)–6, 161, 176, 180 (2)–1, 183 (2)–4, 189, 191, 196, 198, 200–1 (2)–2, 205 (2)–7.
......, Katherine, 139, 140
......, Mary, 64, 65
Barnsley, co. York, 21
Barrow, Esther, 54, 56–7 (2), 66, 77–8
Bathurst, Elizabeth, 19

Beacock, Michael, 3, 13
Bell, Leonard, 101, 102, 164, 181, 187
Beltoft [in Belton par.], co. Linc., 14 (2), 17 (3), 21, 23 (2), 33 (2), 35, 37–8 (3), 40–1, 47, 56–7, 71 (2), 75 (2), 103, 131, 140, 154, 159, 160 (3)–1 (4), 175 (2), 186 (2), 188, 204–5
Belton, co. Linc., 4 (3), 73–4, 100, 102, 104, 155 (2)–6 (2), 175
Bennington, John, 132, 180, 190, 193
Berrier, Joan, 48–51
......, John, 155–6, 168, 176
......, Joseph, 27, 45, 47–8 (3)–9, 51–2 (3)–4, 61–2, 80, 83 (2), 85, 133, 135, 167–8, 173, 183, 185
......, Mary, wife of Robert, 20, 33, 38, 39 (2), 41, 42, 45, 49, 70, 71
......, ..., 125
......, Robert, 3 (2), 5, 33
......, William, 40 (2), 41, 62
Bethel, Jabez, 18 (2), 27, 47 (2)–8 (2), 51, 55 (2), 58 (2), 61 (3), 65–6, 68, 71, 73, 83 (2)–4 (2)–6
Birkes, William, 8, 9
Birket, William, 146, 148, 184–5, 189–90 (2)–91, 199
Bishop, John, senior, 70–1, 78, 111, 156, 162 (2), 168, 172, 177, 186, 200
......, ..., junior, 168–9, 171, 173
......, Mary, 74, 77–8, 84
Blyth, co. Nott., 15–6, 67
Bogg, William, 98
Bourn, co. Linc., 149, 156
Bradley, Nicholas, 79
Brigg, co. Linc., passim
Bristol, co. Glos. and Som., 203
Broadhead, Mary, 22, 28–9
Brown, Ann, 138
......, Appelline, 3 (2), 5
......, Elizabeth, 36, 37
......, Hannah, 171
......, Isaac, 140, 142, 181
......, Jane, 126, 127
......, John, 7 (4), 11–2, 17, 20, 22, 24, 29 (2), 31, 34 (2), 38 (4), 39 (2), 40–2 (2), 45, 47–8 (2)–9, 55 (2), 58, 61 (2), 65–6, 71, 83 (2)–4 (2)–6.
......, Rachel, 188
......, Samuel, 97 (3), 141, 143, 164, 179
......, Sarah, of Partney Mills, 40, 41
......, ..., of West Butterwick, 155
......, Thomas, 41, 97
......, William, 27, 38, 42, 52
Bugg, Henry, 102
Burringham, co. Linc., 6, 9, 11
Burton, Gate, co. Linc., 119, 121

Burton—*cont.*
......, Thomas, 189–90, 198, 206
Butterwick, West, co. Linc., 2 (3), 3,
  11–3 (2), 30 (2), 40–2 (2), 50 (2),
  58, 63 (2), 69–70, 97 (2), 102, 137,
  141, 143, 155, 168–9, 204–5

Cambridge, 1
Cambridgeshire, 1
Carnell, James, 97
......, Jane, 5–6, 15, 21–2 (2)
Castlethorpe [in Broughton par.], 40–1,
  59, 67–8, 73, 76 (2), 78 (2)–9,
  88 (3), 96, 104 (2), 111 (2), 120
  (2), 133 (2), 146, 148, 161 (2),
  176 (2), 187 (2)
Champion, John, 105 (2)
......, Sarah, 15–6
Chapman, Alice, 110
......, Cassandra, 5, 6, 15, 24, 113,
  118, 125, 185, 187, 202
......, Judith, 39 (2)
Chesman, Josiah, 205
Clarborough, co. Notts., 191–2
Clark, Ann, 30 (2)
......, Henry, 136, 138, 203
......, Joan, 40–1
......, John, senior, 15–6
......, ..., junior, 30–1, 40 (2), 46,
  68 (2), 88, 104 (2), 105–6 (2),
  113 (2), 115–6 (2)–23 (2)–4, 126–
  37, 139–45, 148–155, 157–8, 160
  (2)–2, 164–5 (2), 167–9, 171–3
  (2)–6, 178 (2)–2, 184 (2)–6, 188–
  93, 195–6, 198–9
......, Richard, 88, 95, 118 (2)–9, 124,
  138, 140, 156
Coakes, James, 30 (2), 54–5, 74, 76 (2)–7,
  84, 92, 125 (2), 127, 137 (3), 141–2
  (2)–4, 146, 148, 155, 159, 162,
  164–5 (2), 167–8, 171 (2), 173
  (2), 178, 181 (2), 186–91, 196–8,
  201, 205
......, Robert, 27, 52 (3), 70 (3), 97,
  99, 102 (2)–3, 106–7, 113 (2),
  126, 143, 168–9, 171, 173, 179,
  192, 203–4
Cockerill, Richard, 85–6
Codd, Mary, 4 (5)–5 (3)–7, 11, 13, 15 (2),
  19, 22 (2), 24, 27, 32–3 (5)–4 (2)–
  5 (2)–6 (2)–8 (2), 40
Collier, Elizabeth, 175, 199
......, Hannah, 205
......, Robert, 11, 22, 25–6 (3), 31,
  37–8, 40, 42–3 (2), 46, 50 (3),
  58, 65–6 (2)–7 (3), 69 (2), 70
  (2)–1, 73 (2), 78, 81–2, 90–1,
  94–5 (3), 98, 108–9, 111, 114 (2),
  117–119, 125–6 (2), 128 (2), 133
  (2), 135 (2), 138 (2)–9 (2), 143
  (2)–5, 148, 150–1 (2)–2 (2)–3 (2)–

Collier, Robert—*cont.*
  5 (2)–6 (5)–7 (2), 159–60 (4)–8
  (2)–9, 171 (2)–3 (4)–4 (3)–6 (2)–
  7 (4)–8 (3)–9 (2), 181–4 (2)–5
  (2)–6 (2)–7 (3)–90 (4)–3, 195–8
  (2), 200–1 (2)–5 (2)–6
......, Sarah, 142, 149, 195, 203
Coningsby, co. Linc., 18 (2)
Cook, John, 111–2
......, Phoebe, 111–2
Cornwell, Elizabeth, 74, 125
......, Gervase, 75–7, 79, 188–9, 201,
  207
Cotley Hall [in Althorpe par.], co. Linc.,
  32 (2), 35, 54, 56, 59 (2), 87 (2),
  102 (2)
Cox, Richard, 99–101 (2)
Crane, John, 159–60, 174, 189
Crispin, Elizabeth, 191–2
Croftsread, Sir Charles, 2
Crook, Thomas, 205
Crosby, David, 4, 6 (2)–7, 9 (2), 11–4 (2),
  16–7, 21 (5)–2, 40–2, 47–8 (2)–9,
  51 (3), 60 (2)–2 (4)–3 (2), 69–70,
  72 (2), 75 (3), 79 (2), 81 (2)–2
  (2)–3 (4)–6 (2)–7 (3)–8 (2), 91,
  94 (3)–6 (3), 103–4 (2), 109 (2),
  122–3 (7)–4 (2), 141, 161–2, 176,
  184, 186 (2), 206
Crosby, Sarah, 50
Crowle, co. Linc., 2–3, 5, 7, 14–5, 17–8,
  20, 22, 24 (2), 27, 32–3, 47, 51–2
  (2), 54–5, 59–60, 62, 66–7, 72,
  79, 81, 110–1, 114, 116, 118, 126,
  137, 139 (2), 162, 168–9, 183
Cutsforth, Thomas, 51 (2), 95, 136–8
  (2)–9 (2)–41 (2)

Davis, Isaac, 73–4, 101, 103, 105, 114,
  122, 131, 137, 140, 145, 157,
  159–60, 165, 171 (2), 173 (4),
  175 (3)–6 (2)–7, 182, 185–7,
  190–3, 200–2 (2)
......, Jacob, 104 (2), 119, 160, 178,
  196, 198
......, Jane, 4 (4)–6 (2)–7
......, Susanna, 100–1
Dent, Francis, 15–6, 27, 74, 78, 86, 90,
  99, 100–3, 109–10, 114–5 (2)–6
  (3)–7 (3), 119–20, 122 (2), 124–9
  (4)–30, 133 (2)–4 (3)–5 (2), 137,
  143, 199 (2)–205
......, John, 63 (2), 67 (2), 95, 98,
  143 (2), 155, 160, 164, 166,
  177–9, 181 (2), 184, 187, 192,
  195, 203 (2)–5
......, Phoebe, 60, 64 (2)
......, Sarah, 101, 154, 156
Derbyshire, 79
Dixon, Paul, 190
Duckworth, Mary, 37 (2)

Ealand [in Crowle par.], co. Linc., 3, 33, 40, 41, 47, 70, 84, 139, 141, 155, 156, 168, 183
Earott, Robert, 42–3 (2), 47–9 (2), 52–3 (2)–4, 63, 69–71, 88–9 (2)–90
Elloughton, co. York, 144, 171
Elsham, co. Linc., 19, 21, 126–7
Empson, Amor, 89–90 (3)–93
Epworth, co. Linc., 4, 6 (2), 15–6 (3), 19 (2)–20, 22–3 (5), 25 (2), 27, 32–3, 38–9 (3), 41 (3)–2 (3)–3 (3), 47 (2), 50–1, 56 (2)–7, 60 (2), 62, 69 (3)–70, 77–8 (3)–80, 87 (2), 90, 95 (2), 98–100 (2), 102–3 (3)–4, 110–11, 117, 120 (2), 130, 136–7 (2)–8, 164–5, 174, 189 (2), 191, 201 (2)
Everatt, Thomas, 130, 146

Faucourt, —, 116
Fisher, Thomas, 61
Fishlake, co. York, 74 (2)
Fockerby, co. York, 58–9, 159, 171–2
Foster, Ann, 38, 126 (2)–7
......, Thomas, 81, 87, 111
Fox, George, 16 (2)–7, 126, 129, 161 (2), 196
Frow, George, 63, 99, 100, 107, 112–3, 124, 126, 137, 144, 151, 153, 158–61, 163, 166, 168, 170, 172, 174, 182, 185, 199–200, 203–4
......, Mary, 125
Frost, William, 112, 158–9 (2), 193

Gainsborough, co. Linc., passim
Garthorpe, co. Linc., 2, 3 (2), 5, 7, 9 (2), 11 (2), 13–5 (2)–8 (3), 20, 22 (2), 24–5 (2)–7 (2), 29–30 (3)–1 (3)–3, 35 (2)–6, 38, 40 (4), 42–4 (2)–6 (2), 49, 51, 53–4, 57–8, 60, 62–4, 66, 68 (3), 71, 74–5, 77, 79–82, 84 (2)–5 (2)–6 (2)–7 (2)–8 (2)–9, 91–5, 98, 100–1, 103–4 (2)–5 (2)–7 (3)–8 (2)–10 (2), 112–3 (2)–5 (2)–6 (2)–7 (3)–9, 122 (2), 124–5 (2)–7, 134, 144, 190
Gibbons, Rebecca, 204–5
Gibson, Thomas, 79–80
Gilliatt, Edward, 9 (2), 10–3, 18 (2)–9 (2)–20, 24–5, 27–8 (2), 30, 35–6 (2)–7, 41–3 (2)–5 (2), 49, 51–2, 54–6 (2)–7, 61, 63–5 (2)–6 (2)–8 (2)–70, 72 (3)–3 (2)–5 (2), 77–8, 80 (2)–1 (2)–2 (2)–3, 90 (3)–2 (2), 98 (2), 112 (3), 114, 121, 127–9 (2)–33 (2)–5 (2)–7 (2)–8 (6)–41, 150 (2)–2, 154, 156 (2), 159–60, 171, 180–1

Gilliatt—cont.
......, Isabel, 59, 74, 175
......, Joseph, 125
Godfrey, Mary, 35–6
Goxhill, Mary, 15, 26–7, 36, 98, 110, 114–5, 121–2, 124, 135, 145, 154 (2), 160, 166
Graham, Ann, 97 (2)
Grantham, Richard, 56–7 (2)
Grimsby, co. Linc., 61–2
Gunness [in West Halton par., but detached], co. Linc., 4, 6 (2), 16–7, 21 (2), 41–2, 47–8, 51 (2), 62 (2), 69–70 (2), 72, 79 (2), 87 (2)–8, 96, 104 (2)
Gunthorpe [in Owston par.], co. Linc., 52–4, 56–7

Haldenby, co. York, 79 (2)
Halliwell, John, 77 (2)–9 (2)–80, 83–4 (2)–5 (2)–6 (2)–7, 89, 94, 98, 102, 111–2, 115, 117, 127–8, 131–2, 134 (2)–5, 137–9, 163, 166
Halton, West, co. Linc., 38–9
Hardy, Mary, 105 (2)
Harrison, Frances, 104 (2)
......, John, 100–1, 163, 199
......, William, 4 (2)–5, 39, 62
Haslehurst, Mary, 46–50 (2), 52
Hastings, Francis, 81
Hatfield, co. York, 111–2
Haxey, co. Linc., 54, 57 (2), 79–80
Headon, co. Nott., 101–2
Heck, co. York, 66, 88
Heptonstall, Mary, 134
Hiblin, Alice, 206
Hicks, Rachel, 30–1
Hirst Hall [in Belton par.], co. Linc., 39, 61–2
Hobson, Ann, 62
......, James, 163–4
Hogg, John, 19 (2)–20
Holbeach Marsh, co. Linc., 139–40
Holderness, co. York, 195
Holland, 109
......, Thomas, 2
Holme on Spalding Moor, co. York, 171–2
......, Benjamin, 109
Holmes, Mary, 93 (2)
Hopkins, Thomas, 61–2
Howell, John, 5 (2), 27, 37 (2), 121
Hudson, Ellen, 74, 77, 102–3
......, Henry, 6, 8 (2)–9, 42 (2), 53, 63 (2), 69 (2), 70 (3)–1
Huntsman, Thomas, 144, 149
......, William, 78 (2)
Hutchinson, Thomas, 58–9, 74, 77, 79, 92, 95, 100, 105, 107, 113, 117 (4), 119 (2)–20 (2)–1 (2)–3 (3)–5 (2)–6, 129–30 (2)–1 (2)–3 (2)–4,

Hutchinson, Thomas—*cont.*
136, 140 (2), 143 (2)–4 (2), 146,
148–9, 152 (2)–4, 157, 159 (2)–
60 (2), 162 (2)–4 (2)–5 (3)–6,
168, 172–4, 177–8 (2), 180–1,
184 (3)–5 (3)–6 (2)–90 (3)–1,
198 (2)–201, 203, 206

Ireland, 24–5 (2)

Jackson, John, 165, 180, 182, 193, 195,
199, 204, 206
Jackson, Matthew, 76 (2)–7, 91–2, 98,
185–6

Keelby, co. Linc., 61–2
Kent, Abraham, 176–7, 179–80, 203,
205, 207
Kexby [in Upton par.], co. Linc., 61
Kingston upon Hull, co. York, 39, 112
Knight, Robert, 196, 198, 201, 204

Lambert, Rebecca, 101 (2)–2
......, Ruth, 67 (2)
Lancashire, 151
Lancaster, 37
Laneham, co. Nott., 191–2
Lea, co. Linc., 15, 34, 39 (2), 57–8, 139,
141
Leeds, co. York, 163
Lincoln, 23–6, 38, 54, 57, 65, 70, 80,
88, 91, 97 (2), 119 (2), 130–2, 140,
152, 193
London, 26, 29, 37, 62, 94, 97, 157 (2)–8,
169, 174, 177, 188 (2), 195, 197,
203
Lower, Thomas, 37
Luddington, co. Linc., 111, 115, 127, 146,
159

Malton, co. York, 30
Mansfield, co. Nott., 184–5 (2), 190
Markham, Jane, 61
......, Thomas, 8–9 (2)–12, 23, 25–6
(3), 34, 41
Marshall, (Ann), widow (of John, of
Gainsborough), 58, 62, 72 (2),
81 (2)–3 (2), 98–9 (2)
......, ..., of Winteringham, 99–100

Marshall—*cont.*
......, John, senior, of York, 60, 94
......, ..., junior, late of London,
94–6 (2)–7, 114, 116, 128, 135,
159 (2)–60 (2), 162–4, 173, 176,
185–6 (2)–7, 190, 199, 200, 202
......, Stephen, 114
......, Thomas, 65, 72, 83–86, 95
......, —, apprenticed to Isaac
Davis, 103, 145
Marshland (sic., for Adlingfleet), co.
Linc., 95, 167
......, William, 201–3
Martin, Margaret, 109, 114–5
......, William, 12–13, 179
Marton, co. Linc., 1
Massey, John, 139–40
Maxfield, co. Chester, 163–4
Mexber, Hannah, 66–7
Middleton, Ellen, 142
Mitchell, Ann, 12–13
Montague, Lord Chief Baron, 1
Moody, Mary, 52–60, 63
Morfitt, Mary, 139, 141
Morley, Jane, 5 (2), 23 (3)–5, 27–8,
48 (2), 50–1, 74, 77 (2), 94 (2),
110 (2), 125
......, John, 132–3
......, Joseph, 160, 166, 172, 184, 191
......, Margaret, 94, 96
......, Mary, 89–90 (2)–3, 145–6
......, Thomas, 46 (2), 56, 77 (2), 79–80,
84, 90–2 (2)–3, 95, 104–5, 111–3,
118 (4)–9 (2)–20 (2)–1 (2), 123
(2)–4, 128 (2)–9 (2)–31 (3)–2
(3)–5 (2)–8 (2)–41 (2)–2 (2)–3
(2)–4 (3), 148 (2)–9, 151 (2)–5,
157–8 (2)–9 (2)–60 (4)–2 (4)–3
(2)–4 (2)–5 (3)–6 (2)–7 (3), 170
(2), 172 (2)–3 (3)–4 (2)–6, 178–
80 (2)–1 (2)–2 (2)–3 (2)–4 (2)–5
(3)–6 (3)–8 (2)–9 (2)–90 (2)–2
(2)–3 (3), 195 (2), 198–9 (2)–200
(2)–3 (2)–4
Morris, Abraham, 70, 84, 98, 114, 116
......, Anthony, 12–14, 16, 35–6
......, Mary, 20, 58–9
Mosley, Bridget, 32, 35, 38–40, 42,
49 (2), 51–3, 60, 71–3, 75, 78,
80, 87, 89, 91, 110, 118, 122, 135,
153, 156, 166, 173, 185, 197, 203
Mumby, co. Linc., 96 (2), 199–201

Nainby, Elizabeth, 76–7
......, Jane, 145, 149
......, John, 40–1, 59–60, 67–8 (2)–
70 (2)–2 (2)–3 (3), 75, 78 (2)–9,
88 (4), 89 (2)–90, 92, 96 (2), 104
(2), 111 (2), 120 (2), 129, 133 (2),
146, 148, 150, 161, 172, 174,
176 (2), 187 (2), 188, 195, 198

Nainby—*cont.*
......, Mary, 78 (2)
......, Miriam, 132-3
......, Sarah, 60, 74, 125, 134
......, Thomas, senior, 27, 50, 65-6
  (2)-7, 72, 81-2, 90, 153, 155,
  157-8 (3)-9, 161-2, 164-6, 178
  (2)-9, 181, 189-90 (2)-3 (2),
  198-9, 202
......, ..., junior, 199 (2)-200
Naylor, Peter, 28-9, 34, 38-9, 44, 46-7,
  51, 56-7 (4), 61, 63, 73 (2)-4,
  79-80, 82, 85, 88, 90-1 (3), 95,
  122-3, 125, 129-30, 146, 151,
  155, 157, 160, 162-3 (2), 168,
  171, 173, 175, 179, 182-3, 188-9,
  198, 201-2
......, Sarah, 74, 125
......, Thomas, 107, 110, 161, 164,
  166, 172, 174 (2), 178, 186, 191,
  193 (2), 195 (2)-6, 198-9
Newbold, Godfrey, junior, 21
Nicholson, Elizabeth, 61-2
Norfolk, 204, 206
Northen, Abraham, 14 (2), 64-5, 79, 85,
  91-2, 97-8, 107, 113, 117, 122,
  128, 135, 142, 153, 163, 170, 177,
  183
......, E., 71
......, Martha, 73, 76 (2)
......, Mary, 30, 66
Nottingham, 76, 97, 101, 119
Nottinghamshire, 184 (2)

Odlin, John, 8 (2)-10 (3), 12-13
......, Sarah, 10
Ousefleet, co. York, 70-1
Owstwick, co. York, 110 (2)-2
Oxley, John, 185, 188, 202
Oyle, Elizabeth, 42, 53, 68, 135

Parish, Hannah, 54, 56
Parker, John, 186
Parkinson, Mary, 142
......, William, 114, 117, 142-3 (2)-4,
  146-7 (2)-8, 205
Parsons, Elizabeth, 56
Partney Mills, co. Linc., 40-1, 93
Pease, Elizabeth, 34-5
Petty, Ann, 73-4
Pickhaver, Dorothy, 40, 49, 75, 78, 89,
  91 (2)-2, 95, 100, 103, 107, 110,
  117-8, 125, 128, 135, 142, 145,
  150, 160, 173, 180, 187, 189, 193,
  206
Pickworth, Henry, 102
Pilsworth, Alice, 43

Pilsworth—*cont.*
......, John, senior, 3-4 (3)-5 (2)-6
  (2)-7 (5), 12-3 (2), 15, 17, 20 (4),
  24, 29 (2), 31, 34 (2), 38-40, 42
  (2)-3 (5), 50 (2)
......, ..., junior, 16, 19 (2)-21 (2)-
  3 (3)-5, 27-8 (2), 43 (6), 50 (2)
......, Joseph, 4, 11, 15 (4), 46
......, Mary, 42-3, 79-80
Poe, Peter, 197
Pontefract, co. York, 205
Potter, John, 15, 34, 36
......, Joseph, 19, 77-8, 93 (2), 107,
  109, 150, 158, 166, 181, 201
......, Thomas, 1, 24, 35, 47-9, 64
  (2)-5, 75, 95 (3), 100, 113 (2),
  117 (2), 129-31, 133, 135, 141-2
  (2), 150-1, 153 (2), 155-6 (2)-7,
  160-1, 163 (2), 165, 167-8, 170-1
  (2), 173, 176-7 (2)-8, 180, 182-3
  (4), 188-9 (4)-90, 193, 195-7
  (2)-8 (2)-9, 202 (3)-3 (2)-4

Raines, John, 188
Rasen, Middle, co. Linc., 93 (2)
Reckitt, Susanna, 78, 80, 91-2, 100,
  105, 108, 113-4, 117, 125, 128,
  142, 145, 150, 153, 163, 166, 170,
  183, 193, 197, 200, 206
......, Thomas, 39 (2), 49, 57-8 (2)-9
  (2)-60, 62 (2)-3, 65-70 (2)-3,
  75, 85-7, 89, 95, 98, 109-10, 113,
  122
Reed, William, 90, 98-100 (2)-4 (3)
Reeder, Hannah, 59, 161, 164-7, 169,
  171 (2)-2 (2)-3 (2)-6 (2), 178,
  182 (2)-5 (3)-6 (2)-7 (2), 193,
  200 (2)-3.
......, Joshua, 54, 56, 78, 87 (2), 100,
  102, 115, 118-20 (2)-1, 123 (3)-4,
  126 (2)-7, 129, 161-2 (2), 170,
  177
......, Robert, 32 (2), 168
Reedness, co. York, 89
Richardson, Ann, 199
......, Elizabeth, 130, 132
......, John, 115
......, Joseph, senior, 2, 5-6 (2)-8 (2)-9
  (2), 11, 12 (4)-3 (2)-5 (3)-6
  (2)-7 (2)-8 (2)-9 (4)-20 (2)-1
  (2)-2 (3)-3 (3)-4 (2)-5, 27 (4)-
  31 (2)-2 (2)-3 (2)-4 (2)-5 (3)-6
  (4)-7 (3), 39 (2)-40 (2)-1 (2)-2
  (3)-3 (2)-4 (2)-5 (3)-6 (3)-8
  (2)-9 (2)-50 (2)-1 (2)-2 (3)-3
  (2)-5 (5)-8 (2)-9 (2)-61 (2)-3
  (2)-5 (4)-6 (2)-8 (2)-9 (4)-70
  (3)-1 (2)-2 (2)-3 (4)-4 (2)-5
  (2)-7 (2)-8 (4)-81 (3)-2 (2)-3
  (2)-4 (2)-5 (4)-7 (3)-8 (2)-9
  (3)-90 (4)-1 (2)-2 (4)-4 (3)-6 (2)

Richardson, Joseph, senior—*cont.*
      –8 (4)–9 (3)–100 (2)–2, 104 (2)–5
   (2)–6 (2)–7 (2)–8 (5)–9 (3)–110
   (2)–1 (2)–3 (3)–5 (2)–7 (3)–8
   (4)–20 (2), 122 (2), 124–5 (2),
   127 (2)–30 (3)–1 (6)–2 (3)–3
   (2)–5 (2)–8 (2)–41 (2)–2 (4), 144
   (2)–5 (4)–6, 149–50 (3)–3 (3),
   155–6 (2)–7 (2)–8 (2)–9 (3)–60
   (4)–1 (4)–2 (3)–3 (4)–4 (3)–5
   (3)–6 (4)–7 (2)–8 (3)–71 (2)–2,
   174–6 (4)–8 (2)–9 (2)–80 (3)–1
   (7)–2 (4)–3 (3)–4 (2)–6 (3)–7
   (4)–8 (2)–9 (2)–90 (3), 192–3,
   195–8, 200–2 (2)–3 (2)–4 (2)–5
   (3)–6 (4)–7
......, ..., junior, 185, 195, 203
......, Robert, 61
......, Samuel, 117–9 (2)–20 (2)–4,
   126–33 (2)–5, 137 (2), 139–41,
   143 (2)–4, 146–7 (2)
......, Susanna, 149, 163–4
......, Thomas, 113
Robinson, Thomas, 91–2, 149 (2), 150–4,
   162, 167, 169
Rockhill, Susanna, 61–2
Rogers, Joseph, 53
Roxby, co. Linc., 15, 33–4, 63–4 (2),
   67 (2)
Rumley, Robert, 66–7

Sayner, Richard, 175, 177
Scotland, 78, 142, 149
Scotney, Aquilla, 81
Scotter, co. Linc., 104, 155
Scrooby, co. Nott., 64 (2)
Searby, co. Linc., 93 (2)
Seaton, Francis, 155–6, 198, 204–5
......, Sarah, 155–6
Selby, co. York, 54, 56, 175, 177
Sharp, John, 138, 166 (2), 171, 173,
   182–3 (2)–4 (4)–5 (2), 187, 199,
   200
Shields, Oakley, 15
Simpson, Henry, 1, 3, 4, 8 (2), 11, 13–5,
   17, 19, 21 (2)–2 (2), 30 (2)–1,
   37–9, 42–3 (2), 46 (3)–7 (2)–50
   (3), 56 (2)–7 (2)–8 (4)–61, 63 (2),
   65–6 (2)–7, 69, 71, 74–6 (2)–7,
   79, 85, 89, 93, 97, 100 (2), 110,
   117 (2), 121, 125
......, John, 94, 96, 114, 117, 125,
   129–30 (2), 145, 151, 157–9, 163,
   174, 185, 187, 200, 202
......, Margaret, 125
......, Mary, 93 (2)
......, Rebecca, 94–6 (2)–7
Skirm, Abraham, 45
Smith, Elizabeth, 155–9, 174–6, 178,
   185–6
......, John, of Nottingham, 76, 97 (2)

Smith, John—*cont.*
......, ..., of Scotter, 104
......, Martha, 14 (2)
......, Samuel, 174, 189
......, William, 27, 36, 50 (2), 66–7
   (2), 74, 90, 94–5
Snowden (Snowdall), Margaret, 83–5,
   87, 89 (2), 92, 107
Spalding, co. Linc., 8, 81 (2)–2, 171
Spavin, Josiah, 107–8
Stanley, Rachell, 140–1
......, Robert, junior, 56
Stephenson, Esther, 19 (3), 21–2, 26–7,
   35–6, 98
......, Joseph, 126–7, 175, 177
Stittenham, co. York, 30
Stovin (previously Berrier), Joan, 51–2
   (2), 54–5 (2)
Stuttin, —, widow, 6, 8 (2)–9 (2),
   11–14
Suffolk, 2
Sykehouse, co. York, 74

Taylor, Judith, 86
......, William, 38–9
Theaker, Ann, 18 (2)
......, Richard, 45 (3), 84 (2)–5
Thealby (in Burton upon Stather par.),
   co. Linc., 4 (2), 15 (2)–7, 22 (2),
   31 (2), 39 (4)–41, 46 (2), 56,
   59–61, 63, 67 (2), 76 (2), 82,
   94 (2), 114, 118 (2), 126, 142, 145,
   154, 156, 158 (2)–9, 174 (2), 181
   (2)–2, 184 (2)
Thorne, co. York, 99 (2), 154, 156
Thornholm [in Appleby par.], co. Linc.,
   102–4, 109–10, 117, 122 (2),
   129 (2)–30, 134 (2)
Tickhill, co. York, 67 (2)
Torr, John, 64 (2)
Tranmore, Elizabeth, 171–2
Trouton, Samuel, 198–9, 201 (3)
Tuke, Hannah, 168–9
Tumby [in Kirkby upon Bain par.],
   co. Linc., 31–2
Turner, Anthony, 1–2, 4 (2)
......, Mary, 40–1
......, Richard, 70 (3)–1, 76 (2)–9,
   88–9 (4)–90 (4)–3, 106 (2)–7, 125,
   128
......, Susanna, 39 (2)

Urry, John, senior, 4 (2)–6 (2), 16 (2),
   23 (2), 32–3, 38 (2)–9, 41 (2)–2
   (3)–3, 47 (3)–8, 51 (3), 53 (2)–4
   (2)–6 (2)–7, 60 (2), 62, 65–6,
   68–9 (4)–70, 74, 76 (2)–8 (2),
   87 (2), 89–90 (3)–1, 95 (3), 97,

Urry, John, senior—*cont.*
    100–2 (2)–3 (3), 110–1, 117, 119–
    20 (2), 125 (2)–30, 138, 157,
    160–1 (2)–2 (2), 164–5, 174–5,
    181–4, 186–9 (2)–90, 201 (3)–2,
    205 (2)–6
......, ..., junior, 52, 54, 98, 100–2,
    104, 106, 129 (2), 136 (3)–8 (2)–9,
    160–2, 175, 181, 188, 191–2, 202,
    206

Vesse, Ellen, 125
......, Robert, 74, 77–8, 83–6, 90–1, 94,
    102 (2), 104, 113, 115–6 (2)–7
    (3)–8 (3)–9 (3)–20 (2)–1 (2)–3
    (4)–5 (3)–8, 139, 142–3, 145–6,
    151, 155 (2), 157–8 (2)–60 (2),
    162 (2), 165 (3)–6 (3), 168, 171 (3),
    173 (4)–5 (2)–6 (3)–7, 179 (3)–80,
    182 (2), 186, 192 (2)–3, 195, 199,
    202, 205
......, ..., junior, 161, 167
......, William, 102–3

Waddingham, George, 99, 100
......, John, 100–1 (2), 125, 139–40,
    143 (2)
Waddington, co. Linc., 56, 64–5, 140–1
Walker, Ellen, 75, 153, 160, 166, 170
......, Sarah, 88 (2)
......, Seth, 151, 170, 179, 203, 205
......, William, 88
Wallace, Penelope, 137, 141
Ward, Elizabeth, 132
Warmsworth, co. York, 66 (2)–7, 74,
    111 (2), 199
Watson, Thomas, 171–2
Webster, Rachel, 175, 177
West, Julian, 166
......, Mary, wife of William, 74
......, ..., daughter of William, 119,
    121
......, William, 8, 27, 95, 119, 177, 184
Westoby, Anthony, 23–4, 53, 59 (2)–60,
    63, 81, 85–6, 96, 130, 144 (2),
    146, 148, 160
......, Elizabeth, 74, 125
......, Isaac, 130, 132, 163 (2), 167,
    175, 181, 193, 200, 204
......, Mordicai, 96–7, 130, 157, 159,
    162, 168, 179, 186, 200, 203, 205
Weston, co. Nott., 119, 121
Whitehead, Hannah, 110 (2)–1 (2)–2
    (2)–3
......, John, 9, 11, 18–9, 27, 50–1,
    54–6, 59–60, 107–8, 117, 133 (2)
Wilkinson, Elizabeth, 115–6 (2)
......, Robert, 119
......, Nicholas, 25–6 (2), 28 (2)–9 (2)

Williamson, Elizabeth, 107–8
......, John, 34–5
......, Thomas, 93 (2), 176
......, William, 27, 127, 157, 163,
    188–9, 201, 205
Wilson, Christopher, 46, 49, 62, 68
......, Jane, 168–9
Winder, Thomas, 47, 114 (2)–7, 139,
    141, 152, 154, 162, 166, 175 (2),
    177, 193
Winteringham, co. Linc., 2–3, 5, 7–8,
    11–15, 17 (2)–8 (2)–20, 22–4 (2)–5
    (2)–7 (2), 29, 31 (2)–3, 35 (2)–6,
    38–40, 42–4 (2)–6, 49, 51, 53 (2)–4,
    57–9 (2)–60 (2), 62 (2)–3 (3)–4,
    66, 68 (2)–9, 71–5 (2), 77, 79–
    81 (2)–2 (3), 84–5 (2)–6 (2)–7
    (2)–91 (2)–4 (2)–5 (2)–100 (3)–1
    (2)–5 (4)–8 (2)–9 (2)–10, 112,
    115–6 (3)–8 (2), 121–2, 124–5
    (3), 127–30 (2)–1 (3)–4, 137–8,
    142–3, 145 (3), 147–8 (2), 150–1
    (3), 153, 155–9 (3)–60 (2)–1
    (2)–3 (4)–6 (3)–8, 170–1 (2)–2
    (3)–3 (2)–4 (2)–7 (2)–9 (2)–80
    (3)–1 (3)–2 (2)–3 (2)–5 (2)–6
    (2)–7 (3)–90 (3)–2 (4)–3 (2)–5
    (2)–6 (3), 198 (2)–9 (3)–200 (2)–1
    (3)–2 (2)–3 (3)–6 (2)–7 (2)
Wood, Dinah, 15
Woodhouse, co. York, 21
Wootton, co. Linc., 61
Wrawby, co. Linc., 34–5, 107
Wresle, Elizabeth, 38 (2), 50 (2)
......, John, senior, of Thealby, 4 (2),
    9, 15 (2), 22, 31, 39, 46, 52–3,
    67–8, 74, 94, 125–6, 158–9 (2),
    174 (2), 181 (2)–2
......, ..., junior, of Brigg, 36–7,
    50 (2)–6, 65–7 (2)–70 (2)–2 (2)–5
    (2)–6, 81–4, 108–9, 111–2, 121–34
    (2)–5, 137–8, 150 (2)–5, 157–9,
    161 (2)–2, 164–5, 168–9 (2)–
    70, 176, 178 (2)–9, 181 (2)–2,
    184 (2), 186–91 (2)–2, 194 (4)–7
    (2)–8
......, Joseph, 63, 107, 139–40, 143–4,
    160–1, 165–7, 175, 178
......, Richard, 114–5, 143, 151, 158,
    163, 172, 186, 199
......, Stephen, 133, 145–6, 153, 155,
    157, 162, 167, 171, 173 (2), 176,
    178, 180 (2), 182–6, 192–3 (2),
    196, 198–9 (3)–205, 207
......, Susanna, 74, 101, 125
......, Thomas, senior, of Beltoft,
    2 (2), 4 (2)–5 (4)–6 (5)–7 (2)–8
    (3)–9 (3), 11–3 (2)–4 (3)–7 (3),
    21 (3)–2 (2)–3, 33 (2), 37, 38
......, ..., junior, of Beltoft, 40–1,
    47–8, 52, 54, 56–7, 71 (2), 75 (2),
    99, 103, 107, 118, 131, 137 (2)–8
    (2)–41, 143–4 (2)–6, 148, 153, 155,
    158–9, 161 (2), 165–6, 168 (2),

Wresle, Thomas, junior—*cont.*
    172, 174–5, 180–1, 184, 187–9,
    193, 198–200, 203 (2)–5 (2)
......, ..., of Winteringham, 8, 19, 27,
    38–9 (2), 42–3 (2)–5, 52–3, 62–3
    (2), 68 (2)–9, 74 (2)–5 (2), 80, 87,
    94–6, 99 (2)–101 (3)–2, 112, 114
    (2)–5 (2)–6 (3)–7 (2), 119–20 (2)–1
    (2)–2 (2)–3 (2)–7 (2)–8 (2)–9,
    133 (2)–5 (2), 137 (2), 143

Wright, Stephen, 159
......, Thomas, 203
......, William, 91, 200, 206

York, 94, 144, 154
Yorkshire, 179, 206

INDEX OF SUBJECTS

Affirmation, approach to Members of Parliament, concerning, 41, 52-3

Briefs, 186
Burial grounds, see under Property, real.

Children :
apprenticeship, 3, 5, 13, 47-8, 55, 58, 60-1 (3)-2, 65-6, 68, 71-2, 81 (2)-3 (3)-4 (3)-5 (3)-6 (2), 95, 98 (2)-9 (2), 103, 105, 114, 131, 145, 155-60, 171-4 (3)-5 (2)-6 (3)-8 (2), 182 (2), 184-5 (2)-6 (2)-7, 189, 200, 202
trial period, " alikeing ", 47
boarded with Friends, 3-4 (3)-5 (2)-6 (2)-7 (4), 11-3, 15 (2), 17, 19-20, 22 (2), 24, 27, 29, 32-3 (3)-4 (2)-6 (2)-8 (3)-9 (2), 45, 49, 76, 97, 183
clothing provided for, 3-5 (2), 7, 11, 13, 19-20, 22 (2), 24, 27, 29, 31 (2), 33 (2), 34 (2)-5, 38, 40-2 (2), 48, 51, 55, 65, 73, 187
education of, 7, 151-2
schoolmaster's salary, 151, 154-5, 157-8, 170, 172
interests of, safeguarded, on re-marriage of widow, 6, 8 (2)-9 (2), 11-14
orphans, care of, 1-3 (2)-4 (2), 19 (2), 38, 76, 162 (2), 164-7, 169-172, 185
Correction, house of
lunatic sent to, 58
for vagrancy, 135, 139

Disciplinary proceedings :
by :
admonition, at Monthly Meet-ing, 28, 76, 83-4, 91, 100, 104, 106, 120, 138-40, 143, 150 (2), 177, 194
by letter, 10, 26-7, 48 (2)-9, 55, 72-3, 92-3, 104, 139, 148
by visitation, 8 (2)-9, 12, 19 (2)-21 (2)-2 (2)-3 (3)-5 (3), 27-8 (4), 46-7 (2)-8 (2)-9 (2)-50 (5)-1

Disciplinary proceedings, by—cont.
admonition, by visitation—cont.
(2)-2 (4)-3 (2)-4 (3)-6 (2)-60, 63, 65-7 (3)-9 (2)-70 (4)-5 (2)-6 (3), 78, 81-2, 90 (2), 94 (2), 96, 99 (3)-100 (2)-1 (3)-5, 108-9, 111 (2)-3 (2), 115 (2)-7 (2)-8 (3)-9 (3)-20 (4)-1 (4)-2 (2)-3 (6)-4 (4)-6 (4)-7 (3)-8 (3)-9 (4)-30 (3)-1 (3)-2 (2)-3 (5)-4 (3)-5 (3)-7 (5)-8 (2)-9 (2)-41 (2)-2 (2)-3 (3)-4 (3), 146, 148-50 (2)-1 (2)-2 (2)-3 (2)-4 (2)-5 (2)-7 (2)-8 (2)-60 (2)-1 (3)-2 (2), 164 (2)-5 (3), 167-8 (2), 171-3 (2)-6 (2)-8 (2)-9 (2)-80 (2)-1 (3)-2, 184 (4)-6 (2)-8 (2)-9 (2)-90 (2)-1 (2)-2 (2)-3, 195 (2), 198-9
disownment, 29 (2)-30, 52, 126-7, 129, 146-8, 196-8 (2)
inquiry into dispute, 47-8, 70-1, 88-9 (2), 137-41, 176
testimony against self (con-fession), 55, 96, 101, 106, 116 (2), 119, 132, 136, 143, 146-7, 169-70, 194
withdrawal of meeting, 16, 154
for :
apostacy (Mary Moody), 52-60, 63
carriage and dress, disorderly (Mary Haslehurst), 46-8 (2)-50 (2)-2
debt (John Odlin), 8 (2)-10, 12-13
debt, sexuality, lying (Nicholas Wilkinson), 25-8 (2)-9 (2)-30
" differences ", 88-9 (2)-90 (2)-3, 106 (2)-7, 121, 123
drunkenness (John Wresle), 50 (2)-6, 65-7 (2)-70 (2)-2 (2)-5 (2)-6, 81-4, 108-9, 111-2, 121-33 (2)-5, 137-8, 150 (2)-5, 157-9, 161-2, 164-5, 168-70, 176, 178-81 (2)-2, 184 (2), 186-92, 194 (2)-8 (2)
drunkenness, wife-beating (Samuel Richardson), 117-20 (2)-4, 126-33 (2)-5, 137 (2), 139-41, 143 (2)-4, 146-7

Disciplinary proceedings, for—*cont.*
  marriage, " disorderly " (John
    Urry, junior), 129 (2), 136–8
  " out of the Society " (Joan
    Berrier), 48–52 (2), 54–5
    (Richard Cox), 99–101
    (2)
    (— Crosby), 94 (2)–6
    (William Parkinson)
    142–3 (2)–4, 146–8
    (William Reed), 98–9
    (2)–100 (2)–4
  " miscarriages " (Elizabeth
    Wilkinson), 115–6 (2)
  neglect of attendance at meet-
    ings (Josiah Chesman), 205
    (Robert Earott), 69–70
    (Mary Pilsworth), 16, 19
    (2)–21 (2)–2 (2)–3 (3)–5
    (2), 27–8 (2)
    (John Urry, senior and
    junior), 160–1 (2)–2
  payment of tithes (Joshua
    Reeder), 118–21, 123 (2)–4,
    126–7, 129
    (Richard Clark), 156
  removal certificate, non-pro-
    duction of (Richard Turner),
    70, 76 (2)–9
  vagrancy (John Halliwell), 78,
    111, 115, 127, 134–5, 137–9,
    163
  " walking disorderly ", neglect
    of attendance at meeting
    (John Clark), 104 (2)–6,
    113 (2), 115–23 (2)–4, 126–
    37, 139–46, 148–55, 157–8,
    160 (2)–2, 164–5 (2), 167–8,
    171–3 (2)–5, 177 (2), 179–81,
    184–6, 188–93, 195, 198–9

Illiteracy, case of, 104

Legislation, penal, against papistry,
  used against Quakers, 1–2

Marriage :
  appointments to inquire into
    " clearness ", 97, 102–3, 137, 168
  broken engagement, 91–3
  intentions of, publication :
    Alcock—West, 119, 121
    Annon—Stanley, 140–1
    Atkinson—Dent, 154, 156
    Bell—Lambert, 101–2
    Benington—Ward, 132

Marriage, intentions of, publication
                                      —*cont.*
    Berrier—Clark, 40–1
    Berrier—Rockhill, 61–2
    Berrier—Seaton, 155–7
    Bethel—Theaker, 18 (2)
    Bishop—Berrier, 70–1
    Bishop—Wilson, 168–9
    Browne—Graham, 97 (2)
    Champion—Hardy, 105 (2)
    Clark—Hicks, 30–2
    Clark—Walker, 88
    Coakes—Clark, 30 (2)
    Coakes—Tuke, 168–9
    Coakes—Wallace, 137, 141
    Cornwell—Nainby, 76–7
    Crook—Collier, 205
    Davis—Harrison, 104 (2)
    Davis—Petty, 73–5
    Dent—Champion, 15–6
    Dent—Lambert, 67–(2)
    Empson—Morley, 89, 90 (2)
    Gibson—Pilsworth, 79–80
    Harrison—Davis, 100–1
    Hobson—Richardson, 163–4
    Hopkins—Nicholson, 61, 62
    Howell—Duckworth, 37 (2)
    Huntsman—Nainby, 78 (2)
    Huntsman—Nainby, 144–9
    Hutchinson—Morris, 58–9
    Marshall—Simpson, 94–6 (2)–7
    Martin—Mitchell, 12–13
    Massey—Barlow, 139–40
    Morley—Cook, 111–2
    Morley—Nainby, 132–3
    Morris—Godfrey, 35–6
    Nainby—Barlow, 199–200
    Nainby—Brown, 40–1
    Newbold—Atherton, 21
    Northen—Smith, 14 (2)
    Potter—Barlow, 64–5
    Potter—Simpson, 93 (2)
    Reckitt—Turner, 39 (2)
    Reeder—Parish, 54, 56
    Rumley—Mexber, 66–7
    Sayner—Webster, 175, 177
    Seaton—Brown, 155–6
    Seaton—Gibbons, 204–5
    Simpson—Morley, 94, 96
    Spavin—Williamson, 107–8
    Stanley—Parsons, 56
    Stephenson—Brown, 126–7
    Taylor—Chapman, 38–9 (2)
    Torr—Dent 64 (2)
    Urry—Crispin, 191–2
    Vesse—Hudson, 102–3
    Waddingham—Marshall, 99–100
    Watson—Tranmore, 171–2
    Westoby—Austin, 23–4
    Westoby—Austin, 96–7
    Westoby—Richardson, 130, 132
    Williamson—Holmes, 93 (2)
    Williamson—Pease, 34–5
    Winder—Morfitt, 139, 141

Marriage, intentions of, publication
—*cont.*
    Wresle—Brown, 36–7
    Wresle—Martin, 114–5
    Wresle—Morley, 145–6
    Wresle—Turner, 40–41
Meeting(s):
  'allowed' at:
    Adlingfleet, 144
    Butterwick, West, 69–70
    Epworth, 162, 164–5, 174
    Gunness, 4, 7, 14, 21, 32, 40–2,
      47–8, 59–61, 63, 69, 87 (3),
      103
    Luddington, 146, 173
    Scotter, 104
    Thealby, 17
    Thornholm, 102–4, 110, 117,
      130
  houses, see under Property, real
  Monthly, day changed, 90
    Minutes to be read in, 61
  Preparative, establishment of, 101–2,
    186–8
    Minutes to be kept, 186, 188–93,
      195–6, 198
  Quarterly, to be followed by Meet-
    ing for Worship, 115–6
  weekday, 21 (2)–2, 80, 82, 101–3
    (2), 117–9 (2), 179 (2)
  women's, 4–6 (2), 57, 92, 116, 168
Money, light, 65

Persecution (Thomas Winder), 114 (2),
  115–6, 152, 154, 162, 175 (2)
Property, real:
  burial grounds, deeds of, 44 (3)–5,
    59–60 (2)–1 (2)–3, 88 (2)–90 (2)–2,
    181 (2)–3
    fencing of, 45–6 (2)–8, 68–70
      (2)–2 (2)–3 (2)–7
  meeting houses, licensing of, 81, 86
    provision of, 69–70, 146 (2),
      148, 154, 177, 188–9

Quaker Practice:
  arbitration, 42 (2)–3, 50 (2), 136–41
  books, Robert Barclay's apology,
    93–4, 105–6 (2)
    Elizabeth Bathurst's, 19
    circulation of, 19 (2)–22, 102
    epistle circulated, 136
    George Fox's, 16 (2)–7, 126,
      129, 161 (2), 196
    John Hogg's, 19 (2)–20
    provision of, 59–60, 88, 98,
      107, 109 (2)–10, 112, 125,
      131–2, 135–6, 138, 153, 163,
      166, 173, 183, 197

Quaker Practice, books—*cont.*
    John Whitehead's, 107–8, 117,
      133 (2)
  membership, 76 (2)–9, 111–2
  ministry, visiting in the, 109 (2),
    139, 142, 149 (2), 179, 188 (2),
    195 (3), 197, 199, 203–4, 206 (2)
  overseers, appointment of, 69–70,
    74, 125, 143, 151 (2)
    duties of, 78–80, 95–6, 121–4,
      162, 182 (2)–3, 189, 196–7,
      206
  removal certificates, 171, 184–5,
    189
  representatives, absence of, dis-
    approved, 101–2, 145, 190, 204
  wills, advice to make, 25
Quakerism:
  testimonies, 25 (2)–8, 30

Recording of:
  births and burials, 135, 188
  history of introduction of Quaker-
    ism, 164, 167–9
  licences of meeting houses, 157–9
  marriages, 134–5, 157, 171, 173
  representatives, to monthly meet-
    ings, 154–5, 157–68, 171–90 (2)–3,
    195–6, 198–202 (2)–3 (2)–5
    to quarterly meetings, 135, 139,
      141, 150, 153, 156, 160, 163,
      166, 171, 173, 177, 180, 183,
      186, 189, 193, 197, 207
  sufferings, 8–9 (2), 11, 17, 18 (2)–19,
    25–7, 34 (2)–5, 43–4, 52–5, 63–4,
    71–2, 81 (2)–2, 90–2, 106, 115–6,
    123–5, 136–8, 151 (2)–2, 164–7
    (2), 177–81 (2), 191–3, 195, 204–5,
    207
Relief:
  assessment to poor rate, exemption
    to be sought, 54, 56–7 (2)
  bedding provided, 102
  cash, 5–6 (2)–7, 11–12 (2)–3 (2),
    15 (4), 17, 19, 21–2 (2), 24, 26–32,
    35 (2)–6, 38–40 (2)–2 (3), 45–6
    (3), 49 (3), 53 (3), 55, 58, 60,
    63–5 (3)–6 (3), 68 (5), 71 (2)–3
    (2), 75 (4), 77–8 (4)–80 (3),
    83–5 (2)–7, 89 (4), 91 (5)–2 (3),
    95 (2), 97–8 (2), 100, 103, 107
    (2), 109–10 (6)–2 (2)–3 (3)–5,
    117 (3)–8 (3), 122 (3)–5 (2), 128
    (3), 131, 135 (5), 138, 142 (2),
    145 (2), 150, 153 (3)–4, 156, 160
    (3), 163, 166 (5), 170 (2), 173 (3),
    177, 180, 183, 185 (3)–7 (2), 189,
    193, 197, 200–1 (3)–3 (2), 206 (3)
  clothing provided, 38, 89, 98, 112,
    132, 193
  employment, provision of, 85–6

Relief—*cont.*
fuel provided, 51–2, 92, 128, 145, 163
funeral expenses paid, 21–2 (2), 36, 60, 107
insanity, during, 49, 57–8 (2)–9 (2)–60, 62 (2)–3, 65–70 (2)–3, 75, 78, 80, 85–7, 89, 91–2, 95, 98, 100, 105, 108–10, 113–4, 117, 122, 125, 128, 142, 145, 150, 153, 163, 166, 170, 183, 193, 197, 200, 206
lodging, provision of, 77 (2), 79 (2), 80, 83–4 (2)–6 (2)–7, 94, 134
negotiations with creditors, 126
prisoner(s), for, 166, 177, 193
family, advice on business, 175
room for, in Lincoln Castle, rented, 140–1, 152 (2)–3
rent paid, 98, 108, 110, 125, 128, 193, 200

Subscriptions for :
general purposes, 2, 3, 5, 7, 11–5, 17–8, 20, 22, 24, 27, 29, 31 (2)–3, 35–6, 38, 40, 42, 44, 46, 49, 51, 53, 58, 60, 63–4, 66, 68, 71, 73, 75, 77, 79, 82, 84–7, 89, 91–2, 95, 98, 100, 103, 105, 107–10, 112–3, 116, 118, 122, 125, 128, 131, 134, 138, 142, 145, 150, 153, 156, 160, 163, 166, 170, 172–4, 177, 180, 183, 185–7, 189, 192, 196, 200–1 (2)–3, 206

Subscriptions for—*cont.*
Richard Grantham, 56–7
Irish friends, 24–5 (2)–6
losses by fire, 8–9, 45 (2), 81 (2)–2, 95–6 (2), 126–7, 146, 148, 191
Meeting House at Bourn, 149 (2)–54, 156
at Tumby Woodside, 31–2
Mumby Monthly Meeting, 96 (2), 199–201
national stock (Yearly Meeting Fund), 17, 79–80, 113 (2), 114, 204, 207
Scottish Friends, 78
Richard Theaker, 84 (2)–5
Samuel Trouton, 198–9, 201
Quarterly Meeting, to repay money borrowed from a legacy, 54
routine contributions, 3, 5, 7, 11, 13, 17, 19 (2), 20, 22, 24, 27, 30–2, 34–6, 38, 40, 42, 46, 49, 51, 55, 58, 60, 63, 65–6, 68, 71, 73, 75, 78, 80, 82, 85, 87, 89, 91–2, 95, 98, 100, 103, 105, 107–8, 110, 113–4, 117–8, 122, 125, 131, 135, 138, 145, 150, 153, 156, 160, 163, 166, 173, 177, 180, 183, 189, 193, 197, 203, 206

Testamentary matters :
advice to make wills, 25
legacies to Monthly Meeting, 37, 39, 100, 130 (2), 144 (2), 146 (2), 148, 160, 199–205 (2)–6 (2)